STO

COMPUTERS
AND THEIR USES

Prentice-Hall

Series in Automatic Computation

George Forsythe, Editor

PRENTICE-HALL INTERNATIONAL, INC., *London*
PRENTICE-HALL OF AUSTRALIA, PTY, LTD., *Sydney*
PRENTICE-HALL OF CANADA, LTD., *Toronto*
PRENTICE-HALL OF INDIA (PRIVATE) LTD., *New Delhi*
PRENTICE-HALL OF JAPAN, INC., *Tokyo*
PRENTICE-HALL DE MEXICO, S.A., *Mexico City*

COMPUTERS
AND THEIR USES

WILLIAM H. DESMONDE

Research Staff Member
IBM Corporation

PRENTICE-HALL, INC.
ENGLEWOOD CLIFFS, N.J.

Current printing (last digit):

14   13   12   11   10   9   8

Library of Congress Catalog Card No. 64-12555
Printed in the United States of America
16560 C

1568791

PREFACE

The main purpose of this book is to give the reader a glimpse into the essential characteristics of digital data processing machines and their uses. It does not offer specialized instruction in design, programming, and applications, but explains the concepts basic to all of these areas by means of simplified examples. Because of its comprehensiveness, this book should be useful as a general introduction to the field for the intelligent layman, for college or graduate students, and for beginners in the data processing industry.

A number of people have assisted me in the preparation of this manuscript by providing me with information or by reading parts of the book. I would like to acknowledge, with thanks, the assistance of R. Beeman, H. H. Goldstine, W. Heising, H. H. Herrick, A. MacAuley, K. Martin, J. Morrissey, D. Newton, D. Quarles, and J. Siegfried. I hope I haven't forgotten anyone. I have made use of some material from various departments in the International Business Machines Corporation. If there are any errors in this book, they are, of course, my own responsibility.

William H. Desmonde

TABLE OF CONTENTS

7 THE ALGEBRA OF AUTOMATA, 88

8 THE ELEMENTS OF PROGRAMMING, 105

13 ADVANCED DATA PROCESSING, 197

14 THE FULFILLMENT OF SOCIAL GOALS, 224

1 THE ERA OF INTELLIGENT MACHINES

Many philosophers have regarded creative intelligence as the greatest power in the universe. Through this force humanity has transformed the surface of this planet and is now reaching to outer space for further conquests. These achievements have been made possible by machines which man has devised to augment the working of the natural laws which govern the cosmos.

The great technological accomplishments of the last few centuries have centered largely about the harnessing of physical energy to control our environment. Our fabulously increased ability to move about and manipulate objects can be viewed mainly as the result of the development of tools for improving upon our unaided muscular and sensory apparatus.

The electronic computer is a radically new type of machine—not simply an extension of our limbs and our senses. It can be conceived, in a sense, as an appendage to our central nervous system. Automatic data processing machines assist us in remembering and organizing external stimuli, in coordinating the tools which give us power over our environment, and in probing more deeply into the foundations of the sciences.

But the import of computers is far more than technological. These machines are serving an ever-increasing function in the rational organization of social effort. An army comparable in size to the military forces of a major world power has as its daily mission the recording, processing, and analyzing of the information generated by American industrial, professional, and governmental organizations. This army of clerical workers, consisting of about 15 million people, does not manufacture or distribute goods or services, but is occupied mainly with the handling of the data related to these productive activities in our complex civilization.

1

With the advent of the industrial revolution, the ratio of clerical personnel to directly productive labor has been growing continually. The invention of calculating equipment has, to a large extent, been motivated by the need for faster, cheaper, more efficient methods of processing data. Although the automatic computer was devised mainly in response to scientific needs, the requirements of business and government data handling have been a major stimulant to the further development of this machinery. The fact that about 1.5 billion lead pencils are sold yearly is perhaps some indication of the enormous area of information-processing activities which have yet to be mechanized.

So fast is the pace of modern science and technology that it now seems incredible that in 1931 it took 3 days for a passenger to fly from New York to Los Angeles in the Fokker F10. Should a modern air traveler, who can now make the trip in less than 6 hours, be subjected for some reason to such a long flight, he would feel this as an intolerable hardship. Yet, 50 or so years previously the same trip in a covered wagon took months of arduous toil under extreme physical danger.

The technology of data processing has advanced with similar rapidity. When the IBM Electronic Calculating Punch, type 604, was announced in 1948, it was greeted with tremendous enthusiasm as a "brain" capable of advanced computational feats. This machine had an electronic memory capacity of 50 digits, and had a normal input rate of 2100 digits per minute. In 1953, when the writer entered the data processing field, he was astounded to learn that electronic computers could perform several thousand additions per second. But within 10 years it was no surprise to hear of machines which could execute a quarter-million additions per second, and new equipment was in the offing which would be even faster. Input-output speeds, too, have increased from the order of tens of thousands of characters per second to hundreds of thousands. Electronic memories have grown from units which can store thousands of numbers to devices with capacities for storing hundreds of millions. Components retaining billions of characters will probably be available within several years.

The ability of electronic computers to play chess and checkers, translate languages, prove mathematical theorems, and perform such popular exploits as election tabulation and prediction has stirred the imagination even more than the fantastic speeds at which the machines operate. The significance of these machines for commercial data processing has been equally exciting. The early applications of electronic computers were for scientific and engineering calculations. Here they could sometimes accomplish, in a matter of hours or days, work which would take humans years or even centuries to complete. Later, when employed in a widespread way for business information systems, such accounting procedures as payroll, billing, and inventory control could be carried out with greatly increased speed and efficiency. A rapidly growing science of management rests upon the use of computers for supplying fast, complete, and reliable information.

The advent of high-speed data processing machines capable of remembering vast quantities of information has enabled many industrial, military, and state functions to be executed with greatly increased productivity. Of major significance has also been the use of the immense new computational facilities in rendering possible scientific and engineering advances in many spheres of technology. The exploration of interstellar space relies heavily upon computers, both on the ground and as instrumentation in the space vehicles themselves.

The present state of business data processing may well turn out to be comparable to that of the airlines in 1934 when, with a combination of the DC-2 and the Curtiss Condor, passengers crossed the United States in 21 hours. Future commercial accounting will probably rely on electronics instead of paper handling. Huge regional computational units, similar to bank clearing houses, will be established. In and out of these units, messages will flow continually from thousands of different business enterprises within the area. Every place of business will have small, inexpensive terminal devices combining the functions of cash registers, typewriters, two-way television, and telephones. From these units, transactions such as sales and purchase orders will be entered into the remote computer via telephone lines or microwaves. These messages will be identified automatically and processed according to contract. The data handling will include the storage of millions of characters of information, the statistical analysis of transactions, the sending of messages (such as bills) to other firms, and the compiling of management reports.

The very nature of money may well be transformed, for data processing centers will no longer handle physical checks and currency. They will simply receive messages to add or subtract from subscribers' records. Such communications and information-digesting networks may ultimately be extended into such diverse fields as the post office and home entertainment. Letters may be transmitted electronically. Personal libraries may be replaced by dialable memory banks which will transmit visual images of the pages of books to special viewers installed in the home. For services of these types, transmission and display units will be developed to suit the needs of citizens or subscribers.

Electronic data processing machines will be used increasingly for the control of complex, dynamic systems. Where a situation is composed of a large number of rapidly changing, interrelated factors, it is difficult for humans to make decisions fast enough to be effective. The regulation of aircraft movements near airports is an example of such a circumstance.

Automobile traffic in metropolitan areas constitutes another situation where no human can sense everything going on at a particular time, and how all of the variables affect each other. This task may someday be performed by automatic computers which will decide when and how to activate the available regulatory devices. Many problems faced by business management in planning financial operations, production, and distribution are equally complicated. The use of high-speed data processing machines to control manufacturing plants has been extensively publicized. Important contributions have already been made by electronic computers in all of these areas requiring decision making in complex situations.

The electronic data processing machine has created the new profession of *systems engineering*. This work consists of the analysis, design, and programming of automatic information-handling systems. The requirement for such a career (except in mathematical applications) is simply the possession of a keen, logical mind. A large number of universities have their own machine installations and offer regular courses in data processing. Many seats of higher learning have graduate programs in this field. The Massachusetts Institute of Technology, to cite one example, has granted a doctoral degree based on a dissertation on artificial intelligence.

The technology of data processing is still in a rapid state of growth, and a whole new engineering art has developed around electronic computing. This has enabled a number of alert and progressive companies of medium size to expand into corporate giants, and has enabled foresighted individuals to make highly successful investments. New careers have opened for tens of thousands of people, and data processing has become big business. From an origin traceable to the erudite abstractions of a few mathematical philosophers, the ideas underlying automatic computers have grown into a billion-dollar industry.

It is fascinating to dwell upon the approaching epoch of space travel, automatic factories, and giant information-processing centers. Yet an uneasy note enters into these speculations about the world of the future. Certainly the increase in man's knowledge and the conquest of the universe are goals which express two of our finest instincts: the enjoyment of creative work and the call to high adventure. What worries some people, however, is the sociological effect of intelligent machines. Professor Norbert Wiener, who has been a major contributor to the art of automatic control, has ceaselessly urged that this science be applied for "the human use of human beings."

Will electronic data processing machines be employed to enrich man's existence, enhance his self-respect, strengthen his integrity, and provide for justice in social life? Or will they be used for nonhumanitarian purposes? Will these developments initiate a trend toward the regimentation of the individual under the bureaucratic control of colossal state machines?

A crisis in human values has been developing during the last three centuries, resulting from the steadily increasing application of the concepts of the physical sciences to man and his society. The medieval conception of the universe, from which modern science arose, was an integrated world view which gave meaning to life and value to man's finer aspirations. It was believed that a deity had created the world, set it in motion, and continued to sustain all things in their courses through his will and divine love. Not a single stone could fall unknown and unplanned by the Creator. The aim of human life was to blend with these cosmic purposes. The fundamental purpose of wisdom and learning was not to predict physical processes, but to comprehend the meaning of the divine scheme. This philosophy gave sanctity to human life, furnished the ethical basis for justice and human dignity, and inspired humans to consecrate their lives to higher causes.

The splendid intellectual and technological triumphs of recent centuries, however, have as yet failed to produce a world view to make life meaningful and to provide the moral foundations for a peaceful and productive international society. What is needed are new conceptions to restore these values to our outlook on the universe.

Possibly this challenge will be met by ideas arising in the sciences of information flow and artificial intelligence. These conceptions are throwing new light upon the nature of determined systems, memory, learning, and biological growth. The age-old problems of free will versus determinism, the origin of life, and the emergence of mind in the cosmos can be approached anew from the fresh viewpoints provided by these theoretical advances. Perhaps the next few centuries will be the era of biology, just as the past few hundred years have been the era of the physical sciences.

The development of electronic computers has been heralded as the beginning of a second industrial revolution as tremendous in scope as that initiated by the invention of the steam engine. These predictions appear to be coming true. Automatic data processors are in no sense "brains." However, in noncreative operations they are far superior to the human mind in speed, accuracy, information storage, and freedom from error. They are devices for controlling other machines, for organizing economic and social information, and for acquiring new knowledge of our environment.

2 THE EVOLUTION OF DATA PROCESSING

AUTOMATIC SEQUENCES OF ACTION

The simplest automatic machines are incapable of self-control. Once a pendulum is set in motion, it continues to swing back and forth unless disturbed by an outside force such as air friction. Similarly, a water wheel invariably turns in the same way, affected only by changes in the rushing water.

A clock is more complex in that this system of gears contains more than one level of control. The movement of the hour hand is regulated by the number of revolutions made by the minute hand. An alarm clock is still more advanced for it includes an adjustable control which humans can set to any desired time. However, it has no capacity for self-control; once the timer is positioned, the machine proceeds in its fixed sequence of behavior. The tea-kettle is a higher type of mechanism, possessing a valve which governs the boiling water. One of the most modern of self-regulatory devices is the gyroscopic stabilizer which keeps rockets in a predetermined position.

The more complicated a machine, the greater its capacity for executing long and complex chains of actions under its own control. The evolution of computers has taken this course in response to practical needs. What, in general, are these requirements?

Whether carried out manually or by machine, the processing of information involves a sequence of operations upon data. Each step usually uses the results of previous calculations in the sequence. The computation of a paycheck, for example, requires the solution of numerous arithmetic problems. Each solution is used by later steps in the calculation. Such solutions are called *intermediate* results.

Box No. 1 of Fig. 2-1 consists of a series of additions. The employee's daily time records are accumulated to obtain the total weekly hours worked. This total is now used to compute the gross pay. This calculation is a multiplication of the total weekly hours worked by the employee's wage rate. Box No. 4 makes use of gross pay, as well as the tax percentage obtained in box No. 3.

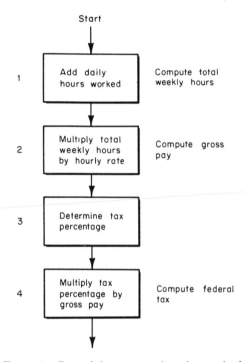

FIGURE 2-1 Part of the computation of a paycheck.

Most problems involve alternative sequences of calculations. In preparing a payroll it is necessary to compute a social security deduction. This is done by deducting 3.625% of the employee's gross pay from each paycheck. There is, however, an upper limit on the amount which must be paid every year. When the total deduction reaches 3.625% of $4800 ($174) no further payments are made.† Hence, whenever a payroll is prepared, it is necessary to test whether this upper limit of $4800 has been reached. This test enables a decision to be made: whether or not to deduct an additional amount for social security. Figure 2-2 shows, in a simplified way, this choice between alternative series of operations, or *branches*.

† The percentage deducted and the total deductions may be changed at the end of a year. The above figures are those used in 1963.

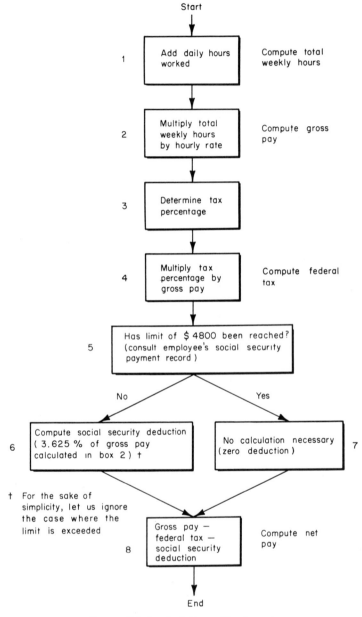

FIGURE 2-2 A calculation with a branch.

Box No. 5 decides which branch is to be executed. Net pay is computed in box No. 8 by the subtraction of federal tax and social security tax from gross pay. Box No. 7 can be considered as computing a social security deduction of zero.

A third common characteristic of data processing is the *iteration* or *loop*. (See Fig. 2-3.) This is a sequence of operations repeated again and again until the right answer is obtained.

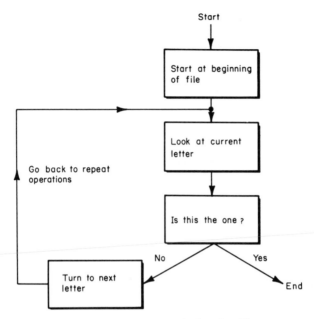

FIGURE 2-3 A loop process in data handling.

Suppose we are searching through a pile of unordered correspondence for a letter from John Smith. One way to find the letter we want is to examine each item in turn. We begin by comparing the name on the first letter with "John Smith." If this name is not present we place the letter to the side and look at the second item of correspondence. Again we compare names. If this is still not the letter we want we place it to the side and examine the third letter. This process is repeated until the comparison yields the item for which we have been searching.

Data processing problems almost always involve long sequences of operations with branches and loops. Such a sequence is called a *program.* The graphic presentation of a series of steps is called a *flow chart,* and is frequently a labyrinth of hundreds or thousands of interdependent operations. These characteristics are present whether the problem is carried out by manual labor or by electronic computers.

Many of the steps required in either scientific or commercial data handling are not mathematical. A good deal of time is spent in gathering and organizing the basic information needed, and in writing down intermediate results. It is often necessary to look up facts in a list or in a file, as in the case of an employee's hourly rate of pay. As we have seen, searching for information frequently involves nonarithmetic activities such as comparisons. The last step in a sequence of operations is writing down the results. Sometimes these answers must be typewritten or printed in a tabular form, or else placed in special parts of documents such as paychecks.

EARLY COMPUTERS

Man's first data processing tools were devices to facilitate counting. Like the lever, one of the earliest machines, the most primitive calculating instruments were completely nonautomatic. Indeed, many of the rudimentary methods used by primitives for counting were simply pebbles, notched sticks, and knotted ropes.

The abacus was invented independently by the Greeks (the Greek word *abax* means *sand tray*) and the Chinese. This instrument, in various versions, is still used by over half of the world's population, chiefly in the Far East. There are two groups of beads in a typical device: the lower group contains four beads, and the upper group has one. Starting from the 0 position (see Fig. 2-4), the number 1 is formed by moving up one

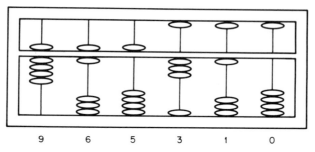

| 9 | 6 | 5 | 3 | 1 | 0 |

FIGURE 2-4 Representation of numbers on an abacus.

of the lower beads. Counting continues by successively moving up a lower bead. When 4 is reached, the next number, 5, is formed by returning the four lower beads to their initial position and moving down one of the upper beads. The digit 6 is now obtained by moving up a lower bead. When 9 is reached, the next number, 10, is produced by carrying a 1 to the next position and returning the original position to 0.

The counting board (Fig. 2-5), used extensively in medieval Europe, is of great antiquity. It operates on the same principle as the abacus. Small disks are placed on, or between, lines on a board to represent numbers. Each digit position consists of two rows. If a disk is present in the upper row, a 5 is added to the disks in the lower row to produce the desired number.

The disks used on these boards came to be called *counters,* and the term *counting house* designated the room in which commercial transactions were calculated and recorded. The display counter in the retail store has its origin in the counting board. The names *carry* and *borrow,* which we use in addition and subtraction, stem from the actual moving of disks when calculating with the old-time counting boards.

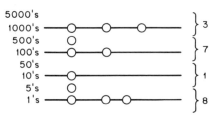

FIGURE 2-5 Representation of the number 3718 on a counting board.

There is reason to believe, by the way, that the game of checkers may have originated in the counting board. Similarly, some authorities have sought to trace the history of the game of backgammon to the ancient abacus. The playing pieces used in both games are often called *counters,* and they greatly resemble the ancient Roman *tesserae* which were used as coins, computational units, and as pieces in board games.

The first calculating device to perform an automatic carry was invented by Pascal, who used wheels with 10 teeth to represent numbers. Each tooth stood for a particular digit. Addition was executed by stepping the gears a number of intervals equal to the digit to be added. The art of mechanical calculation was extended by Leibniz, who utilized Pascal's methods to develop a machine which could multiply and divide. Multiplication and division are, in actuality, long sequences of additions, subtractions, and tallies. The completely automatic execution of these operations, as in our modern desk calculators, requires a high level of self-control.

But even our contemporary adding machines and desk calculators are primitive from the standpoint of automatic data processing. The solution of problems is largely manual, and the operator can perform only one step at a time. To execute a calculation he must manually store information in the keyboard, and then press other keys to activate the desired operation. Only two numbers can be handled at the same time. Intermediate results not used in the next step must be written down by the operator and re-entered later in the procedure.

TABULATING EQUIPMENT

Punched-card machines are usually traced to the patents of Dr. Herman Hollerith. His predecessors, whose ideas we will discuss later, were Babbage and Jacquard. Hollerith's plan was used in 1889 for the punching, sorting, and tabulation of data for the United States census of 1890.

Another machine was developed in 1907 by James Powers for the 1910 census. The punched-card equipment, produced in later years by the International Business Machines Corporation (IBM) and by the Sperry Rand Corporation, stem largely from the work, respectively, of Hollerith and Powers.

Enormous amounts of human labor can be avoided through the use of punched-card machines. Once information is keypunched into a card, this card can be used again and again in a series of calculations. It is not necessary to enter manually the same data more than once into the information-handling system. The same punched card can also be used for many different problems. Furthermore, the equipment can be instructed to punch out new cards containing the results of calculations. These results can then either be printed out automatically or used for further computations. Thus, where the same operation must be carried out on a great mass of data, stacks of punched cards representing hundreds or thousands of items of information can be processed without human intervention. Once the cards are placed in the machine's input device, called the *hopper,* all the required calculation and printing is executed automatically.

Punched-card machines are electromechanical devices which perform a relatively fixed type of operation. A tabulator, for example, can add, subtract, and print out lists of items with their totals. Other punched-card machines can execute multiplication. It was recognized early that special equipment was necessary for getting input cards in order, for merging card files, and for separating cards into different categories. *Sorters* and *collators* were developed to carry out such activities. These devices automatically read in cards, sensed the information, and shifted the cards to their appropriate pigeon holes. Most punched-card installations consist of a variety of machines such as sorters, collators, keypunches, tabulators, and multipliers.

One of the main disadvantages of most punched-card machines is that they can perform only one operation at a time. A degree of flexibility is provided through control panels which can be changed whenever necessary. These units are plugboards into which wires can be inserted, as in a telephone switchboard. By employing such devices, it is possible to vary somewhat the manner in which a machine executes its range of functions.

Even with this flexibility, however, it is usually necessary to have a separate pass of punched cards through a machine for each operation in a sequence. At most, only a few steps can be performed at a time. The handling of intermediate results is clumsy; these answers must be punched out on new cards which are saved for later entry into the machines. Such procedures require a staff of machine operators for the physical handling of the cards. Punched-card equipment in most instances have no capacity to execute loops; they cannot repeat a sequence of operations without the re-entry of cards into the machine. The performance of branching operations usually involves cumbersome additional procedures.

The same motivation which gave rise to the automatic carry, and to automatic multiplication and division, spurred the invention of *stored program* machines. Equipment was needed which could perform long sequences of operations with branches and loops without human intervention. Three of the machine characteristics required for this technological advance were: the presence of *memory* for storing intermediate results and constant factors used in the computations; the ability of one machine to execute a wide variety of operations; and the control capacity necessary to enable a machine to execute in succession a series of calculations.

It is true that all three of these factors are present in a rudimentary way in simple equipment. The electromechanical counters, which keep a running total when a list of numbers is added, constitute an information storage unit. As has been stated, punched-card machines can perform a narrow range of different operations under the control of the plugboards. And finally, tabulating machines also have the capacity to perform several steps in sequence when preparing and printing subtotals and totals.

THE HISTORY OF STORED PROGRAM MACHINES

The IBM type 604 is illustrative of the evolution of the stored program principle. This equipment is a punched-card machine which has the ability to execute a program of 20 or more steps between the successive reading-in of cards. The wiring of the control panels determines which operations are to be performed in each step. The wiring of the control panel also enables the machine to suppress certain operations under specified conditions. This enables branching to occur. The program can include tests on the results obtained by its past calculations, and can thereby loop back to repeat a series of calculations.

In the IBM 604 the program is fixed in advance by the wiring of the plugboard. A different control panel is needed, therefore, for each problem. The Card-Programmed Calculator (CPC), a more advanced machine, included the IBM 604 as one of its units. In the CPC the sequence of operations was determined by the reading-in of a deck of *instruction cards*. Each card contained an instruction code which actuated the required operation.

Although archaic in comparison with ·modern equipment, the Card-Programmed Calculator represented a significant step forward in data processing technology. The initiation of each machine operation by codes on punched cards introduced great new flexibility. Instead of inserting a different plugboard whenever another problem was to be handled, the user of the equipment had merely to employ a different deck of instruction cards. The same control panel, more or less, could be used for all applications.

Many of the ideas underlying such early computers as the CPC stemmed from the famous work of Professor Charles Babbage of Cambridge University in England, during the period from about 1822 to 1833. Babbage conceived of an *Analytical Engine* which can be regarded as the predecessor of all later automatic computers. Unfortunately, the equipment was never completed, largely because its design was in advance of the engineering technology of the time. The projected machine was composed basically of a data processing unit, aptly called the *mill*. Part of this unit was a *store*, a memory device consisting of groups of 50 counter wheels.

The punched card can be traced back to the Jacquard loom in which cards with holes were used to control the weaving of complicated patterns composed of different color threads. In this control equipment the cards were connected together. It seems, however, that Babbage planned to utilize cards which were not in any way linked.

Machine steps in the Analytic Engine were to be actuated by punched cards. The sequence to be executed was, hence, determined by the order in which the cards were fed into the equipment. Data could be entered into the machine either by cards or by the setting of dials. Information such as intermediate results could be placed in the store and obtained again when needed. The capacity for branching was envisaged, and advanced techniques were devised for the arithmetic units.

The first programmed computer to operate successfully, the Automatic Sequence Controlled Calculator, or Mark I, contained many of the ideas conceived by Babbage, and there is reason to believe that the design of this machine was inspired to some degree by the Analytic Engine. The Mark I was built by Professor Howard Aiken of Harvard University, in conjunction with the International Business Machines Corporation. The construction of this equipment, started about 1939, was completed in 1944. It was composed largely of standard IBM electromechanical devices such as relays, counters, and cams, and reading, punching, and printing units. The sequencing of instructions was mainly by means of a paper tape input. Only a limited capacity for program branching was available.

THE ENIAC

A number of other relay calculators, including the Bell Laboratories machine designed by Dr. George Stibitz, were under construction or completed during the approximate period 1938-1944. However, the decisive breakthrough in the computational art is generally associated with the ENIAC. This machine did not, in its original form, constitute a major logical advance over the Mark I. Nevertheless, it was the first electronic computer, and in this respect was a great stride forward in engineering technology.

The ENIAC was built under the pressures of World War II at the Moore School of Engineering at the University of Pennsylvania. Its purpose as originally conceived was to produce mathematical tables required for the firing of projectiles. These tables involved the numerical integration of differential equations; hence the name *ENIAC* (*E*lectronic *N*umerical *I*ntegrator *a*nd *C*alculator).

Firing or bombing tables are computed by the solution of equations which describe the trajectory of each type of shell with different values of muzzle velocity and angle of fire. Each ballistic table requires the computing and processing of hundreds of trajectories. For these purposes the Army Ordnance Department maintained well over 100 college graduates on the campus of the University of Pennsylvania, along with several hundred hurriedly trained Army employees. In addition, about 100 members of the Women's Army Corps were serving in these duties. These groups, centered at the university, comprised about one-half of the computational center, the remaining part of the organization being located at Aberdeen, Maryland.

Despite the fact that this staff constituted one of the largest computing centers in the world, it soon became apparent that it was far too small to handle the volume of computations needed for the necessary ballistic tables. Professor J. G. Brainerd, now dean of the Moore School, suggested that the Moore School build a digital computer. A contract for the ENIAC was signed, with funds supplied by the Army. The machine was designed by Dr. J. Presper Eckert and Dr. John Mauchly of the Moore School, in cooperation with Major Herman H. Goldstine of Army Ordnance. Numerous other individuals who have since distinguished themselves in the computer field were major contributors to the design of the ENIAC. Among the first to join this group was Arthur Burks, who had received his Ph.D. in philosophy at the University of Michigan. Burks (now a professor at the University of Michigan) came to the Moore School to take technical courses, and was an Assistant Professor of Electrical Engineering when ENIAC was started.

The designers of the machine were young men—Eckert, for example, was in his early twenties, and Goldstine, 32. The actual construction of ENIAC consisted mainly of the wiring of electrical circuits, and a large part of this work was done by housewives. Many of the networks were checked out by employees of the telephone company during their off-hours. About half a million dollars was spent for the development and manufacture of ENIAC. The machine, completed in 1946 after three years of work, was moved to the Ballistic Research Laboratory at the Aberdeen Proving Grounds. At the time the equipment was built, electronic engineering techniques were in their early stages, and the failure rate of tubes was very high. Since every tube in the machine had to be operative at the same time, ENIAC could be used only when all of its 18,000 tubes (and 1500 relays) were functioning properly. Despite these difficulties, however, the machine was a success. A skilled human operator using a desk calculator can compute in about 20 hours the trajectory of a shell which is in the air for 60 seconds; ENIAC could perform this computation in 30 seconds.

Two types of circuits existed in ENIAC: lines for the transmission of numbers, and lines for carrying control signals. As originally designed, a problem was set up on the calculator by making several hundred manual adjustments. The equipment consisted of a number of different processing units, each of which had its own set of controls. The control system for a given unit was impulsed by a signal from another unit. When this operation was completed, an output signal was sent to other units to initiate their operations. This method of computing was called *local programming*. To prepare ENIAC for a calculation it was necessary beforehand to set up manually all of the connections for the transmission of data from one unit to another. Each unit had to be wired to recognize when it was to start and to recognize which operation it was to perform. The sequence of processing was determined by the input and output signals between units. All of the units operated in synchronism with each other, and it was possible for several units to operate simultaneously.

The major theoretical advance in computer design resulted from the work of John Von Neumann, one of the greatest mathematicians of the twentieth century. Born in Budapest in 1903, he was a child prodigy, reading Latin and Greek at the age of five. Von Neumann received his doctorate in 1926, and joined the staff of Princeton University in 1930. Shortly afterwards he became a professor of mathematics at the Institute for Advanced Study, in which position he remained for the duration of his life. In 1955 he became a member of the U.S. Atomic Energy Commission, where he served until his death from cancer in 1957. Among his many achievements were important contributions to quantum mechanics. In mathematical logic, he was a forerunner to the great logician Goedel. Von Neumann was the founder of the theory of games, a mathematical analysis of human strategies in such social situations as the distribution of economic goods in a market.

Von Neumann early recognized the importance of computing machinery for mathematics, scientific computation, economics, and for industrial and military problems. While the ENIAC was being built, Von

Neumann, in conjunction with others, made an extensive study of the logical design of computing machines. It was in this period that he suggested the use of a stored program. This brilliant conception was to revolutionize the technology of automatic data processing. The idea stemmed both from practical necessity and previous theoretical developments. There was an urgent need for extensive scientific and engineering computation. These calculations involved numerous *loop* sequences, and a new technique was required to enable this iterative data processing to be carried out by machine.

Early studies in pure logic made by A. M. Turing, it is believed, influenced Von Neumann at this point to suggest the stored program as an answer to this problem. The notion, basically, was to store instructions in a machine in the same manner as data. This would enable machine commands to be manipulated by arithmetic and logical operations. In this way, a machine would have the ability to change and modify its instructions. This capacity opened up vast new horizons in flexibility and self-control.

One of the first reports in which these ideas of Von Neumann appeared was a 1945 study defining a proposed machine called EDVAC (*E*lectronic *D*iscrete *V*ariable *A*utomatic *C*omputer). Eckert and Mauchly had begun to design this equipment while the ENIAC was still under construction. In 1946 another paper followed, discussing these conceptions in greater detail. This report was published in collaboration with Goldstine and Burks, who had joined Von Neumann at the Institute for Advanced Study for development of another machine.

Neither the EDVAC nor the Institute machine were completed for several years. The former was placed in operation in 1950, and the latter in 1952. Meanwhile, in 1947, Von Neumann suggested a method for converting ENIAC into a stored program machine. Previously, as has been stated, this equipment consisted of a number of different units, and a large number of wires had to be plugged manually to prepare each unit for executing its operations. The sequence in which units executed their operations was determined by signals sent from one unit to another during the running of the machine.

Under the scheme proposed by Von Neumann, the operation carried out by each unit was fixed by permanent wiring. Each unit was placed under a central control. An arrangement was made to enable codes to be stored in memory for the actuation of the necessary operations. The sequence of commands necessary for solving a problem was given to the machine in the form of a list of coded instructions stored in the memory. The central control system was designed to obtain and execute commands in the same order in which they were stored. Special instructions enabled the machine to perform branching and looping by modifying the sequence in which instructions were obtained from memory. These methods have now become basic to all data processing machines, and we shall discuss how they work in a later chapter.

The converting of ENIAC into a stored program machine was carried out by a group including Adele Goldstine (wife of Dr. Herman H. Goldstine), B. Bartik, R. Clippinger, and A. Gehring. Von Neumann played a major role in implementing the details. Since ENIAC was the first stored program machine in operation as well as the first electronic computer, it can in large measure be regarded as the prototype of all later equipment.

The advantages of the new ENIAC were fourfold:

1. It became much faster and easier to prepare problems for the machine. Previously, much more elaborate specifications had to be set up. These involved the plugging in and out of cables, and the setting and resetting of switches. With the centralization of control, more complex operations could be called for and the amount of human effort needed could be reduced.

2. Problems of greater complexity could be handled as a result of the increased flexibility afforded by stored program techniques. Problems about four times longer could also be prepared.

3. The manual time for readying the machine for its next problem was reduced tremendously. Under the old system it was a day's work to set up the equipment. It now became possible to enter a problem on the machine in about an hour by setting switches in the memory unit. Checking the wiring for accuracy, formerly an arduous task, was now much simpler.

4. Engineering tests became easier under central rather than local programming.

THE RISE OF THE MODERN COMPUTER

The EDVAC report stimulated the design and production of two computers in England. The EDSAC (*E*lectronic *D*elayed *S*torage *A*utomatic *C*omputer), completed at the Mathematical Laboratory at the University of Cambridge in 1949, under the direction of M. V. Wilkes, was actually the first machine with a stored program to be completed and put into use. This machine utilized mercury delay lines as storage, and input-output was by teletype tape read photoelectrically. Another computer, designed in 1945 and completed in 1950 at the National Physical Laboratory by Womersley, Turing (the logician), and Colebrook, was called the ACE (*A*utomatic *C*alculating *E*ngine).

During the period between the definition and physical completion of the EDVAC and the Institute for Advanced Study machines, a number of other computers were built and placed in operation. The IBM Selective Sequence Electronic Calculator (SSEC) was put into use in 1948. This machine had both electronic and electromechanical circuits, the former being used for arithmetic, storage, and control. Instructions were entered into the machine by means of punched tapes. The SEAC (Bureau of Standards Eastern Automatic Computer) was placed in service in Washington, D.C., in 1951. Jay Forrester at the Massachusetts Institute of Technology was responsible for the production of Whirlwind I, using cathode-ray storage. Another type of cathode-ray storage machine was developed by F. C. Williams at the University of Manchester in England.

Early utilization of the magnetic drum as a memory unit is associated with SEC (Simple Electronic Computer) at the University of London, the ERA 1101 computer (built by Engineering Research Associates), and Mark III and Mark IV at Harvard. The UNIVAC (Universal Automatic Computer) was built by Eckert and Mauchly, who left the University of Pennsylvania to form their own company. This machine used mercury delay lines for storage, and magnetic tapes as input-output devices. Information was placed on tape by means of a card-to-tape converter and by direct transcription on to tape by the Unityper. The Eckert-Mauchly company (as well as Engineering Research Associates) later became parts of the Sperry Rand Corporation.

One of the first successful electronic devices for handling business information was the Reservisor, a magnetic drum machine operated by American Airlines for tallying flight reservations. Agents of the airline could interrogate the drum at any time to ascertain the availability of seats on future flights. However, the Reservisor was a special-purpose machine with a fixed sequence of built-in processing steps.

With the advent of UNIVAC and such machines as IBM's Card-Programmed Calculator, the 650, 701, and the 702, a pioneering era came to a close, and electronic data processing began to emerge as a major industry. Farsighted individuals had long envisaged the use of this machinery for the needs of business and government. Their prophecies were now fulfilled by a vast market for such applications, running into billions of dollars. However, despite the development of many sophisticated techniques in logical design and programming, it seems reasonable to assert that no radical change has occurred since Von Neumann suggested the stored program. The equipment used at the end of a decade was still heavily influenced by conceptions which had originated from the needs of scientific computation. It may be that the next great advance will stem from the development of machine systems which are capable of artificial intelligence and instantaneous response to many simultaneous inputs.

See page 213

3 PUNCHED-CARD MACHINES

PUNCHED CARDS

The punched card is the medium most commonly used for entering information into data processing systems. Many billions of these cards are produced every year by various manufacturers.

The IBM punched card contains 80 vertical columns, each having

Card columns	Name of field
1-2	date (month)
3-4	date (day)
5	date (year–last digit)
6-7	number of entry
8-29	customer name
30-31	invoice date (month)
32-33	invoice date (day)
34-38	invoice number
39-43	customer number
44-45	location (state code)
46-48	location (city code)
49-51	trade class
52-53	branch code
54-56	salesman number
57-58	date paid (month)
59-60	date paid (day)
61	date paid (year–last digit)
62	reason code
63-67	discount allowed
68-73	amount paid
74-80	invoice amount

positions (rows) numbered 0, 1, 2, 3, 4, 5, 6, 7, 8, 9. Each column represents one character. Figure 3-1 shows a punched card with columns one through eight punched to represent the number 36214901.

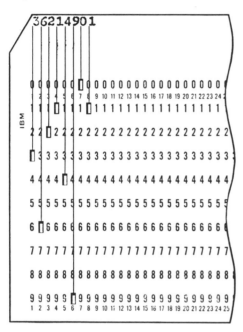

FIGURE 3-1 Punched card with columns 1-8 punched to represent the number 36214901.

Above the 0 row there are two unmarked positions called the 11 and 12 rows, which are also available for punching (Fig. 3-2). The 0, 11, and 12 rows are called the *zones*. By combining a numerical (digit) punch with a zone punch, a code for an alphabetic character is produced.

A group of columns used for the representation of a particular item of information is called a *field*. A number of fields may be placed on the same card. The capacity of a punched card is 80 columns of information. Often all 80 of these columns are used to represent fields. Figure 3-3 shows an accounts receivable card completely packed with information. Certain basic data punched into the card has been printed on top of the card to facilitate the use of the card by humans.

When a numerical field is negative, the usual convention is to place an 11 punch (called an *X* punch) over the unit's position of the number. In the absence of an *X* punch, the field is assumed to be positive. Punched-card processing equipment can be instructed to distinguish between negative numbers and the alphabetic characters J-R, which use an 11 punch as their zone.

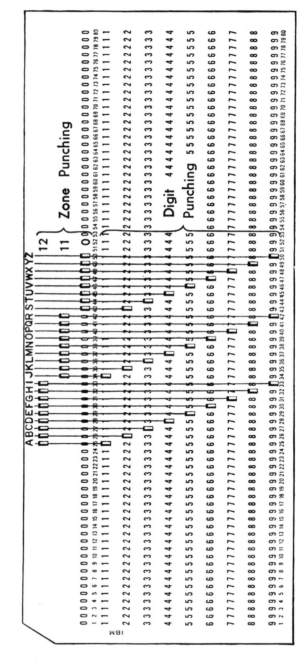

FIGURE 3-2 A punched card combining zone punches and numerical punches to produce codes for alphabetic characters.

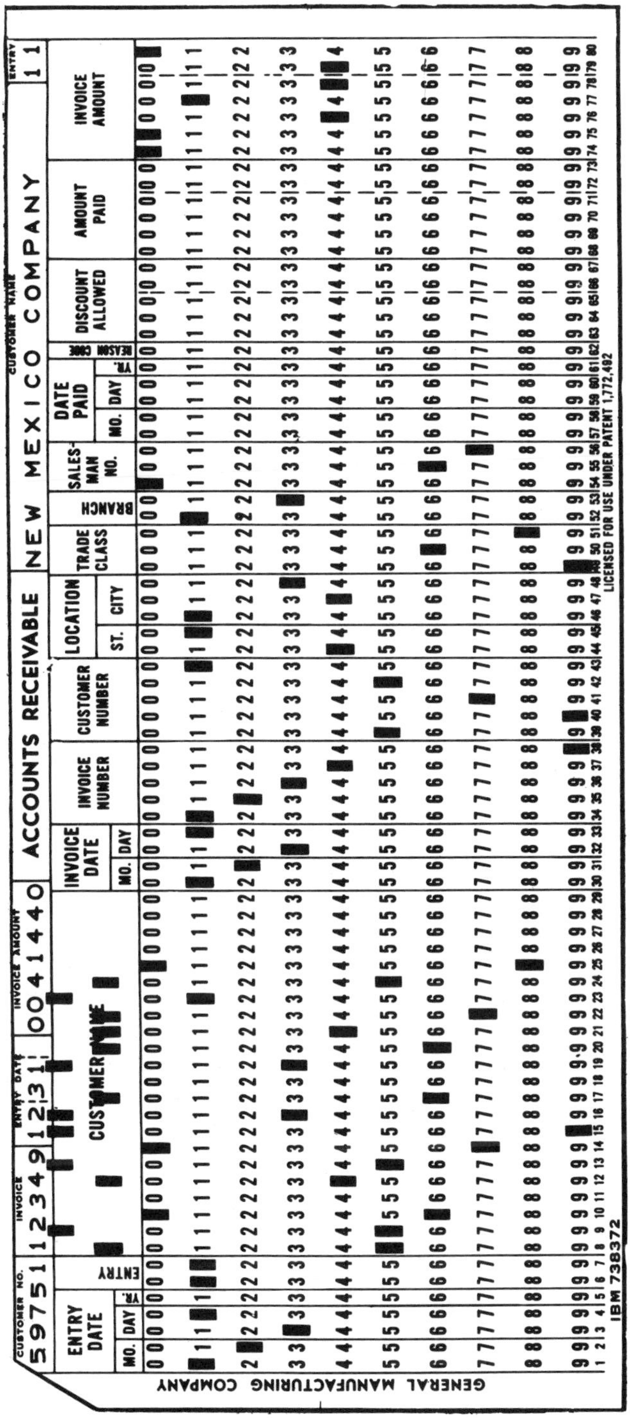

FIGURE 3-3 A punched card filled with accounts receivable information.

23

Information is punched into cards by operators of keypunch machines, who obtain the data from source documents. These documents are usually paper forms, such as checks, bills, purchase orders, or credit memoranda, prepared by humans when originating a business transaction. In scientific and engineering computations the source documents are data sheets containing physical observations. A typical commercial application is based on thousands of paper forms. The information on each of these forms is converted to punched cards. The keypunch operator punches the information from each source document into the specified columns in each card. In this way, thousands or even millions of standard unit records can be created to serve as the input for the data processing machine.

The keypunch machine is similar to a typewriter in that it has a keyboard. In most instances there is an automatic feeding mechanism which moves blank cards into a position for punching. Various conveniences are present, such as the ability to skip over columns which are not to be punched.

SENSING PUNCHED CARDS

Punched-card machines are electromechanical. They are driven by gears connected to an electric motor. The cards to be processed are placed in a receptacle called a *hopper*, which can hold several hundred cards. The rotation of a central shaft within the machine is called a *cycle*. At the end of each such time period the next card to be processed is mechanically grasped from the hopper.

How does the machine sense what information is contained in a card? The cycle, analogously to a clock, is divided into 12 parts, known as *1-time*, *2-time*, etc. At each of these moments a timing signal is produced. When a card enters the machine from the hopper, it passes over an electrically charged roller. A metallic brush connected to a source of electricity passes over each card column. The card acts as an insulator between the brush and the roller. Whenever a hole is present in the card, a brush comes in contact with the roller, and an electric current flows. This impulse represents information.

Each punch position in the card passes over the roller in synchronism with the timing signals produced during the cycle. For example, as the brush passes over the 2 position, the 2-time signal is emitted by the machine. If a hole is present in this position, the resulting electrical impulse will occur at the same time as the 2-time signal. In this way the machine can recognize what information is present in every column of a punched card.

TABULATING MACHINES

Tabulating machines still perform a large part of the data processing carried on throughout the world. Despite their elementary nature, the problems involved in utilizing this equipment most effectively often present a challenge to clever and resourceful people.

One of the simplest of these machines is the punched-card sorter. The sorter has pockets corresponding to each of the punching positions on a punched card. There are receptacles labeled 0, 1, 2, 3, 4, 5, 6, 7, 8, 9 for the digit punches. In addition, there are 11 and 12 pockets for the zone punches, as well as a reject pocket for unpunched cards.

The cards to be sorted are first placed in the hopper of the machine. A start button actuates the machine to grasp the lowest card in the hopper. This card is moved automatically to a "sensing station" where brushes pick up the information in the column. The electrical impulse resulting from a punched hole in the column represents one of the digits 0-9. This signal initiates a mechanical movement of the card into the corresponding pocket. The particular pocket to which a card is sent is thus determined by the punch in the column.

Each successive bottom card in the hopper goes through this process during every machine cycle. The output cards pile up in the 10 pockets. Processing continues until no input cards are left in the hopper.

The sorter described here is completely single-purpose—all it can do is sort. The machine has only one type of flexibility, the ability to sort on different columns of a punched card. The operator can adjust a handle before starting the machine, which instructs the equipment which of the 80 columns to sense.

PLUGBOARDS

The most important output from a punched-card machine is a printed report. The simplest output is a listing of the information contained in a stack of punched cards. Figure 3-4 shows the print-out of some of the information on a punched card.

Note that the data on the card is re-ordered on the listing, and that some of this information is omitted from the print-out. Each print position in a row of type is assigned a number, and the user of the machine has the option of placing printed characters anywhere he wishes in this horizontal line. For example, the words ABBOT BRASS in Fig. 3-4 occupies print positions 1 through 11, as follows:

A	B	B	O	T		B	R	A	S	S
1	2	3	4	5	6	7	8	9	10	11

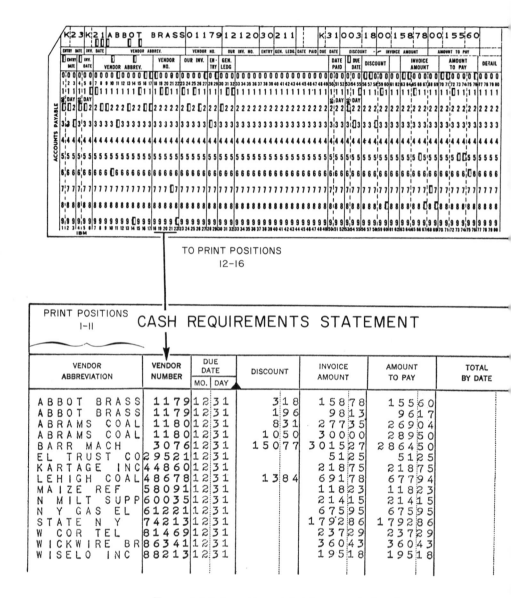

TO PRINT POSITIONS
12-16

PRINT POSITIONS
1-11

CASH REQUIREMENTS STATEMENT

VENDOR ABBREVIATION	VENDOR NUMBER	DUE DATE MO.	DUE DATE DAY	DISCOUNT	INVOICE AMOUNT	AMOUNT TO PAY	TOTAL BY DATE
A B B O T B R A S S	1 1 7 9	1 2	3 1	3 1 8	1 5 8 7 8	1 5 5 6 0	
A B B O T B R A S S	1 1 7 9	1 2	3 1	1 9 6	9 8 1 3	9 6 1 7	
A B R A M S C O A L	1 1 8 0	1 2	3 1	8 3 1	2 7 7 3 5	2 6 9 0 4	
A B R A M S C O A L	1 1 8 0	1 2	3 1	1 0 5 0	3 0 0 0 0	2 8 9 5 0	
B A R R M A C H	3 0 7 6	1 2	3 1	1 5 0 7 7	3 0 1 5 2 7	2 8 6 4 5 0	
E L T R U S T C O	2 9 5 2 1	1 2	3 1		5 1 2 5	5 1 2 5	
K A R T A G E I N C	4 4 8 6 0	1 2	3 1		2 1 8 7 5	2 1 8 7 5	
L E H I G H C O A L	4 8 6 7 8	1 2	3 1	1 3 8 4	6 9 1 7 8	6 7 7 9 4	
M A I Z E R E F	5 8 0 9 1	1 2	3 1		1 1 8 2 3	1 1 8 2 3	
N M I L T S U P P	6 0 0 3 5	1 2	3 1		2 1 4 1 5	2 1 4 1 5	
N Y G A S E L	6 1 2 2 1	1 2	3 1		6 7 5 9 5	6 7 5 9 5	
S T A T E N Y	7 4 2 1 3	1 2	3 1		1 7 9 2 8 6	1 7 9 2 8 6	
W C O R T E L	8 1 4 6 9	1 2	3 1		2 3 7 2 9	2 3 7 2 9	
W I C K W I R E B R	8 6 3 4 1	1 2	3 1		3 6 0 4 3	3 6 0 4 3	
W I S E L O I N C	8 8 2 1 3	1 2	3 1		1 9 5 1 8	1 9 5 1 8	

FIGURE 3-4 Information printed from punched card.

26

In accounting machines 80 brushes are provided at the station where the punched card is sensed. The entire 80 columns are thus read simultaneously. A hypothetical nonflexible machine would simply take information from each column of the input card and would print it out directly at the corresponding position on the output report, as shown in Fig. 3-5.

```
Card column                          Print position
sensed            Internal  wiring   actuated
   1  ──────────────────────────────▶ 1
   2  ──────────────────────────────▶ 2
   3  ──────────────────────────────▶ 3
   4  ──────────────────────────────▶ 4
   5  ──────────────────────────────▶ 5
```

FIGURE 3-5 Print-out of columns in corresponding print positions on a report.

Such a one-to-one direct connection would be impractical, for flexibility in the rearrangement of input information is necessary. Therefore, instead of connecting each reading brush directly to a print position, the circuit is broken and two separate wires, one from each sensed card column and one from each print position, are brought to a plugboard. This unit consists of terminals (hubs) placed near the side of the machine.

In the center of Fig. 3-6 we see the hubs brought from print positions and the sensing stations. Any print position hub can be connected by wire to any sensing station hub. Here we see the plugboard wired so that the field in card columns 18-22 is printed out in print positions 12-16.

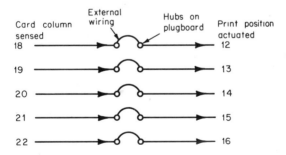

FIGURE 3-6 Plugboard wired across hubs so that field in card columns 18-22 will be printed out in print positions 12-16.

The plugboard is also known as the *control panel*. By using this device the user of the equipment has complete flexibility in rearranging input data when it is printed out. Connections on the plugboard are made in a manner similar to the insertion of plugs in the hubs of a telephone switchboard.

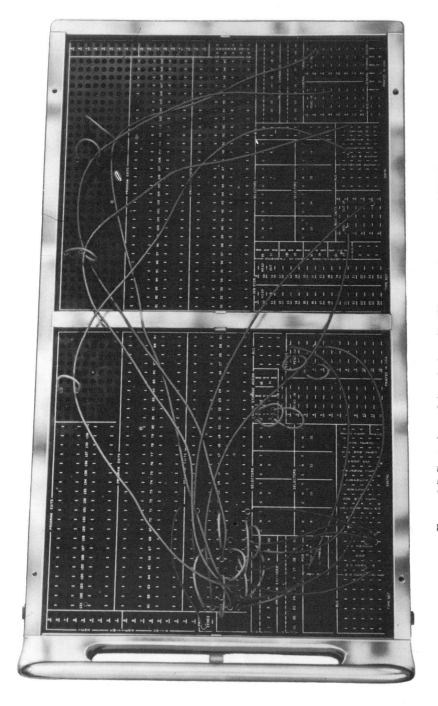

FIGURE 3-7 Control panel (or plugboard). (Photograph courtesy of IBM)

The plugboard (Fig. 3-7) performs a large number of complex control functions. In many instances the plugboard becomes a highly involved pattern of numerous intertwined wires. The wires have plugs at both ends. When both ends of the wire are plugged into hubs, these hubs are connected and an electric current can flow between different internal parts of the machine.

The same machine must frequently be used for a variety of applications within a few hours. It would be inefficient if the control panel had to be rewired for each different problem. Therefore, plugboards are designed to be detached easily from machines. Installations keep a number of plugboards permanently wired. In this way the control system of a machine can be changed rapidly.

REPRODUCING MACHINES

What has been said about flexibility in printing also applies to machines which reproduce punched cards. It is often necessary to duplicate some or all of the information in one card into another card. In so doing, rearrangements of the data are frequently needed. The reproducing machine has two hoppers—one feeds in the original punched cards, the other furnishes blank cards to be punched as outputs. Electromagnets

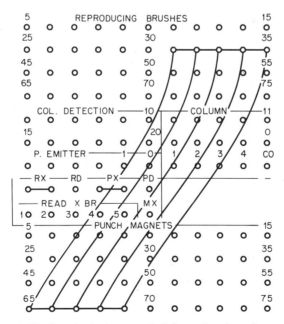

FIGURE 3-8 Plugboard wired to punch information from input card columns 31-35 into columns 65-69 on output cards.

control the punches which make holes in the specified rows and columns of the blank cards. The plugboard routes input information from the reading brushes to any desired punch. We see in Fig. 3-8 a plugboard wired to punch the information in columns 31-35 of input cards into columns 65-69 of blank output cards.

Punched-card machines usually have the capacity to produce information which is not in the original input card. For example, in reproducing a deck of cards it may be desirable to include today's date in every new card. This is accomplished by making the timing signals produced at 1-time, 2-time, etc., available on the control panel. These signals can be used to actuate the punch magnets to punch a date in any specified columns of the new cards. A 6-time signal, for example, produces a 6-punch when wired through the plugboard to the punch for a particular column.

COMPARISON TECHNIQUES

In conventional punched-card equipment comparisons are carried out by a thin metallic strip called an *armature*. The armature is placed between two electromagnets. When two columns are to be compared, the reading brush of each is wired through the control panel to an electromagnet. If both columns have punched in them the same information, both electromagnets are energized simultaneously, and exert equal but opposite pulls on the armature. The armature therefore remains stationary. However, if the punches in the columns are different, the armature will be attracted away from its neutral position. The armature is like a switch in that its movement opens or closes two possible circuits, thereby telling the machine whether or not the columns are equal. Any number of columns can be compared if enough devices of this type are available.

How does the machine discern which of two fields is larger? When two columns are unequal, the armature will move toward each electromagnet at different times. Suppose card A, column 43, contains an 8, and the same column in card B contains a 3. The card enters the machine in such a way that the order of sensing is 9's row, 8's row, 7's row, etc. Therefore, the 8 in card A will be read first, and the comparing magnet to which card A is wired will attract the armature before card B's electromagnet. The first circuit activated by the armature indicates which column is higher.

Any two fields of data can be compared by means of control panel wiring. The hubs from the reading brushes are wired to the comparing magnets. These magnets, arranged in pairs, enable any two columns to be compared with each other. Figure 3-9 shows the reading brush for column 43 of both card A and card B wired to a pair of comparing magnets.

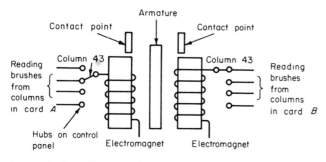

FIGURE 3-9 Control panel hubs wired to compare two columns of data.

The comparison of fields on the same or on different cards plays an important role in the ordering, summarizing, and selecting of data. The result of a comparison is an impulse which can be used for control purposes. In this way the machines can make decisions. Such choices are, to a large extent, the basis for the capacity of the equipment to "think" and to possess "intelligence."

THE COLLATOR

The collating machine is based upon the utilization of comparing magnets. One of the main uses of this equipment is to merge two sets of cards, each of which is already in sequence. The sequence is constituted by a number in each card, for example:

set No. 1 cards	4, 8, 9, 23, 29, 101
set No. 2 cards	3, 6, 7, 38

After collation, the resulting deck of cards appears as

3, 4, 6, 7, 8, 9, 23, 29, 38, 101

It is true that this function could be carried out by the sorter. However, since the cards are already sequenced within each group, it is more efficient to perform an interfiling activity. The collator compares cards from two input hoppers containing, respectively, set No. 1 cards and set No. 2 cards. The signals resulting from the comparisons are sent to the plugboard. The selection of the next hopper to read from is under the control of the plugboard, as is the output of cards into the stacker. In this way the signals from the comparing magnets can be used to place the incoming cards in sequence.

SELECTION

One of the most powerful decision-making capacities available in punched-card machines is the ability to select certain cards for special processing.

Selection is carried out by means of a relay. A relay is an electromagnetic switch. When the electromagnet (Fig. 3-10) is actuated, an armature is attracted. This closes an electric circuit, thereby causing current to flow. When the electromagnet is not actuated, the armature is pulled back by springs. This opens the circuit, making it impossible for electric current to flow.

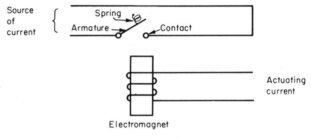

FIGURE 3-10 Relay.

Suppose a tabulating machine is processing a deck of cards. Let's assume that a special calculation must be carried out on certain of these cards. The special cards have an X-punch in column 80. What we do is to wire the plugboard so that, whenever a card is sensed with an X-punch in column 80, an impulse is sent to actuate the electromagnet. This closes the relay's circuit, which causes the special calculation to be executed. All cards lacking this special punch do not actuate the electromagnet and, hence, are processed normally.

ADDITION

In conventional punched-card equipment, addition takes place by means of groups of *counter* wheels (Fig. 3-11). Segments of the circumference of each wheel represent the digits 0, 1, 2, 3, 4, 5, 6, 7, 8, 9. When a hole in a card column is sensed, an impulse is routed, via wiring on the control panel, to the counter, causing it to turn until 0-time occurs. It will be recalled that the 9 position of a card is sensed at 9-time. Next comes 8-time, during which the 8 position is sensed. This continues until 0-time. The counter wheel will therefore turn a number of positions equal to the number punched in the card column.

Consider the addition $4 + 3 = 7$. Assume the counter originally is in state 4, and a column with a 3-punch is read. The wheel is immediately actuated to move at 3-time, and will continue to turn during 2-time and 1-time. When 0-time occurs, the wheel comes to a stop in position 7.

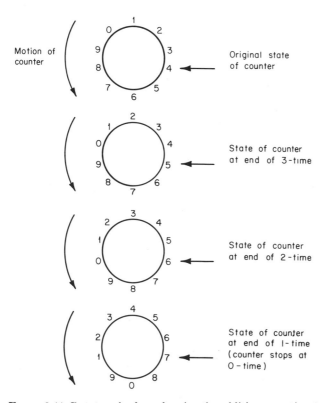

FIGURE 3-11 Counter wheels performing the addition operation $4 + 3 = 7$.

Each wheel in a group represents one of the digits in a number. When any wheel passes from its 9 position to its 0 position, the wheel to its left automatically turns one position forward. In this way carries from each digit position to the next are achieved.

Counters are controlled by plugboard wiring. Each card column in fields to be added must be wired to a counter, and every counter whose sum is to be printed out must be wired to a print position.

The resetting of counters to zero and the printing of totals are under the control of relays available at the control panel. This feature enables the machine to print various levels of subtotals and grand totals. Let us suppose that the input cards are arranged in three sequential groups, represented by the number 1, 2, or 3 in column 30. By comparing column

30 in every input card with its successor card, an unequal signal is obtained when one group ends and the next starts. This impulse is used to initiate the printing of a subtotal. A grand total is obtained by wiring the control panel to add subtotals (from each counter group) into another higher-level counter group.

"PROGRAM START" CONTROLS

An unequal comparison obtained in an accounting machine provides a signal which can be used for controlling the machine's functions. To clear counters containing subtotals, as well as to print these numbers and to add them into other counters for accumulation of higher-level totals, the unequal signal is wired to a *program start* hub. This hub, in turn, is wired to other contacts on the plugboard. When the program start

City	Office	Salesman	Product	Amount and total by salesman	Total by office	Total by city
1	1	1	A	12.40		
			B	6.28		
			C	14.82		
			D	12.45		
				61.95*		
		2	A	28.64		
			B	4.26		
			C	42.63		
				75.53*		
					137.48*	
	2	1	A	10.16		
			B	4.22		
				14.38*		
	2	2	B	42.50		
			C	53.72		
			D	10.81		
				107.03*		
					121.41*	
						258.89*
2	1	1	A	48.21		
			B	33.33		

FIGURE 3-12 Use of program start controls to produce subtotal and grand totals. (Machine inserts asterisk when it produces a total.)

hub is energized, the machine ceases reading in more cards until one or more activities called *program cycles* occur. During these program cycles the wire from the program hub actuates a sequence of processes. Generally, the program hub is connected to hubs which activate the subtotaling and resetting of counters, as discussed above.

Accounting machines have different program start hubs available for each level of subtotaling required. In the simplest case, three program starts are available, called minor, intermediate, and major, corresponding to the level of totaling required. In Fig. 3-12 the minor total is by salesman number, the intermediate by office number, and the major total by city code. It is apparent that three totals are needed when city changes, two when office changes, and one when salesman changes. When the comparing magnets indicate that there is a change in salesman, the minor program start makes one program cycle available for the salesman subtotal. When office changes, the intermediate program start provides two cycles and when city changes, three program cycles are available for the three totals which are needed at this point.

CONTROL OF INPUT DATA

1568791

One of the ways in which tabulating equipment is used in conjunction with electronic data processing machines is in readying data for input into the computer. No matter how well a problem is understood, and regardless of how carefully the machine solution is organized, a computer cannot produce correct results if the input data are fallacious.

This fact is particularly prominent in business data processing where the volume of input data is extremely large. In a big commercial installation there are rooms in which dozens and dozens of keypunchers are perpetually at work preparing punched cards to be used as input into a computer. It is unavoidable for a small percentage of mistakes to be made by these keypunchers in transcribing information from source documents to punched cards. Verifying machines are used to catch such errors.

The operator of a verifying machine makes use of a stack of cards previously punched, along with the source documents from which they were prepared, and operates her keyboard as if repunching these cards. A signal appears if there is any disparity between the original keypunching and the repunching done on the verifier. Certain types of errors result not so much from keypunching mistakes as from ambiguity in the source document. For example, the number 1 may be very similar to the number 7 when handwritten. Sometimes the alphabetic O is confused with the number 0.

Despite careful keypunching and verification, errors in the transcription of source data nevertheless occur. Therefore, it is necessary to set up *controls* on the input data, to the extent that this is possible.

One way of establishing control upon the data entered into the system is to take an adding machine total of the quantity fields in each of the source documents, along with a tabulating machine total of the same fields in the punched cards. These totals should obviously be equal. Should a keypunching mistake have been made, a disparity would occur, except in the unlikely case of compensating errors. A short consideration indicates that it is necessary to classify the source documents by small batches, each with its own total, and to compare these sums with the totals from the punched cards. Otherwise, if there are a large number of source documents and punched cards, finding an error would be like looking for a needle in a haystack. With an input of, say, 20,000 source documents, it would obviously be impractical to compare each card with each document, in the attempt to locate an error.

An easier way to locate an error might be to break the 20,000 source documents into batches of 20, each with a subtotal. Batches of 50 batches would have their own subtotals, and the grand total would be a total of 20 of the latter batches. When the punched cards are prepared, they can then be listed and totaled on tabulating equipment. If there is a disparity in the grand total, it is simple enough to narrow the error down to a group of 20 cards. When a mistake is located, a correct card is prepared and the erroneous card destroyed.

This above method of control also takes care of the possibility of source documents or cards being lost or mislaid, in which case the machine would, of course, produce incorrect results. This type of control can also be achieved by establishing a count of the number of source documents, and by comparing this count with the number of punched cards prepared. A disparity means either that some source documents were misplaced somewhere enroute to the keypuncher, or that some duplicate cards were produced. Batching for the control count is, obviously, also necessary in this method.

Another problem in control is the possibility of mistakes in nonquantitative fields such as names and codes. The keypuncher may prepare a card for Mr. John E. Doe instead of Mr. John F. Doe, or may prepare a card specifying the shipment of stock item No. BG583E instead of No. RG583E. Such errors result in irate customers and unnecessary expense. One way of averting these mistakes is to take a "hash total" of alphanumeric fields, that is, simply to add the fields together, arriving at totals which are themselves meaningless, but which serve to check on the transcription from source documents to punched cards.

In actual practice there are many problems in batching input data for the purposes of control. To make comparisons of subtotals practical, for example, it is necessary to identify the punched cards which belong to each batch, and to keep these cards in the same order as the original source documents. One solution to this problem is to staple batches together with a tag containing the batch number. When the cards are prepared, the batch number is actually keypunched into each card. This method involves a great deal of additional keypunching, and it is therefore preferable, if possible, to use codes which happen to be in the cards as the basis for batching.

In punched-card data processing systems, it is necessary not only to establish controls on the input, but also to keep track of the flow of information as it passes through the system. These procedures are often extremely complicated, involving scores of machine runs during which information is moved around, sorted, filed, retrieved from files, tabulated, etc. It is therefore customary to take accounting controls after most processing steps on the machines, for when tens of thousands of cards are handled it is easy for cards to become misplaced or in some way mishandled.

KEEPING THE MACHINES BUSY

In installations of punched-card machines there are often complicated scheduling problems. All of the machines comprising an installation must be kept as busy as possible, for this equipment represents either a rental expense or a capital investment. For economic reasons, therefore, it is desirable to minimize the number of machines needed in the installation to do the required processing jobs with the necessary speed and efficiency. To keep the machines busy, it is often necessary not to wait until all of the cards have been processed in one type of machine before going on to the next step. Rather, the cards which have already been processed by machine No. 1 will be placed, if possible, in machine No. 2, so that processes No. 1 and No. 2 can be overlapped, thereby cutting down the time required for the entire job. The result is that there is often a bewildering amount of card handling taking place, and only a person well acquainted with the installation can know what any given stack of cards represents in terms of the procedures taking place at a given time.

Similar problems exist in electronic computer installations. Here, there is usually subsidiary equipment in operation while the computer itself is running. This equipment, which we will talk about later, is concerned with such processes as the printing or punching out of the information on magnetic tape, or with the converting of punched-card data to magnetic tape. The operations of the computer and these subordinate devices are often interdependent. Sometimes one machine run cannot take place until a processing has been completed on another unit. Proper scheduling is, hence, necessary to avoid having any machine idle because it is waiting for other equipment to finish. The optimum situation, of course, is where all machines are busy all of the time.

In some businesses a problem is created by the late arrival of source transactions at the data processing installation. This may disrupt a carefully planned schedule of equipment usage.

Generally, an installation is used for a number of different applications. It can be ascertained how long each machine run will take, and when outputs such as paychecks, bills, and management reports must be ready. The schedule is based upon these facts.

It is sometimes possible to devise special procedures for entering late information into a processing system. However, when data is unexpectedly tardy, it often becomes difficult or impossible to meet output deadlines. A commercial data processing installation is, of course, part of a going concern, and its problems are always subordinated to the actual activities which enable the business to survive and grow.

4 THE ORGANIZATION AND FUNCTIONS OF A MODERN COMPUTER

APPLICATIONS

The main value of electronic data processing machines is that they are faster, cheaper, and more reliable than humans. Applications may be classified as information handling or computation. Business and governmental record keeping usually centers around some systematic way of storing, adjusting, summarizing, and making reference to information. In science and engineering, on the other hand, the task consists primarily of the evaluation of mathematical functions, rather than maintaining files.

There are many applications, however, where communication facilities are of equal importance to processing and computing capacity. These are situations where an immediate response to a problem is required. For example, in an airline reservation system, passengers' inquiries concerning the availability of seats must be answered at once. Precise, timely records must be kept of the unfilled seats on all present and future flights. The inquiries enter the reservation system from a large geographical area. To handle situations of this type, machine systems consist of a central intelligence at the center of a communication network. Information pours in continually from remote input terminals, and reports are transmitted back immediately to display units.

In many instances communication-based data processing equipment is used not simply to receive, process, and transmit information, but also to perform a control function. Such machine systems are used in situations which are so fast moving and complex that humans cannot make the necessary decisions with sufficient speed. The SAGE-BOMARC system, for example, monitors all airplane flights around the United

States, and is always ready to dispatch missiles to intercept enemy aircraft. The regulation of industrial processes, such as oil refineries, is another type of application where electronic computers can handle a problem too difficult for unaided humans.

Both conventional and communication-based machines will probably be utilized increasingly for understanding and optimizing complicated problems of a sociological or economic nature. High-speed data processing has made it possible for mathematical and logical techniques to be applied to many of these situations. A wholesaler, for example, must maintain a certain inventory in order to supply his retailer customers promptly. However, if he keeps too large a stock of goods on hand, his operating costs become excessive. There is always a delay when he orders replacements from manufacturers. Computers can be used to study the most profitable inventory level and re-order point. Problems in the allocation of resources on a national scope can also be analyzed with data processing equipment.

To what extent will computers ultimately be capable of bettering the performance of their human masters? Is there any limit to the construction of machines with artificial intelligence? Later on we will discuss whether machines can perform such mental activities as learning and solving logical problems. This has been the aim of research on programming computers to play chess and checkers. An abstract branch of mathematics, the theory of automata, is concerned with the theoretical limitations of machines.

THE INNER WORKINGS OF ELECTRONIC COMPUTERS

The solution of a problem by an electronic computer requires an automatic sequence of machine steps. Hence, to understand an application in detail it is necessary to study the manner in which the equipment is programmed.

What enables a machine to carry out these instructions? Underlying each command a computer executes is a network of switching and memory devices. The manner in which these elements are organized is called *machine logic*. The physical basis for these elements is the actual electronic components of which the machine is comprised.

Let's examine these inner workings in greater detail. The purpose of data processing machines is to transform patterns of information. The transformation requires a sequence of logical and arithmetic steps. Basically, all information handling takes the form shown in Fig. 4-1.

If we look inside this box, we find that all input data is first entered into the memory (Fig. 4-2). The data processing unit obtains information from this memory, performs the required operations, and then

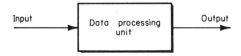

FIGURE 4-1 A progressively more detailed explanation of over-all machine logic.

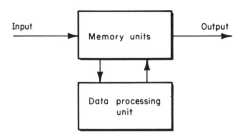

FIGURE 4-2

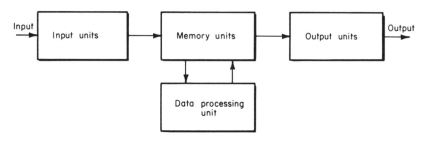

FIGURE 4-3

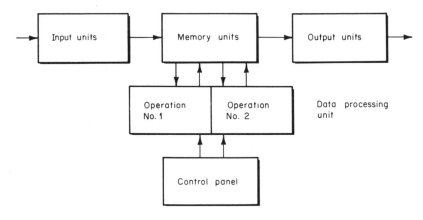

FIGURE 4-4

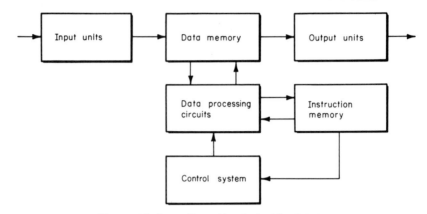

FIGURE 4-5 Over-all machine logic (simplified).

returns the data to the memory. The results become the *output* from the machine. The memory also holds intermediate answers which are used later in the calculations. Constant factors, such as tax percentages, are also retained in memory units for use in the computations.

Special units are used to sense input data and transmit it into memory. Similar devices are needed for output. (See Fig. 4-3.)

The data processing unit can carry out a number of different operations upon data stored in memory. Punched-card machines contain a control panel. This unit sends out signals which activate the operation which is needed. The control panel is manually wired before the machine is used. This wiring determines which control impulses are sent to the data processing unit. Figure 4-4 is a simplified representation of this arrangement.

In a stored program machine, as has been stated, the sequence of operations is governed by coded instructions placed in the memory units. The control circuits obtain these codes in succession, and actuate the corresponding operations. Figure 4-5 shows these concepts schematically. All of the possible instructions which can be executed are contained in the data processing circuits. The control system selects which operation is to be actuated by sending an appropriate signal to the data processing circuits. The diagram indicates that the codes contained in the instruction memory can themselves be operated upon by the data processing circuits. The equipment can thus modify or change the commands given to it by humans.

The input for any application is based upon source data. This information must be placed into a form which can be sensed by the machine. Almost always the data is put into punched cards. These cards are usually sorted into an order convenient for machine processing. It is frequently advisable to list and summarize all of the information on the cards. This provides what accountants call an *audit trail,* a procedure for tracing back all later results to the original data. This procedure is necessary to make sure that all of the data was entered into the machine properly. Sometimes mistakes occur in the punching or handling of cards. In business applications it is necessary to check against the possibility of deliberate fraud. Finally, in the unlikely event of a machine breakdown, the audit trail furnishes a way of starting all over again with the application.

Punched-card machines are used for the preprocessing of data to be entered into electronic computers. These simple machines, by the way, are still used for a large number of elementary applications where the vast speeds and capacities of modern equipment are not necessary. For these reasons, we have included a section on the basic principles of punched-card machines.

To carry out an application, a sequence of instructions is prepared by a programmer. These are placed in memory in coded form. (In reality, both instructions and data are stored in the same memory units.) Memory is composed of a large number of pigeon holes, each with a number. An instruction consists of a code designating the operation to be performed, along with a number indicating where the data to be used is kept in memory.

The control system operates in two phases. First, it gets the next instruction to be executed from memory. It interprets the operation code. Secondly, it sends out signals actuating the required command. The needed information is now routed from memory into the data processing circuits. These two procedures are repeated continually, whenever the machine is running. In this way an entire sequence of instructions is interpreted and executed automatically.

If we peer inside of the boxes representing the control system, data processing circuits, memory, input units, and output units, what we find are *switching circuits.* These networks comprise the machine logic. They are of two types: *combinatorial,* and *sequential.* Combinatorial circuits transform information in a fixed way. Sequential networks employ a feedback principle. Their output depends not simply on their present input, but is also a function of their history of past inputs. Combinatorial and sequential circuits are studied by *switching theory.* This science uses mathematical logic to understand the behavior of these networks.

Switching circuits can be designed to transform information in any desired way. Some of the fundamental operations in a computer are addition, shifting, comparison, and counting. More complex operations, such as multiplication and division, can be based on these procedures.

The logical networks are composed of physical components. The early machines used electromechanical devices. In modern machines, however, there are no moving parts, apart from input and output units. All that occurs is the passage of electrical impulses from one storage unit to another through data processing circuits. These electronic signals are coded to represent information.

HOW TO UNDERSTAND DATA PROCESSING

How deeply is it necessary to go into these details to understand computers? Many expert programmers know very little about machine logic or electronics. Moreover, it is possible to have a good conception of how well a machine can handle many applications without knowing very much about programming. There are four levels (Fig. 4-6) at which the subject of electronic data processing could be approached.

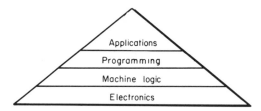

FIGURE 4-6 Levels for approaching a study of electronic data processing.

The procedure we shall follow in this book is to start at the bottom of this pyramid and to work our way up. In following this course, we present to the reader a broad picture of the entire data processing technology. However, if the reader is primarily interested in the top of the pyramid, it will suffice if he merely attains a general grasp of the lower levels.

Our first undertaking is to explain how information is represented in computational equipment. In so doing we will obtain some glimpses into the engineering technology underlying the machines. This comprises the first level of the pyramid.

5 THE REPRESENTATION OF INFORMATION

INFORMATION PATTERNS

Many physical media can be used to represent information. A melody, for example, can exist in the form of notes in a musical score, as grooves in a phonograph record, as sound waves produced by an orchestra, as radio (electromagnetic) waves, or in the form of a haunting refrain which runs around the brain. The same pattern, or organization, of messages exists in all of these instances.

It may be objected that music cannot be equated with mere information. It is of interest, however, that by amplifying certain electrical circuits, a computer can be made to emit noises characteristic of various internal states. Certain repeated sound patterns, for example, may indicate the presence of that programmer's error known as an *endless loop*. One machine operator once asserted that he could detect the convergence of a mathematical series by such sounds.

Actually, through programming, it is not difficult to produce thin, piping sounds which correspond to the notes of the musical scale. The demonstration of a newly purchased million-dollar computer to top executives has been known to include a rendition of popular tunes by the machine. In a similar manner, a computer service bureau once entertained the public with Christmas carols during one snowy holiday season.

For engineering reasons, most electronic data processing equipment use the binary number system to represent information. This system contains only the numbers *zero* and *one*. It is interesting that in ancient times 0 and 1 represented sexual symbols, and that the sign + was a symbol of eternity—the joining of these sexual principles. Indeed, the notion that "all numbers are generated out of an undifferentiated dyad"

45

runs through pre-Socratic, Platonic, and neo-Platonic philosophy. Odd numbers were thought of as male; even numbers as female. In the language of data processing, 0 and 1 are referred to as *bits,* a contraction of *binary digits.*

NUMBER SYSTEMS

The everyday decimal number system employs the digits $0, 1, 2, 3, 4, 5, 6, 7, 8, 9$. The position of each digit within a number designates that it is multiplied by a power of ten corresponding to its particular location. The number

$$72,479$$

actually stands for the sum of

$$70,000$$
$$2,000$$
$$400$$
$$70$$
$$9$$

This sum can also be expressed in the following way:

$$70,000 = 7 \times 10,000 = 7 \times 10^4$$
$$2,000 = 2 \times 1,000 = 2 \times 10^3$$
$$400 = 4 \times 100 = 4 \times 10^2$$
$$70 = 7 \times 10 = 7 \times 10^1$$
$$9 = 9 \times 1 = 9 \times 10^0$$

Each digit in a number is a multiplier of a power of ten. The succession of decimal numbers is formed by adding 1 to each preceding number. Since there are only nine digits available after 0, whenever a 9 is encountered we obtain the next higher number by a *carry* to the next digit position. Thus, we increase the multiplier of 10 in the next digit position.

This mode of expressing numbers is called *positional notation.* Some authorities believe that it originated in the use of the abacus for performing arithmetic. The value of positional notation is that it facilitates the operations of addition, subtraction, multiplication, and division.

The number 10 is called the *base* of the decimal number system which we use. However, it is possible to construct number systems with a different base.

In the octal number system, for example, the base is 8. The only digits available are $0, 1, 2, 3, 4, 5, 6, 7$. In this instance, each digit is a multiplier of a power of 8. All decimal numbers have corresponding octal numbers, and vice versa.

The base which is used for expressing numbers is a matter of convention, tradition, and convenience. There is a complete correspondence between the numbers in any particular system and the numbers in any other system. From this standpoint, it does not make any difference in what system a machine performs calculations. So long as it consistently does arithmetic by the rules of the system it is using, the machine will arrive at the same result it would have reached in the decimal system.

THE BINARY NUMBER SYSTEM

The correspondence between decimal and binary numbers is:

Decimal	Binary
0	0
1	1
2	10
3	11
4	100
5	101
6	110
7	111
8	1000
9	1001
10	1010
11	1011
12	1100
13	1101
14	1110
15	1111
16	10000
17	10001

As with decimal numbers, the next higher binary number is formed by adding 1 to its predecessor. Whenever we exceed 1, there is a carry to the next position. Each digit position is the multiplier of a higher power of 2.

The addition of binary digits occurs as follows:

$$
\begin{array}{cccc}
0 & 0 & 1 & 1 \\
\underline{0} & \underline{1} & \underline{0} & \underline{1} \\
0 & 1 & 1 & 10 \quad \text{(carry required)}
\end{array}
$$

The binary equivalent to the decimal number 20 is 10100. The binary number takes the form

16	8	4	2	1	Powers of 2
1	0	1	0	0	Binary digits

Hence, the binary number 10100 represents the sum of the decimal quantities

$$
\begin{array}{ll}
1 \times 16 & 16 \\
0 \times 8 & 0 \\
1 \times 4 & 4 \\
0 \times 2 & 0 \\
0 \times 1 & \underline{0} \\
& 20
\end{array}
$$

BINARY CODED DECIMAL REPRESENTATION

Another way in which information is often represented in electronic computers is the *binary coded decimal* system. In this method each digit in a number is symbolized by a four-bit binary number. Some examples are:

Decimal number system	Corresponding binary coded decimal number	
3	0000	0011
9	0000	1001
12	0001	0010
75	0111	0101

The manner in which information is represented within a computer has a very strong influence on its design. Indeed, a piece of equipment is often referred to as a *binary machine* or a *binary coded decimal* machine. Both types of data processing machines have advantages and disadvantages for particular types of applications.

One important factor relates to human communication with data processing machines. It is comparatively easy for a person to acquire facility in recognizing information expressed in binary coded decimal. Whereas in the binary mode, it is more difficult for a person to ascertain what numbers are present.

Another consideration is that decimal numbers are easily converted to binary coded decimal, and vice versa. Where binary computers are used, input data must be converted into binary form to make it usable by the equipment. Output data must be converted back into decimal to be of value for human comprehension.

These are two of the major reasons why machines designed for business information handling have frequently used the binary coded decimal mode. Accountants, controllers, and methods analysts find it easier to work with decimal data. Binary representation is sometimes difficult or repugnant to people without mathematical training. Of greater importance, however, is the fact that the input-output conversions required for binary machines is very time consuming. When millions of characters of information must be entered into machines and printed out, this additional time may seriously reduce the efficiency of an installation.

Binary machines are usually regarded as more useful than binary coded decimal machines for scientific and engineering calculations. Input and output conversion time is less important in these applications, for there is usually a much smaller volume of input and output data. The binary mode also lends itself to faster arithmetic speeds. This characteristic is significant in mathematical work, where there is extensive computation. In business data processing the amount of mathematical calculation is often slight.

Another advantage of binary machines is that in the binary mode four bits can represent all of the decimal digits from 0 to 15, whereas in the binary coded decimal system four bits can represent only the numbers from 0 to 9. In this respect the binary coded decimal mode is less efficient. This factor becomes more obvious when large numbers are involved. For example, the decimal number 255 can be expressed by the eight-bit number 11111111. In binary coded decimal the twelve-bit number 0010 0101 0101 is needed. Since it is expensive to provide memory space for the storage of information, it is often more economical to use the binary system of representing numbers.

REPRESENTATION OF NONNUMERIC INFORMATION

Data processing machines must handle many nonnumeric characters, such as alphabetic letters, punctuation marks, and dollar signs. This information is usually represented by six binary digits. The first two of these bit positions are called the *B zone* and the *A zone*. When these zone positions are 00, the next four bits represent a numeric character in binary coded decimal. If the zones are not both zeros, the six bits stand for some nonnumeric character. Some of the six-bit characters used in the IBM 1401 data processing system are:

Character	Zones		Numeric portion of code
	B	A	
1	0	0	0001
7	0	0	0111
A	1	1	0001
K	1	0	0010
S	0	1	0010

This mode of representing information has largely stemmed from the storing of information on punched cards. As many as 64 different characters can be expressed in a six-bit code. Should future machines need to handle more than 64 characters, additional bits will be added to the code. Each additional bit doubles the number of characters which can be represented.

A *check* or *redundancy* bit is often used with character codes to aid in error detection. In the case of the six-bit code, an extra seventh bit is added automatically when the character enters the machines. This redundancy bit does not affect the character which is represented, but simply causes the sum of the 1 bits to add up to an odd number. For example:

Character	Check bit	Zones		Numeric portion	Number of 1 bits
		B	A		
C	1	1	1	0011	5
D	0	1	1	0100	3
2	0	0	0	0010	1

As information is processed in the machine, the circuits automatically check to see if the sum of the seven bits is odd. If this condition fails to exist, the machine has most probably either erroneously lost or added a 1 bit, and corrective measures are taken. A similar procedure was employed in the first UNIVAC, which used a redundancy bit to make the sum of the bits in the character code an odd number. Also, the arithmetic and control circuits of this machine were duplicated, and were compared against each other continually. If a disparity occurred, an error indication was given to the operator.

ELECTRICAL REPRESENTATION OF BITS

Binary information can be represented by electrical pulses passing along wires. The presence of a signal at a particular time and place represents a 1 bit; the absence of a signal, a 0 bit. Two different voltage levels on a wire can also perform this function. The sequence of pulses shown in Fig. 5-1 stands for the code 0110001. This is the letter A in the IBM 1401 code.

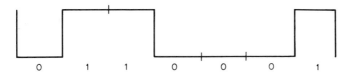

FIGURE 5-1 Binary code 0110001, representing the letter A in IBM 1401 code.

Any physical device which can be switched back and forth between two stable states can be used as an information storage or *memory* unit. Such components are called "bistable." Ordinary light bulbs in a row (Fig. 5-2) could represent binary data. Let a bulb which is turned off

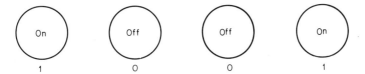

FIGURE 5-2 Using light bulbs to represent binary data.

stand for a 0, and a bulb which is turned on represent a 1. In this fashion the binary number 9 could be expressed as shown in Fig. 5-2.

MEMORY UNITS

Data processing applications may require the storage of thousands, millions, or even billions of bits. A fast growing technology has made such memory devices possible.

One frequently used technique is the magnetic drum (Fig. 5-3). This unit consists of a rotating metallic cylinder divided into many channels. Each channel can retain numerous binary digits. A 1 bit is represented by a tiny magnetized spot.

Information is recorded by *writing heads*. These are electromagnets close to the drum channels. When an electromagnet is energized, the metal on the surface of the drum is magnetized. The retrieval of information is accomplished by coils near the drum, called *reading heads*. A changing magnetic field induces an electric current in nearby wires. Since the drum turns continually, a magnetized spot in a channel will produce a voltage in a reading head. This is how 1 bits are sensed.

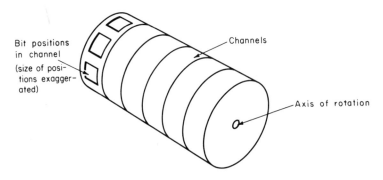

FIGURE 5-3 Magnetic drum memory unit.

The capacity of a drum depends on the density of storage of bits in each channel and how closely bits can be packed along the axis of the drum. Typical densities around the circumference of the drum are of the order of 100 bits per inch. Twenty channels are frequently placed in 1 inch along the axis. One commonly used drum has a storage capacity of about 500,000 bits. About 25,000 characters per second can be read or written.

MAGNETIC CORES

Magnetic cores are often used for information storage. These components—doughnut-shaped devices threaded with two different wires—are less than 0.5 inch in diameter. Made of a ferromagnetic material, they can be magnetized in either of two directions. They are thus bi-stable. Typical memories of this type have a capacity of about 20,000 to 100,000 characters. The time to store a character or to obtain it when needed is usually several microseconds. A microsecond is 1/1,000,000 of a second. The cores are arranged in a matrix, depicted schematically in Fig. 5-4.

A separate wire runs through each row and column of cores. To store information in a particular core, both wires threaded around the ring must be energized. For example, to place a 1 bit in core $B3$, current must be passed both through wires 3 and B. A current in only one of the wires cannot affect any core, but the sum of two currents can change the state of the selected core. The only core which can change state in this instance is *B*3. The direction (to the right and downward, or to the left and upwards) of current flow through the wires in the matrix determines the manner.in which the core is magnetized. Reading information from cores is accomplished by a sense wire (not shown) which passes through all of the rings in the array.

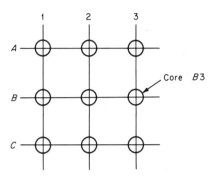

FIGURE 5-4 Matrix of magnetic core memory units.

A memory can be designed either for a *destructive* or *nondestructive* read-out. In the former case, the storage unit is always placed in the 0 state after information is obtained from it. If it initially contained a 1, a second read-out would obtain a 0. In a nondestructive read-out, all subsequent reads will find the original information still present. Since the nondestructive read-out is more practical, whenever the electronic reading of information causes the destruction of a binary digit in a storage medium, a reinsertion of the bit is usually executed by the memory circuitry. This process is automatic so that from a user's point of view the read-out can be regarded as nondestructive. This method is used in magnetic core memories.

DISK MEMORIES

Millions of bits can be stored on horizontally stacked disks which look like records in a juke box. Each disk contains a number of tracks, in each of which thousands of bits can be recorded. A comb of vertical arms moves in and out of every disk simultaneously, stopping at the desired track, and reading or writing information from whatever disk is specified.

Many other techniques for storing information are available or are being studied. The use of mechanical gears for storage purposes is, of course, much too slow to be coupled with the tremendous processing speeds of electronic computers. A promising technique is that of photographic memories in which thousands of clear dots are concentrated on plates an inch or two square. After exposure, these plates must be developed and fixed. Recording or reading of information requires scanning by cathode-ray tubes and focusing by systems of lenses. Information can be rapidly read out, and billions of bits can be stored in a small area.

It is instructive to note that photomemories are nonerasable and, hence, must be used for the permanent storage of information. Ordinarily a computer's memory is used like a blackboard: when a problem is completed, the board is erased to enable it to be used again. However, a very large and cheap memory can be used like a scratch pad, employed only once for recording information, and then filed or thrown away.

It seems certain that within several years memory devices will not only store many billions of bits but will also be faster and much smaller. Future memories, it is predicted, will enable from 30 to 100 million electronic components to be packed into a cubic foot. Wrist watch radios and record players to fit into purses will come into use, and the size of data processing equipment will be reduced proportionately. One of the chief uses of such miniaturization is in the field of airborne equipment and space vehicles.

The science of cryogenics will likewise enable computer components to be smaller, operate faster, and be of greater capacity. At temperatures approaching absolute zero, which is about 459° below zero Fahrenheit, certain metals known as superconductors show no electrical resistance. Here, an electric current lasts indefinitely. This flow of current, sensed through magnetic fields, will enable superconductors to be employed as memory units.

SWITCHING SYSTEMS

A computer operates by switching information through networks. The first modern computers, those built at the Harvard Computational Laboratory, used electrical relays as switching devices.

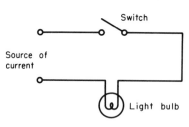

FIGURE 5-5 Simple electrical switch for breaking or completing a circuit.

An electric current consists of the flow of electrons through conductors such as wires. If there is a break in the conductor, electrons cannot pass through the wire. The well-known analogy is that of a water pipe. If the pipe is broken at any point, the water leaks out and cannot reach the end of the pipe. The function of water valves such as faucets is to cut off, or control, the flow of water. Valves are used for analogous purposes in electrical circuits.

The purpose of an electrical switch is to complete or break an electrical circuit. The ordinary household light switch is a manually operated device for performing these functions.

When the switch is closed, the circuit is completed (Fig. 5-5), and electrons flow through the filament of the bulb, producing light. When the switch is opened, the passage of electrons ceases, and the light goes off. Here the representation of 0's and 1's is under the control of a mechanical switch.

RELAY CIRCUITS

As we have seen, a relay is a switch which can be opened or closed by an electrical signal.

The two basic types of relay circuits, serial and parallel, are shown in Figs. 5-6 and 5-7. (The control circuits operating the switches are omitted from the diagrams.)

In Fig. 5-6 the light will be turned on only if relays X and Y are energized at the same time. In Fig. 5-7 current will flow if either X, or Y, or both relays are energized.

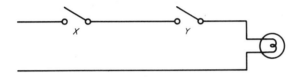

FIGURE 5-6 Serial logic.

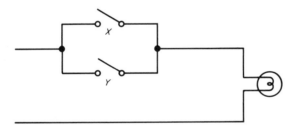

FIGURE 5-7 Parallel logic.

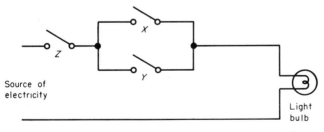

FIGURE 5-8 Combination of serial and parallel logic.

A combination of serial and parallel logic produces the circuit of Fig. 5-8, in which there is an output only if Z is closed, along with either X, or Y, or both.

Suppose we let a closed relay represent a 1, and an open relay a 0. Assume also that the *on* state of the bulb is a 1, and the *off* state a 0. This yields:

Input			Output bulb
Z	X	Y	
1	1	1	1
1	1	0	1
1	0	1	1
1	0	0	0
0	1	1	0
0	1	0	0
0	0	1	0
0	0	0	0

This table represents a transformation of information. It shows the resulting output under eight possible combinations of input.

Relay circuits of tremendous complexity are often needed. The analysis of the conditions under which the networks are open or closed often becomes very involved. This is exemplified in Fig. 5-9.

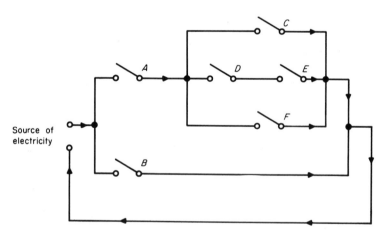

FIGURE 5-9 A more complicated system of relay circuits.

A number of different types of relays can be constructed. A single relay can be built to control several different circuits. Important logical properties can be created by using multiple independent windings of the electromagnet.

SEQUENTIAL CIRCUITS

We have assumed so far that all of the relays in a network are energized simultaneously. If this synchronism does not exist, the circuit may not possess the needed logical characteristics. Such networks are *time dependent*. Here it is necessary to know the time relationships among the relays to ascertain the behavior of the system. Circuits in which there is no time dependence are called *combinatorial;* time-dependent circuits are called *sequential*. Both types of circuits have practical value.

The relays we have been discussing open and close circuits only as long as the electromagnet is energized. As soon as the signal from the control circuit ceases, the electromagnet is de-energized, and the armature returns to its original position. Certain relays are equipped with a mechanical or electrical latch which keeps the relay closed until a special signal releases the latch. Another class of relay opens and closes with every alternate control signal. Relays of these types are used for the storage of information.

ELECTRONIC COMPONENTS

The mechanical motion of the armature of a relay causes a time lag between the energizing of the electromagnet and the closing of the circuit. There is also a delay in the dropping out of the armature when the electromagnet is de-energized.

Despite the fact that the armature moves only a few hundredths of an inch, this interval, called *switching time,* is of the magnitude of milliseconds. One millisecond is 1/1000 second. In many types of automatic control equipment utilizing relays this lag is not significant. It is, however, enormous where modern computers are concerned. Thousands of electronic elements are used in computers. The speed of a machine is to a large extent a function of the switching time of its components. For this reason, among others, electronic equipment has supplanted the use of relays in data processing machines.

Electronic techniques use various physical components for representing, processing, and communicating information. There are no moving parts in such devices. At lower costs, they can be built for greater speed, sensitivity, and reliability. The manufacture of electronic equipment was a small part of the electrical industry before World War II. Today gross electronics sales is in the magnitude of $15 billion, of which a large fraction is for data processing machines.

VACUUM TUBES

The vacuum tube is based on Edison's discovery that the filament, or *cathode,* in an evacuated tube emits electrons when heated. In the every-

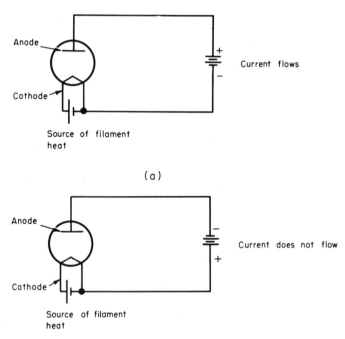

Current flows

(a)

Current does not flow

(b)

FIGURE 5-10 Diode used as an electrical switch.

day electric light the electrons cluster around the filament. However, if a metallic conductor, called a *plate* or *anode,* is sealed into the tube and is given a positive charge with respect to the cathode, the electrons are attracted to the anode, and an electric current flows across the vacuum (Fig. 5-10). The flow of electrons can normally occur only when the anode has a positive charge. If the anode has a negative charge, the electrons are driven back toward the cathode. The anode, of course, does not ordinarily emit electrons. For these reasons, current can flow only in one direction.

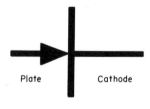

FIGURE 5-11 Symbol representing a diode.

These devices are called diodes, and are represented by the symbol shown in Fig. 5-11. When the plate is positive with respect to the voltage on the cathode (Fig. 5-10a), the diode conducts from cathode to plate. In this instance the diode offers a low resistance, and can be regarded as a closed switch. But when the cathode is positive with respect to the plate (Fig. 5-10b), the diode presents a very high resistance to the flow of electrons. In this case the diode can be conceived as an open switch.

TRIODES

The birth of modern electronics occurred in 1906 when Dr. Lee DeForest placed a wire mesh between the cathode and the anode. In this tube, called the *triode* or *valve*, it is possible to control the flow of current by altering the charge on the grid. If the grid were positive, the electrons emitted from the cathode, being charged negatively, would be attracted by the grid. Because of their high velocity, a large number of electrons would pass through the holes in the wire mesh, and would be collected by the anode. However, if the grid is given a negative charge, the electrons from the cathode tend to be repelled back to the cathode. In this case, fewer electrons are picked up by the anode.

If a sufficiently strong negative charge is imparted to the grid, no electrons at all can penetrate the mesh to reach the anode. The grid thus acts like a valve. It can cut off the current completely, or permit any desired current to flow. In this way, a very small charge on the grid can control a large amount of anode or plate current. This property makes the vacuum triode valuable for the amplification of electrical signals. It is apparent that the grid can control the flow of information in a manner similar to the relay. In practice, vacuum tubes are much more complex. Additional electrodes of various types are placed in the tubes for various engineering purposes.

The cathode-ray tube, which is used as the screen in television sets, was employed as a memory device in some of the first electronic computers. This device consists of a cathode whose electrons are focused and accelerated down the neck of a flask-like tube. These electrons pass through an electromagnetic or electrostatic field which deflects this beam in its passage toward the face of the tube. Combinations of voltages applied to horizontal and vertical deflection plates shoot the electrons with great accuracy to any specified region on the face of the tube. The screen can be regarded as a large number of tiny squares. A charge placed in a square can be retained for a small interval of time. As a memory unit, the cathode-ray tube was often unreliable because of engineering problems. It is now employed only for visual displays of computer outputs.

One of the most important electronic components is the *flip-flop*. It was invented in 1919 by Eccles and Jordan, who called it a *trigger relay*. This device consists of two vacuum triodes connected through an electrical network. The circuit permits only one triode to conduct at a time.

The voltage in the conducting tube prevents the other triode from passing a current, and vice versa. This establishes a bistable condition which is very useful in the logical circuitry of computers. When a signal is applied to the flip-flop, the conducting tube is cut off, and the other triode operates. The next signal received by the system returns the network to its original state.

TRANSISTORS

In recent years, germanium diodes have been used increasingly in computers. The germanium diode (Fig. 5-12) consists of a thin tungsten wire maintained in contact with a germanium crystal. The physical

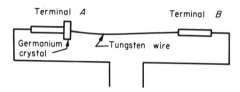

FIGURE 5-12 The germanium diode.

properties of these unlike metals cause a difference in electrical charge to exist between them. This results in a movement of electrons from the germanium to the tungsten, and the wire thereby acquires a negative charge. Unlike regular metallic conductors, the germanium crystal lacks a large number of electrons available to move about freely. Therefore, a small area lacking in electrons develops around the point of contact with the wire. The negative charge on the tungsten prevents electrons from entering this spot, which acts as a blocking layer.

If a source of electricity is applied across the terminals, it can flow only if terminal B is positive with respect to A. If the tungsten is positive, the electrons flow off the wire to the external source of the current, and electrons pass into the germanium from outside to fill up the small positive area, and from there pass to the wire. However, if terminal A is positive, and B negative, the wire becomes additionally negative, and causes the blocking layer to increase in the crystal. As the voltage increases, the thickness of the blocking area is extended. The germanium diode thus has the property of permitting current to flow in only one direction. In the forward direction, its resistance is in the magnitude of hundreds of ohms; in the back direction its resistance is of the order of hundreds of thousands of ohms.

The junction transistor consists of n and p types of germanium. The n type readily loses electrons, whereas the p type readily acquires electrons. The *p* type is placed between two *n* types, as shown in Fig. 5-13.

The slab of *p* type germanium corresponds to the grid of a vacuum tube. The end sections, the *emitter* and *collector*, are to be likened to the cathode and anode. The flow of electrons is controlled by the application of signals to the *base*.

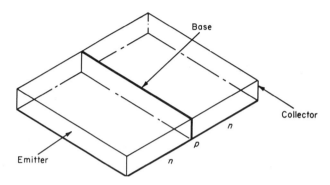

FIGURE 5-13 The junction transistor.

Transistors have several advantages over tubes. In the vacuum tube, power is required to heat the cathode, but in the transistor no such energy is required. Therefore, transistors use much less power than tubes. Secondly, the smaller size of transistors enables computers to be built more compactly. Finally, transistors are more reliable, and last longer than vacuum tubes. For these reasons, transistors have made the vacuum tube largely obsolete in electronic data processing equipment.

Research is continually increasing the speed and reliability of electronic components. Before long, switching and memory devices will be microscopic in size and will be operating in the magnitude of nanoseconds. A nanosecond is a billionth of a second, or 1/1000 of a microsecond. For example, thin film memories can operate in the order of about 60 nanoseconds. With components of such fantastic speed, the velocity of electricity (186,000 miles a second) becomes significant. It takes an electric current about one nanosecond to traverse a wire one foot in length. Excessively long interconnections among components therefore decrease the speed of the machine. Hence, future circuits will be packaged closely together to avoid losing these minute amounts of time.

6 MACHINE LOGIC

BASIC CONCEPTS

All of the complex work which a data processing machine performs is based on the four fundamental operations—*and, or, not,* and *memory.* In electronic computers these functions are executed by circuits called *gates* and *triggers.* The organization of these building blocks into circuits which can carry out programs is called *machine logic* or *logical design.*

And gates (Fig. 6-1) are devised so that they emit a 1 bit as output only when all of the input bits are 1's.

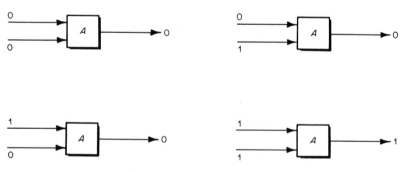

FIGURE 6-1 *And* gate operations.

Or gates (Fig. 6-2) produce a 1 output whenever at least one of the inputs is a 1. A zero output occurs only if both inputs are zero.

The *not* operation is performed by a device called the *inverter.* This component reverses the signal (Fig. 6-3) which is applied at its input. If a 0 bit enters, a 1 output occurs. If a 1 bit enters, there is a 0 output.

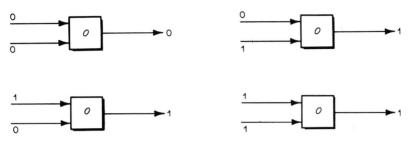

FIGURE 6-2 *Or* gate operations.

FIGURE 6-3 Operations of an inverter.

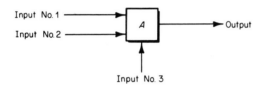

FIGURE 6-4 Operation of *and* gate with three inputs.

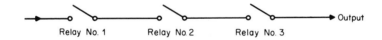

FIGURE 6-5 Three relays in series.

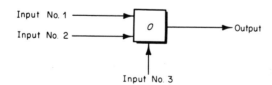

FIGURE 6-6 Operation of *or* gate with three inputs.

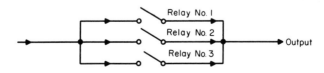

FIGURE 6-7 Three relays in parallel.

And gates and *or* gates may have more than two inputs. However, the same logical principles apply, regardless of the number of inputs.

An *and* gate with three inputs (Fig. 6-4) performs a function equivalent to three relays in series. (See Fig. 6-5.)

Or gates (Fig. 6-6) behave in the same way as relays in parallel (Fig. 6-7).

GATING CIRCUITS

As in the case of relay circuits, gating systems of great complexity can be constructed. (See Fig. 6-8.)

Here there can be a 1 output only if both inputs to *and* gate A_2 are 1's. This can occur only if input D is 0, and if either C is a 1 bit or else if both A and B have 1 signals applied.

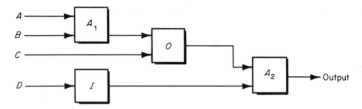

FIGURE 6-8 A more complex gating system, using *and* and *or* gates, and an inverter.

Gates can be used to recognize codes. The letter C, represented by 110011, is uniquely decoded by the gating system of Fig. 6-9. Gate A_1

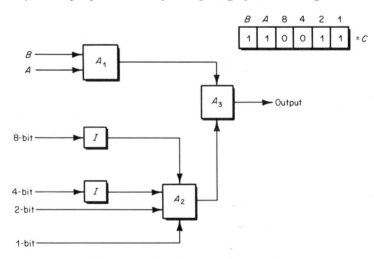

FIGURE 6-9 A gating system for decoding.

will produce an output only if 1 bits enter the system at B and A. If there are 0 inputs to the 4-bit and 8-bit lines, these will be converted to 1's when applied to gate A_2. In this event A_2 will produce an output if the 1-bit and 2-bit input lines both receive the signal 1. Since the output lines of A_1 and A_2 are gated together at A_3, there will be an output only when the letter C enters the gating circuit.

Encoding, the opposite of decoding, converts a character into its binary representation. Such a procedure is necessary for entering information into a computer. A circuit to encode the characters 0, 1, 2, 3, 4, or 5 is shown in Fig. 6-10.

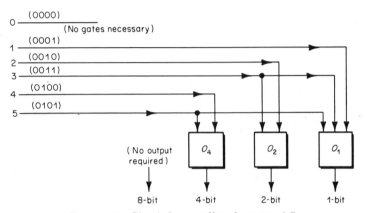

FIGURE 6-10 Circuit for encoding characters 1-5.

Since none of the numbers need an 8-bit, no signal is ever placed on this output line. Each of the numbers goes through a combination of *or* gates to produce the proper output signals. The 3, for example, goes both to gate O_2 and gate O_1. In this way a 1 bit emerges from these two gates. No signal (a 0 bit) comes from O_4.

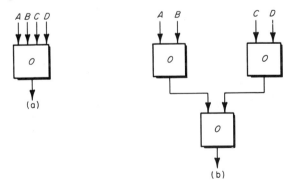

FIGURE 6-11 Single gate arrangement, and use of subsidiary gates to funnel input together.

In actual engineering practice, various limitations exist on the purely logical arrangement of gates to produce desired effects. For example, it may prove electronically unfeasible to have too many inputs converging upon the same gate, as in Fig. 6-11a. This can be avoided by using subsidiary gates to funnel the inputs together (Fig. 6-11b). The logical result is the same in both circuits.

ADDITION CIRCUITS

Addition is executed by gating circuits. If we represent the adder simply as a box whose contents are, for the moment, unspecified, then the operation

$$
\begin{array}{r}
1\,0\,1\,0 \\
+\quad 1\,1\,0 \\
\hline
1\,0\,0\,0\,0
\end{array}
$$

takes the form shown in Fig. 6-12.

The unit is designed so that each pair of bits enters concomitantly. If there is a carry, it is fed back into the adder at the same time as the next pair of binary digits.

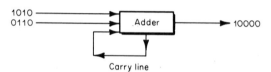

FIGURE 6-12 Over-all machine logic for addition.

There are only four different situations a gating circuit for addition must be able to handle:

$$
\begin{array}{cccc}
0 & 0 & 1 & 1 \\
+0 & +1 & +0 & +1 \\
\hline
0 & 1 & 1 & 0
\end{array}
$$
(with carry)

These functions can be performed by a *half adder* (Fig. 6-13).

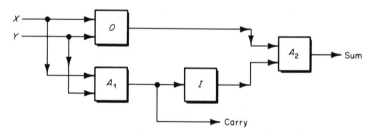

FIGURE 6-13 Gating system for a *half adder*.

If the two inputs, X and Y, are both 1 bits, then there is a 1 bit output from the *or* gate, which is applied at *and* gate A_2. The X and Y inputs also enter A_1. This emits a 1 bit which becomes both a carry pulse and also a 1 input to the inverter I. The inverter produces a 0, which is applied to A_2. *And* gate A_2 is therefore closed, so the sum output is 0.

If X is a 0-bit input and Y a 1-bit input, then the *or* gate emits a signal which is applied to A_2. Gate A_1 emits a 0 bit which becomes a no-carry as well as an input to the inverter. The inverter's output is now a 1 bit. Hence, A_2 produces a 1 output, as required.

If both inputs are 0 bits, A_1 emits a 0 output to the carry line. The inverter causes a 1 bit to be applied to A_2, but this gate is closed because there is a 0 bit output from the *or* gate.

SEQUENTIAL CIRCUITS

The circuits we have been considering so far are combinatorial. The behavior of such networks is determined completely by their present inputs. No time dependence is present.

Combinatorial circuits are used for many important functions. However, it is in sequential circuits that we encounter the fascinating characteristics associated with automata and the capacity for self-determination. A combinatorial network is at the mercy, so to speak, of its present environment, and has no way of reacting in terms of previous stimuli. In a sequential circuit, however, the output of the network is a function, not only of present inputs, but of past inputs as well. The response of the network is determined by its history as well as its present environment. The history of the circuit is represented by memory units, which enable the past to influence the present functioning of the system.

Timing factors may be present in combinatorial networks as the result of faulty operation. For example, the relay circuit of Fig. 6-14 is

A B

FIGURE 6-14 Relay circuit controlled by two switches.

required to produce an output when switches A and B are energized. This logical condition presupposes, however, that the contacts A and B both close simultaneously. In actuality, as we have previously stated, relays may differ in the speed of their mechanical movements. As a result, even if the two electromagnets are energized at the same time, the first relay may close much later than the second. If the two switches do not close simultaneously, the passage of a signal may not be possible. Even if there is some overlapping in the closing of the switches, the output current may not have the electrical characteristics which constitute a proper signal. The speed of closing and release of relays is affected by such factors as the electrical and magnetic properties of the wire windings around the electromagnet; mechanical features of the armature, springs, and air gap; temperature and humidity; and, of course, deterioration stemming from long usage. In a complex logical network composed of thousands of relays, time delays may interfere with the logic of the system.

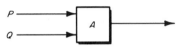

FIGURE 6-15 Multiple input gating circuit.

Similar considerations apply to electronic gating circuits. For example, if in the circuit of Fig. 6-15 the input signals do not fall within the range of amplitude, duration, and waveform specified by the designer, the output may either be incorrect or below requirements.

Another difficulty arises from the fact that it takes time for voltages to reach their proper levels for representing information. Erroneous logic can be avoided by applying repetitive timed signals throughout a machine to make sure that all gates are performing their functions only after information signals are electronically stabilized. These control signals, called *clock pulses,* are emitted from a central device called the *master clock.* Special *and* gates (Fig. 6-16) function as *clock gates* to prevent the passage of information until the permissive clock pulse arrives.

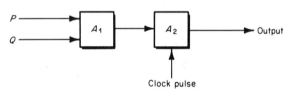

FIGURE 6-16 Clock gate.

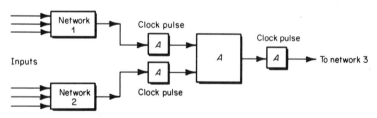

FIGURE 6-17 Clock pulses used to maintain synchronism between two networks.

Any output from A_1 arriving at A_2 when the clock pulse is not present will not be able to pass A_2. By utilizing these timing signals, all of the far-flung logical components comprising a computer can be kept in synchronism with each other. This makes it impossible for the outputs of two gating networks (Fig. 6-17) to cause faulty logic by arriving at a common gate at different times. Here the clock pulses controlling networks 1 and 2 cause the outputs of these networks to enter the *and* gate simultaneously. Without this simultaneity, 1 outputs from both networks might fail to cause an output from the *and* gate.

DELAY CIRCUITS

By deliberately introducing time delays, previous conditions in a network can affect present functioning. Such sequential circuits are represented as in Fig. 6-18.

Any input pulse which enters the unit is delayed one time interval before it emerges as an output. The subscript of D designates the number of time delays undergone by the signal. With a D_2 delay, for example,

FIGURE 6-18 Representation of a time delay circuit.

there can be an output present only if there was an input two time intervals previously. If there is an input at the present time, this information does not emerge immediately, as in a combinatorial circuit, but is emitted as an output after two time intervals have elapsed.

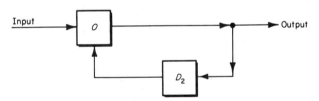

FIGURE 6-19 A delay line used to store information.

A delay line can be used to store information. In Fig. 6-19, whenever a 1 bit is entered into the system there is immediately an output, but at the same time the signal is fed back into the two-interval delay line D_2. Assuming all further inputs are 0 bits, the circuit will emit no output after the very next interval, after which it will put out a 1 bit periodically every two time units. Whenever D_2 emits a signal, this passes the *or* gate, becoming simultaneously an output and a fed-back input into D_2.

CLOCK CIRCUITS

A computer consists of a complex system of interconnected gating and memory networks. To control the flow of information through these circuits, a master clock is necessary in most machines. This device produces timing signals which are sent out along wires to all parts of the computer.

To illustrate this concept, suppose we set up a clocklike system that emits a series of pulses separated from one another by a certain interval. After ticking off seven signals, the pulse returns to the beginning and repeats. We'll call the sequence of pulses $t_1, t_2, \ldots, t_7$. The diagram of Fig. 6-20 represents this system.

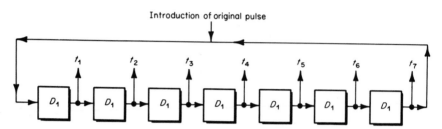

FIGURE 6-20 A clocking system for emitting timed pulses.

The original pulse enters a delay D_1; after the present delay time it emerges as t_1, which in turn is delayed in the next delay box and emerges as t_2, and so on.

With a few elaborations, information can be entered or withdrawn from a delay circuit. Such networks (Fig. 6-21) can therefore be used as memories.

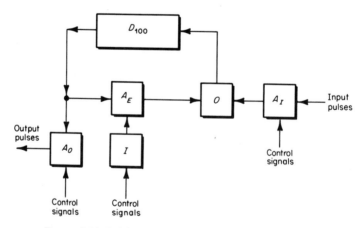

FIGURE 6-21 A delay circuit developed for use as a memory.

Gate A_E is normally open to the passage of information, for in the absence of control signals, the inverter produces a steady train of 1 bits. This permits all outputs from the delay to go through A_E. Information in this network recirculates indefinitely. All signals leave the delay line, pass A_E and the *or* gate, then re-enter the delay.

Information is "erased" by applying control signals to the inverter. The inverter emits a 0 pulse every time the control signal is a 1. This closes A_E, producing no output. The absence of an output is the same as a 0 bit. If a sequence of one hundred 1 bits are applied to the inverter, then all of the information in the system is erased. This leaves one hundred 0 bits in the memory.

Gate A_I is employed for entering pulse trains into information storage. The application of control signals opens A_I, thereby enabling input signals to enter the delay system. Since old information must be erased before new data is entered, gate A_E should be operated at the same time as A_I.

The output arrangement is similar. Normally A_O is closed. When information is needed from memory, control signals open this gate. Information can now pass out to another part of the machine. However, the same data remains recirculating through the delay. This read-out is nondestructive.

Some of the early computers, such as EDVAC and UNIVAC, used acoustic delay lines as memories. These devices consisted of mercury tubes. Information was retained in the form of sound waves vibrating through the mercury. At both ends of the tube there were crystal trans-ducers—components which convert energy from one form to another. When an electrical pulse entered the input crystal, it was converted to mechanical energy in the form of the sound waves. When the vibrations reached the output crystal, they were converted back into electrical energy. The electrical pulses were then amplified and reformed, after which they were re-entered into the mercury delay line. The velocity of the acoustical waves was closely controlled by the maintenance of the mercury at a constant temperature.

TRIGGERS

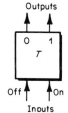

FIGURE 6-22 A trigger.

Modern computers do not use delays as memory units. However, the notion of delay is useful for expressing the conception of memory in a theoretical way. For example, the flip-flop, or trigger, which emits a steady sequence of 1 bits when turned on, can be conceived as a delay memory with a 1 bit capacity. As we shall see in a later chapter, this way of thinking of information storage enables computer circuits to be expressed mathematically. The symbol for a trigger is shown in Fig. 6-22. The trigger is regarded as turned *on* when it is in the state of emitting 1 bits. Otherwise it is regarded as *off*.

Now that we understand the four fundamental operations of *and*, *or, not,* and memory, we will be able to see in a simplified way how these building blocks can be used for several of the basic circuits in data processing machines.

THE BINARY COUNTER

Counting in the binary system can be carried out by means of special triggers. These change state every time an input is applied. However, they emit a signal only when their state changes from 1 to 0. With three of these devices, represented by S_1, S_2, and S_3, a circuit (Fig. 6-23) which can count from 0 to 8 can be constructed.

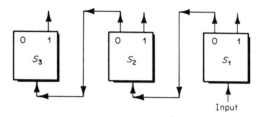

FIGURE 6-23 Trigger system capable of counting from 1 to 8.

Let's suppose that the initial state of the system is 0. This means that all three units are in the 0 state. Hence, we have the binary number 000.

Input pulses	Output		
	S_3	S_2	S_1
0	0	0	0
1	0	0	1
2	0	1	0
3	0	1	1
4	1	0	0
5	1	0	1
6	1	1	0
7	1	1	1
8	0	0	0

The first input causes S_1 to enter the 1 state. Now the network represents the binary number 001. The next signal returns S_1 to the 0 state. However, S_1 now emits an output which places S_2 in the 1 state. So now we have 010. When the third signal enters, S_1 goes into a 1 state, and the system goes to 011, which is decimal 3. In table form, we have the array shown on the opposite page.

THE ADDER

We have seen that a half-adder can be constructed with a combinatorial circuit. A full adder requires a network to take care of carries. It is therefore a system whose output is a function of past inputs as well as present inputs. This unit (Fig. **6-24**) consists basically of two half-adders with a D_1 delay included to handle the carry.

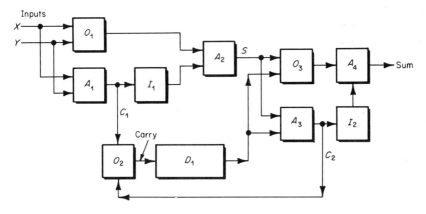

FIGURE 6-24 Full adder constructed from two half-adders and a delay.

Consider the addition

X inputs	010
Y inputs	011
Sums	101

The binary numbers appear at the X and Y inputs as sequences of 0 or 1 bits. Each pair of bits is timed to enter the system simultaneously. In the example above, the 0 from X and the 1 from Y enter O_1 and A_1 concomitantly. One time interval later, the 1 from X and the 1 from Y enter O_1 and A_1 concomitantly.

If there was a carry from the addition of the first pair of binary digits, this carry must be added in with the second pair of bits. The delay's purpose is to hold back the carry one time interval so that its effect is simultaneous with the addition of the second pair of bits.

Pursuing the example through the network, we see that the first pair of bits (0 and 1) causes a sum signal S_1 to emerge from A_2. No carry is produced. The S signal passes O_3 and is applied at A_4. Meanwhile, there is no output from A_3. I_2 now produces a 1 bit which causes A_4 to emit a 1, the first binary digit of the final sum.

When the second pair of bits (1 and 1) enters the system one time interval later, a carry is produced and there is no S output from A_2. This carry is now delayed for one time period. Therefore it cannot affect O_3 or A_3 until that interval has elapsed. Hence, there is no output from O_3 during the second time period. As a result the second digit in the final sum is a 0 bit.

The third pair (0 and 0) produces neither an S nor a carry output but D_1 now emits its output, which passes O_3. At the same time, the inverter converts its 0 bit input into a 1 bit. As a result the final binary digit in the sum is a 1.

The purpose of the C_2 signal is to provide for proper logic in the event of two consecutive carries, as in

$$
\begin{array}{r}
001 \\
\underline{011} \\
100
\end{array}
$$

The addition of the first pair of 1 bits causes a 0 output from A_4 since there is no output from A_2 at this time. However, a C_1 carry is now produced. When the second pair of bits is added, the 1 output from A_2 and the output of D_1 combine to pass A_3. The C_2 signal causes A_4 to emit a 0 and at the same time is fed back into O_2. In this way C_2 is enabled to play its part in the addition of the third pair of input bits. At the end of the next time interval, C_2 emerges from the delay and passes O_3 to produce a final sum bit of 1. By the way, it is not possible for C_2 to be present at the same time as C_1. C_1 can occur only when X and Y are 1 and 1, respectively, whereas C_2 can come into existence only when X and Y are 0 and 1, or 1 and 0.

COMPARISON

Most of the decision-making powers of computers are based upon their ability to compare fields of information. Suppose we set up a simple network called a *comparator* to perform this operation.

Let the inputs to this circuit (Fig. 6-25) be called I_1 and I_2 (not to be confused with Inverter No. 1 and Inverter No. 2). We'll assume that two binary numbers are entering, and that we want to find out which is larger.

The result of the comparison will be signaled by the final state of a trigger T, after both numbers have been processed by the network. We start the procedure by applying a *reset* signal to place T in an initial state 0. The signal emitted by the trigger depends upon its state.

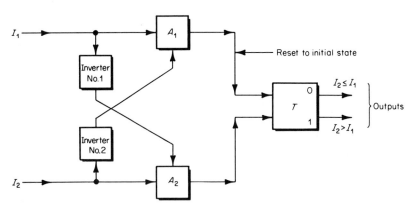

FIGURE 6-25 A comparator network for comparing information.

If the inputs for I_1 and I_2 are both 0's or both 1's, there can be no output from A_1 or A_2. Hence, on an equal condition there is no change in the state of T. If I_2 is a 1, and I_1 a 0, then a signal will pass A_2 to place T in the 1 state, thereby designating I_2 as the larger input. When I_2 is a 0 and I_1 a 1, then T enters the 0 state, for in this case the I_1 input is larger.

Suppose for example, the numbers 6 (0110) and 13 (1101) enter I_1 and I_2, respectively. After the first pair of bits, T enters the 1 state. The trigger returns to the 0 state after the second inputs, and remains in this state after the third pair of input bits. The final set of inputs, however, places T in the 1 state, thus indicating that I_2 is greater than I_1.

Order of entry	I_1 input (6)	I_2 input (13)	T output
1	0	1	1
2	1	0	0
3	1	1	0
4	0	1	1

SHIFTING

For various logical purposes, as well as for multiplication and division, it is necessary to provide the facility for shifting information within a memory unit without altering the data.

Suppose we have a 12-digit storage unit containing the number 73,452. Assume that this information can be shifted two digits to the left. In effect this multiplies the original number by 100.

Before	0	0	0	0	0	0	0	7	3	4	5	2

After	0	0	0	0	0	7	3	4	5	2	0	0

Let's consider a simple gating system (Fig. 6-26) to carry out a right shift operation on three binary digits. We shall store this binary number in three triggers. If a trigger is on, it emits a 1; if off, a 0. The number 110 is represented by the states on-on-off of the three triggers T_1, T_2, and T_3.

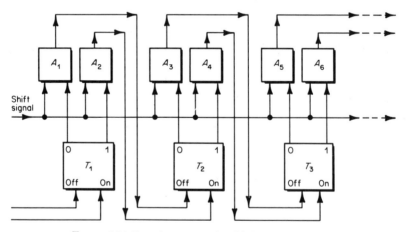

FIGURE 6-26 A gating system for shifting information.

When the shift signal occurs, all of the *and* gates receive a permissive pulse. The output of each trigger passes its associated gate, and is applied to the next trigger on the right. This next trigger is set on or off in accordance with the state of the prior trigger. Thus, if T_1 contains a 1 bit, this passes gate A_2, after which it turns on trigger T_2.

THE ORGANIZATION OF MEMORY

Data processing involves the handling of thousands of items of information. It is necessary to keep track of where each record is stored. Otherwise, data could not easily be obtained when needed. Furthermore, this method of data handling must be devised so that it can be carried out automatically.

This filing problem is solved by dividing the memory into a large number of pigeon holes called *locations,* each of which can store an item of data. Each location has an *address* consisting of a number. In this way every stored record has its own address. When an item of information is needed for an operation, the machine makes use of its particular address to obtain this data from memory. Results of calculations are also stored in memory locations.

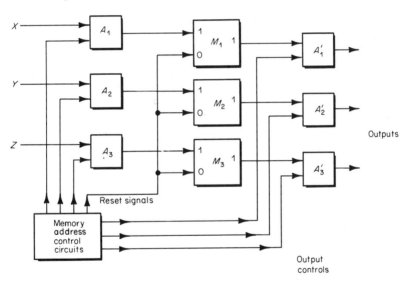

FIGURE 6-27 Memory unit with three locations.

To illustrate simply how this is done, let's assume that we have a memory (Fig. 6-27) consisting of three locations, M_1, M_2, and M_3, each of which can be set to 0 or 1. The addresses of these locations are 1, 2, and 3. Suppose it is necessary for the machine to make use of the information location M_1. The memory address control circuits emit a signal which opens output control *and* gate A_1'. If there is a 1 bit in M_1, this will now pass A_1' and will then be routed to some other parts of the machine. The absence of an output from A_1' means that a 0 bit was present in M_1.

To store a 1 bit in a memory location, say M_2, a similar procedure occurs. The input bit enters on the left. The memory address control circuits apply a signal to *and* gate A_2, which now passes the 1 bit to set M_2 to 1. Prior to storing information in these memory locations, they are reset to 0. This erases all previous data. If the input data is a 0, M_2 simply remains in the 0 state.

CONTROL CIRCUITS

A machine can perform many different operations upon information obtained from its memory. *Routing signals* select which circuit will process the data. These signals are emitted from a central control system which also has under its direction the memory address control circuits. Figure 6-28 shows these relationships schematically.

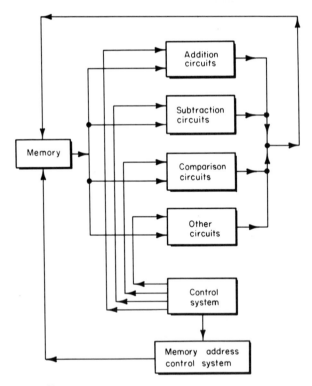

FIGURE 6-28 A control circuit for routing signals.

Here the control system signals a subsidiary circuit, the memory address control system, to obtain information from a specified memory location. This information is then available to be routed through several different gating networks, such as the addition circuits or subtraction circuits. The control system actuates the appropriate circuit for the processing of the data. After being operated upon, the information is returned to the memory.

This principle functions somewhat differently in practice. In building a computer, it is economically very useful to combine gating circuits whenever possible. Machines are cheaper to construct if common circuitry can be used for a number of different operations. Sometimes segments of gating systems can be utilized for this purpose. It is obvious, for example, that addition and subtraction are very similar. Hence, much of the circuitry for these processes can be used in common.

Gating circuits are so designed that, by opening and closing appropriate segments, the various required operations can be performed on data. The actual function of the routing signals dispatched by the control system is to switch information through network segments so as to perform a desired step in a calculation.

THE LOGIC OF THE ARITHMETIC FUNCTIONS

Let's now consider in greater detail how some of the more complex arithmetic operations are executed. The operations of addition, subtraction, multiplication, and division are essentially the same in any number system. The only variation is that the carry takes place at a different point in each system.

The addition in binary of the decimal numbers 3 and 9 takes the form

binary

$$
\begin{array}{ll}
\overset{\frown}{1\ 1} & \text{carries} \\
0\ 0\ 1\ 1 & = \text{decimal } 3 \\
\underline{1\ 0\ 0\ 1} & = \text{decimal } 9 \\
1\ 1\ 0\ 0 & = \text{decimal } 12
\end{array}
$$

When 1 is added to 1 in the first digit position, there is a carry to the second digit position. When this carry is added to 1 in the second digit position, there is a carry to the third digit position.

The rules for binary multiplication are:

$$
\begin{array}{l}
0 \times 0 = 0 \\
0 \times 1 = 0 \\
1 \times 0 = 0 \\
1 \times 1 = 1
\end{array}
$$

The simplicity of these operations enables binary numbers to be multiplied very easily. For example,

$$
\begin{array}{r}
1\,0\,0\,1\,1 = \text{decimal } 19 \\
\times\,1\,1\,0 = \text{decimal } 6 \\
\hline
0\,0\,0\,0\,0 \\
1\,0\,0\,1\,1 \\
1\,0\,0\,1\,1 \\
\hline
1\,1\,1\,0\,0\,1\,0 = \text{decimal } 114
\end{array}
$$

MULTIPLICATION

To understand how arithmetic is automated, we must examine these procedures more closely. Multiplication is basically a way of performing repeated additions. The process

$$214 \times 3 = 642$$

for example, is actually the addition three times of the number 214:

$$
\begin{array}{r}
1 \quad \text{carry} \\
214 \\
214 \\
214 \\
\hline
642
\end{array}
$$

The number 214 is called the *multiplicand* and 3 the *multiplier*.

When the multiplier consists of more than one digit, we are in reality multiplying by a higher power of ten, as in the case of

$$
\begin{array}{r}
126 \\
\times\,21 \\
\hline
126 \\
252 \\
\hline
2646
\end{array}
\qquad \text{which is equivalent to} \qquad
\begin{array}{r}
126 \\
\times\,1 \\
\hline
126
\end{array}
\quad
\begin{array}{r}
126 \\
\times\,20 \\
\hline
2520
\end{array}
\quad
\begin{array}{r}
126 \\
+\,2520 \\
\hline
2646
\end{array}
$$

This procedure consists of successively forming partial products with each consecutive digit in the multiplier.

SUBTRACTION

The two numbers involved in subtraction are called the *minuend* and the *subtrahend*:

$$
\begin{array}{rl}
40 & \text{minuend} \\
-\ 8 & \text{subtrahend} \\
\hline
32 &
\end{array}
$$

Computers usually execute subtraction by forming a *complement* of the subtrahend, and by adding this number to the minuend. A complement of a number is obtained by subtracting that number from 100. The complement of 8 is therefore 92. The operation of subtracting 8 from 40 can be carried out as follows:

$$
\begin{array}{r}
40 \\
+\ 92 \quad \text{complement of 8} \\
\hline
132 \\
-\ 100 \quad \text{(performed by dropping the 1 in 132)} \\
\hline
32
\end{array}
$$

This is based on the fact that

$$
40 + (100 - 8) - 100 =
$$
$$
40 + \quad (92) \quad - 100 = 32
$$

The reason why computers subtract by adding the complement is economic. The circuitry for executing arithmetic operations is expensive to design and build. The complement of binary numbers is obtained very simply, and it is then possible to use the addition circuits for the subtraction operation.

Subtraction and addition, as we have remarked, use much of the same circuitry (Fig. 6-29). Subtraction is performed by routing the subtrahend through a gating network called a *complement generator* before this information enters the adder.

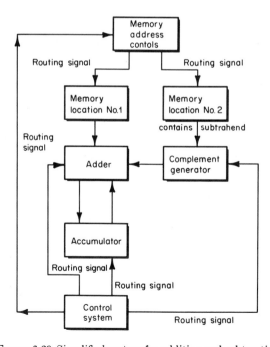

FIGURE 6-29 Simplified system for addition and subtraction.

Suppose the minuend is stored in memory location No. 1 and the subtrahend in memory location No. 2. The control circuits actuate the memory address controls to obtain this information. The control circuits activate the complement generator and the adder. The minuend and complemented subtrahend enter the adder in synchronism. The result of the subtraction is placed in the *accumulator,* a special register used for arithmetic operations.

In the process of addition, the complement generator is not actuated by the control system, and a number to be added from memory location No. 2 passes through this unit unchanged. Actually, the addition of a positive number to a negative number is the same as a subtraction. For this reason whenever the machine initiates an addition, the first step in the procedure is for the control system to test for this condition. If this condition exists, the computer carries out a subtraction.

Subtraction is, in practice, more complicated than we have indicated. In some instances it is necessary to complement the result of a subtraction to obtain the correct answer. In such cases the control system routes the contents of the accumulator through the complement generator to complete the operation.

DIVISION

Division consists of subtracting the divisor from the dividend repeatedly until no more subtractions are possible. The number of subtractions which are possible constitutes the quotient. For example,

$$\frac{\text{Dividend}}{\text{Divisor}} \quad \frac{30}{5} = 6 \quad \text{quotient}$$

actually consists of:

$$
\begin{array}{rl}
30 & \\
-\ 5 & \\
\hline
25 & (1) \\
-\ 5 & \\
\hline
20 & (2) \\
-\ 5 & \\
\hline
15 & (3) \\
-\ 5 & \\
\hline
10 & (4) \\
-\ 5 & \\
\hline
5 & (5) \\
-\ 5 & \\
\hline
0 & (6) \\
\end{array}
$$

tally of number of subtractions

no remainder

It is often difficult to estimate how many times the divisor can be subtracted from the dividend. The test is whether a negative remainder is produced. Consider

$$346\overline{)2421}$$

Is the quotient digit 6 or 7? If we choose 7 we obtain a negative remainder:

$$
\begin{array}{r}
7 \\
346\overline{)2421} \\
2422 \\
\hline
-1
\end{array}
$$

This result is improper, and we see at once that we should have chosen 6 as our answer.

To perform division a machine must be able to recognize when it has executed too many subtractions. This is done by designing the equipment to test each time for a negative remainder. If a negative remainder is sensed, then the machine adds back the divisor to obtain the proper quotient digit and remainder.

MULTIPLICATION BY COMPUTERS

Multiplication consists of a series of steps. Each successive multiplication by a multiplier digit produces a partial product which must be added to the previous partial product. Special auxiliary storage units, such as the accumulator, are usually employed for holding the multiplier and for storing and shifting the partial products. Multiplication is a program in itself. The control system automates the sequence of steps by sending out routing signals at the proper times to initiate each new procedure.

Numerous methods for performing multiplication have been used in computers. Speed of operation, of course, is a prime objective, but this must be balanced against the cost of constructing the required circuits. One of the problems in multiplication is to enable the machine to form the partial products as fast as possible. If this is done simply by repeated addition, multiplication becomes a long, drawn-out procedure. One way of reducing this time is to provide *multiple generators*. These are gating circuits (Fig. 6-30) which prepare partial products without repeated addition. This circuit consists of two doublers, one quintupler, and a multiplicand adder. The doublers each perform the operation 2 × multiplicand; the quintupler executes 5 × multiplicand.

The original multiplicand is available at the *and* gates by itself, and

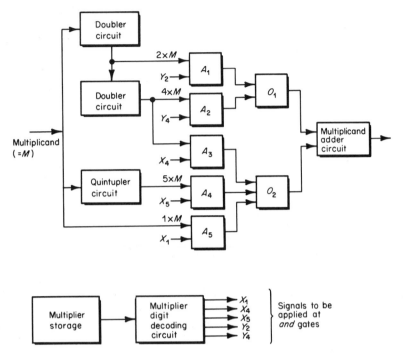

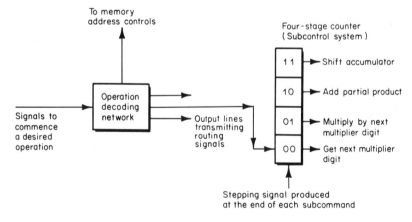

FIGURE 6-30 Multiple generator.

in doubled, quadrupled, and quintupled forms. By opening and closing the proper combination of gates, any multiple can be obtained from the multiplicand adder. For example, the signal X_5 causes only the quintuple to be added, thus producing an output of $5 \times$ multiplicand. The partial product, consisting of $8 \times$ multiplicand, is obtained by using

FIGURE 6-31 Simplified control circuit for multiplication.

signals X_4 and Y_4, the two quadrupled numbers being combined in the multiplicand adder.

The multiplier digit decoding circuit ascertains what multiplier digit is present, and produces the proper combination of signals to be applied at *and* gates.

The control circuits (Fig. 6-31) initiate the steps in a multiplication. Consider the machine procedure for

$$
\begin{array}{r}
753 \\
\times\ 326 \\
\hline
4518 \\
1506 \\
2259 \\
\hline
245478
\end{array}
$$

If a multiple generator is used, the sequence of occurrences is:

Basic cycle of four steps

1. Obtain first multiplier digit (6).
2. Multiply 6 × 753 (= 4518).
3. Add partial product to accumulator (which is assumed to be initially 0000000). The present state of the accumulator is 4518000. (The left-hand digit of each partial product is always added to the left-hand digit in each accumulator.)
4. Shift accumulator one position to the right. The present state of the accumulator is 0451800.

Basic cycle of four steps

5. Obtain second multiplier digit (2).
6. Multiply 2 × 753 (= 1506).
7. Add partial product to accumulator (1506 + 0451800 = 1957800, which now becomes the present state of the accumulator).
8. Shift accumulator one position to the right. The present state of the accumulator is 0195780.

Basic cycle of four steps

9. Obtain third multiplier digit (3).
10. Multiply 3 × 753 (= 2259).
11. Add partial product to accumulator (2259 + 0195780 = 2454780, which now becomes the present state of the accumulator).
12. Shift accumulator one position to the right. (The present state of the accumulator is 0245478).

13. Sense end of multiplier. End operation.

Multiplication, as exemplified above, involves the repetition of four basic steps for as long as there are multiplier digits. Each cycle of four is accomplished by the dispatching of a different set of routing signals from the control circuits. Let's refer to these four-step cycles as subcommands.

To provide for the repetition of these four commands, a subcontrol system is necessary. The control system in a computer contains an operation decoding network. This circuit receives, in coded form, the next command for the machine to execute. The operation decoding network provides the signals which are routed throughout the computer for each particular operation. The control system also receives the address of the memory locations involved in the command, and uses this information to actuate the memory address controls.

In the case of multiplication, the routing signals are not sent out directly. Instead, the control system activates a four-stage counter—a binary counter which counts from 0 to 3. This device is started at 00. In each stage it emits the routing signals required for a subcommand in multiplication. At the end of each subcommand, a *stepping* signal is produced which increases the number in the counter by 1. After the counter reaches 11, it returns to 00 and recommences the cycle. The four-step cycles are repeated until there are no more multiplier digits.

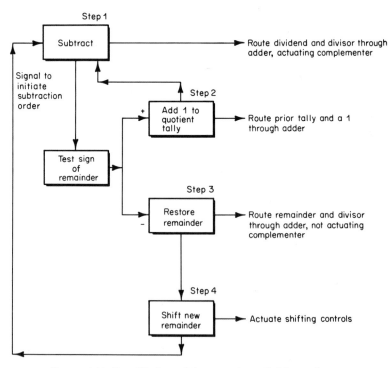

FIGURE 6-32 Simplified control system for a division order.

DIVISION BY COMPUTERS

Actually, even the simplest of the commands in a computer's repertoire usually requires two or more subcommands. One of the most complex
operations in most machines is division. Part of the subcontrol system for
division is shown in Fig. 6-32. As depicted here, there are four basic
steps in the procedure. A test of the sign of the remainder is initiated
after every step 1. This test determines whether step 2 or step 3 will
follow at this point.

7 THE ALGEBRA OF AUTOMATA

SYMBOLIC LOGIC

The everyday language we employ in thinking is far broader than arithmetic, which expresses only quantitative relationships. There are patterns of information in our environment which we cannot understand solely through operations on numbers. Many of these processes involve systematic qualitative relationships whose language we have yet to discover.

Boolean algebra, a discipline which is part of symbolic logic, is one of a large class of abstract grammars which have received extensive attention by logicians and mathematicians in the last few decades. This language was first formulated by George Boole in 1854 in his "Investigation of the Laws of Thought." One of its practical uses has been in the understanding of switching circuits.

The algebra devised by Boole can be regarded as based on three operations: *and, or,* and *not.* These operations are performed upon variables such as p, q, r, or s. The expression

$$pq$$

represents the statement "p and q." This conjunction is true only when both p and q are jointly true. The expression

$$p \vee q$$

means "p or q." This statement is true when either p is true, q is true, or when both are jointly true. It is false only when *both* p and q are jointly false. Finally, we have

$$\overline{p}$$

which symbolizes "not p," that is, the negation of p.

The application of Boolean algebra to switching circuits was suggested by Claude Shannon in 1938. His idea was to express each relay in a network by a variable. Series connections were represented by the operation *and,* and parallel circuits by *or.* In this way relay networks could be expressed algebraically. For example, the circuit in Fig. 7-1 is represented by pq.

FIGURE 7-1 A relay circuit expressed algebraically by pq.

When the logical statement pq is true, then current will flow in the circuit. When false, current will not flow. A variable is true when the relay it represents is closed. Therefore, when relays p and q are both closed, the variables p and q are both true. This makes the statement pq true. Hence, current will flow in the circuit only when both relays are closed.

A parallel circuit (Fig. 7-2) is represented by p v q. This Boolean statement is true if at least one of the relays is closed. Hence current will always flow, except when both relay p and relay q are open.

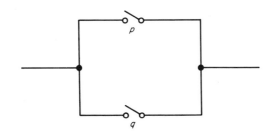

FIGURE 7-2 Parallel circuit represented by p v q.

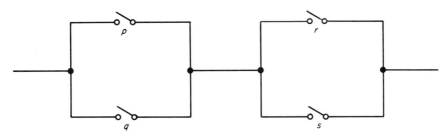

FIGURE 7-3 Two parallel circuits connected in series, expressed as $(p$ v $q)$ $(r$ v $s)$.

Complicated networks are very difficult to understand with unaided common sense. The representation of these logical relations in algebraic form introduces a vastly superior method for manipulating these ideas. Thus, the diagram of Fig. 7-3 is represented by $(p \vee q)(r \vee s)$.

Here we have two parallel circuits connected in series. The parallel circuits are expressed by $(p \vee q)$ $(r \vee s)$. The parentheses act as an *and* between these two expressions.

BOOLEAN ALGEBRA

By algebraic manipulation a Boolean statement can be transformed into an equivalent Boolean statement expressing the same logical relationships. Two such statements are called *equivalent,* and are represented by the symbol $\equiv$. This manipulation makes it possible to obtain two or more relay circuits which perform the same function. For example, by reversing the order of the variables, we have

$$p \vee q \equiv q \vee p$$

Translated into circuitry, we obtain Fig. 7-4a equivalent to Fig. 7-4b.

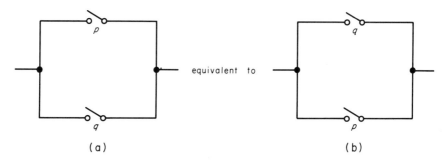

FIGURE 7-4 Equivalent circuits, expressed by $p \vee q \equiv q \vee p$.

This method can often be used to economize on the number of relays in a network. Consider, for example, a circuit (Fig. 7-5) required to transmit current under one or more of the three conditions:

1. p is closed, and q is closed
2. p is closed, r is closed, and s is closed
3. p is closed, r is closed, and t is closed.

The Boolean equation for this system is

$$pq \vee prs \vee prt$$

Notice that the variable p is present in each of the terms of this expression. As in high school algebra, we can factor out this p.

$$pq \text{ v } prs \text{ v } prt \equiv p \,(q \text{ v } rs \text{ v } rt)$$

This yields the simpler network shown in Fig. 7-6.

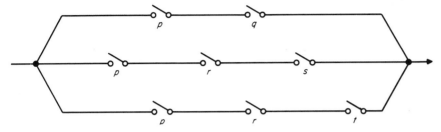

FIGURE 7-5 A circuit expressed by pq v prs v prt.

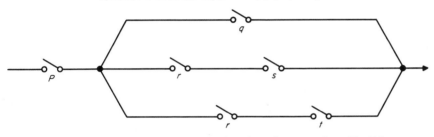

FIGURE 7-6 Simpler network achieved by factoring out p from Fig. 7-5.

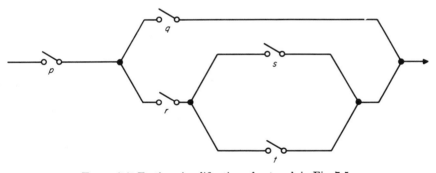

FIGURE 7-7 Further simplification of network in Fig. 7-5.

Further reduction in the number of relays is possible, however, for additional factoring can be carried out on the expression in parentheses by noting that the variable r occurs in two of the terms. We have

$$pq \text{ v } prs \text{ v } prt \equiv p \,(q \text{ v } rs \text{ v } rt) \equiv p \,[q \text{ v } r(s \text{ v } t)]$$

We now have a network (Fig. 7-7) with five relays, as compared with eight in the circuit we started with.

GATING NETWORKS

As we have seen, gating networks have the same logical characteristics as relay circuits. The basic rules for representing gates are illustrated in Fig. 7-8.

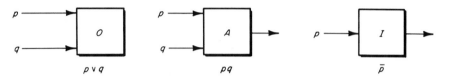

FIGURE 7-8 Rules for algebraic representation of gates.

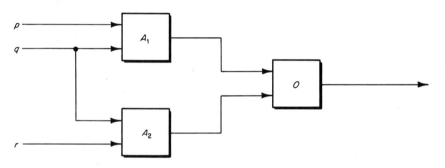

FIGURE 7-9 A gating network expressed as $(pq \lor qr)$.

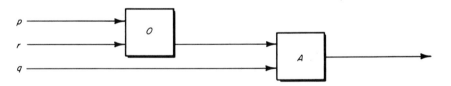

FIGURE 7-10 Simplified form of network in Fig. 7-9.

Any gating network can ·thereby be placed in algebraic form. For example the illustration of Fig. 7-9 becomes $(pq \lor qr)$.

This network, by the way, can be simplified by logical manipulation, in this case by factoring out the q's to give $q(p \lor r)$, which is the circuit of Fig. 7-10.

There are a large number of logical equivalences which are immediately obvious. For example,

$$xx \equiv x$$

$$\text{and} \quad x \lor x \equiv x$$

The symbol 1 is used to designate an expression which is always true, as in the case of

$$x1 \equiv 1$$

This statement says "*x and* 1 are equivalent to 1."

DeMorgan's theorems are particularly interesting. They are:

(1) $$\overline{(xy)} \equiv \bar{x} \text{ v } \bar{y}$$
(2) $$\bar{x}\bar{y} \equiv \overline{(x \text{ v } y)}$$

A bar over a parentheses means that the entire expression is negated. Proposition (1) states that if the conjunction of x and y is false, then either x or y, or both, must be false. Proposition (2) states that if x and y are both false, then the disjunction $x \text{ v } y$ is false.

CIRCUIT SIMPLIFICATION

The design of gating circuits is an art which utilizes intuition and past experience. However, as the level of complexity increases, logical equations become more useful. It is not immediately obvious, for example, that the circuit of Fig. 7-11 can be constructed in a simpler, equivalent way.

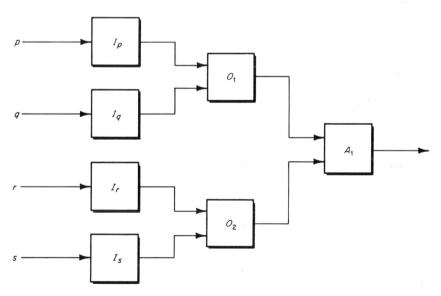

FIGURE 7-11 A network expressed as $(\bar{p} \text{ v } \bar{q})(\bar{r} \text{ v } \bar{s})$.

This network provides an output only when both *or* gates emit a 1 bit to be applied to A_1. The *or* gates in turn must both be fed by at least one 1 bit to produce a 1 output. If both p and q are 1 bits, then I_p and I_q will emit 0 bits; therefore, either p or q, or both, must be 0 bits. Since the circuit is symmetrical, it is apparent that r and s, likewise, must be 0 bits. In summary then, there will be a 1 bit output from the system if either p or q, or both, are 0, and if at the same time either r or s, or both, are 0. This wordy description is easily stated algebraically as

$$(\bar{p} \vee \bar{q})(\bar{r} \vee \bar{s})$$

By two applications of DeMorgan's theorem, this expression can be transformed.

(1) $\qquad (\bar{p} \vee \bar{q})(\bar{r} \vee \bar{s}) \equiv (\overline{pq})(\overline{rs}),$ and in turn

(2) $\qquad (\overline{pq})(\overline{rs}) \equiv (\overline{pq \vee rs})$

The right-hand side of equivalence (2) describes the gating circuit of Fig. 7-12. The performance of this system is identical with that of the original network.

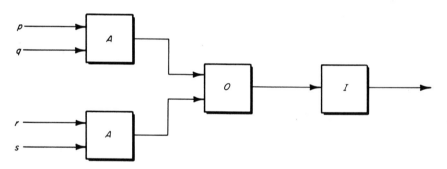

FIGURE 7-12 Simplified form of gating network in Fig. 7-11.

An easy way of finding out whether two networks are logically equivalent is to form their *truth tables*. We'll illustrate this method with the circuits

$$x \vee y \qquad\qquad y \vee x$$

For these two networks to be equivalent, they must have the same output for every set of inputs. What we do is to list all possible combinations of inputs. Then we write down what the output of each circuit is when it has these inputs.

Inputs		Statement		
x	y	$x \lor y$	$\equiv$	$y \lor x$
0	0	0		0
0	1	1		1
1	0	1		1
1	1	1		1

We now can ascertain when $(x \lor y)$ and $(y \lor x)$ are equivalent.

Inputs		Statement		
x	y	$x \lor y$	$\equiv$	$y \lor x$
0	0	0	1	0
0	1	1	1	1
1	0	1	1	1
1	1	1	1	1

It is apparent that the two circuits always have the same output whenever they have the same input. Therefore they are equivalent.

Let's now consider two gating networks (Fig. 7-13) where the equivalence is less obvious. Again we list all combinations of inputs, and ascertain what the outputs would be for each possibility.

Circuit No. 1 $(pq \lor \bar{q})$

Inputs				Outputs
p	q	pq	$\bar{q}$	$pq \lor \bar{q}$
0	0	0	1	1
0	1	0	0	0
1	0	0	1	1
1	1	1	0	1

Circuit No. 2 $(p \lor \bar{q})$

Inputs			Outputs
p	q	$\bar{q}$	$p \lor \bar{q}$
0	0	1	1
0	1	0	0
1	0	1	1
1	1	0	1

An examination of the two tables shows that in both instances the same combinations of inputs produce the same outputs. The circuits are therefore equivalent. It is obvious that circuit No. 2 is more economical, as it does not require the *or* gate which is used in circuit No. 1.

Since a data processing machine consists of a very large number of gating networks, an important aspect of the design of the equipment consists of attempting to simplify these circuits. We have seen that a visual examination of networks cannot achieve this purpose. The ma-

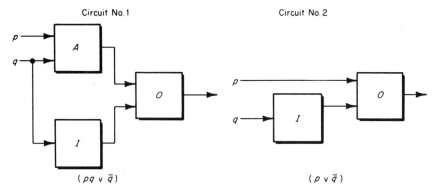

FIGURE 7-13 Two equivalent gating networks.

nipulation of Boolean equations facilitates the minimization of circuits. However, these equations are of great complexity, and even a skilled individual has difficulty in sensing what algebraic transformations are required in many instances. Furthermore, there is no guarantee that the art of the individual will produce optimum results in his manipulations.

THE SYNTHESIS OF SWITCHING CIRCUITS

Boolean algebra can also be used to design circuits from specifications. These specifications consist of a list of all possible inputs, along with the output required in each case.

Let's design a network which will have three input wires, p, q, and r. In any particular instance either a 0 or a 1 could be present on the wire. There are eight possible combinations of inputs. These are listed below, with the output we want the network to have in each case. Suppose we specify that the circuit is to add three binary bits, ignoring carries:

p	q	r	Output
0	0	0	0
0	0	1	1
0	1	0	1
0	1	1	0
1	0	0	1
1	0	1	0
1	1	0	0
1	1	1	1

This network performs the operations

$$
\begin{array}{cccccccc}
0 & 0 & 0 & 0 & 1 & 1 & 1 & 1 \\
0 & 0 & 1 & 1 & 0 & 0 & 1 & 1 \\
\underline{0} & \underline{1} & \underline{0} & \underline{1} & \underline{0} & \underline{1} & \underline{0} & \underline{1} \\
0 & 1 & 1 & 0 & 1 & 0 & 0 & 1
\end{array}
$$

To meet these specifications, the gating network must produce a 1 output in four instances only. We begin by considering the case where the input on p is a 0, the input on q is a 0, and the input on r is a 1. The Boolean expression for this combination of inputs is

$$\bar{p}\bar{q}r$$

We find the logical representations for the other three cases in a similar way. They are

$$\bar{p}q\bar{r}, \qquad p\bar{q}\bar{r}, \qquad \text{and} \qquad pqr$$

By forming an equation from these expressions, we are able to state precisely under what conditions we wish our network to emit a 1 output.

$$\bar{p}\bar{q}r \text{ v } \bar{p}q\bar{r} \text{ v } p\bar{q}\bar{r} \text{ v } pqr$$

The corresponding circuit is shown in Fig. 7-14.

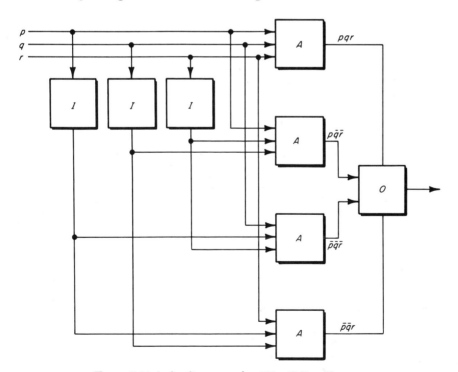

FIGURE 7-14 A circuit expressed as $\bar{p}\bar{q}r$ v $\bar{p}q\bar{r}$ v $p\bar{q}\bar{r}$ v pqr.

In the preceding chapter we said that networks can often be combined so as to reduce the total required circuitry. Figure 7-15 shows an il-

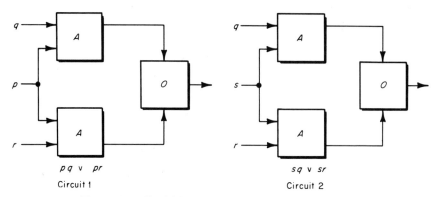

Circuit 1   Circuit 2

FIGURE 7-15 Combining networks to reduce total circuitry.

lustration of this type of simplication. Suppose we have the two circuits (1) and (2). By factoring, we obtain the equations

(1) $$p\,(q \vee r)$$
(2) $$s\,(q \vee r)$$

It now becomes apparent that the required outputs can be produced

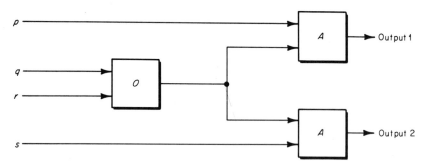

FIGURE 7-16 Combined network from Fig. 7-15.

by the circuit of Fig. 7-16. This circuit is more economical, for if the circuits were uncombined, an additional three gates would be needed.

THE LOGIC OF SEQUENTIAL CIRCUITS

Thus far we have considered the application of symbolic logic only to combinatorial circuits. Let's now see how Boolean algebra can be used to represent sequential circuits.

Suppose we have the delay network of Fig. 7-17. For convenience, we'll designate the output of the circuit by the letter O. The output of the delay will be called K. Inputs are I_1 and I_2.

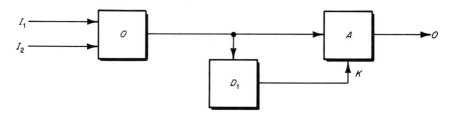

FIGURE 7-17 A sequential circuit with a D_1 delay.

To get an output from this circuit, a signal must pass the *and* gate. This occurs when K is 1 and when there is a 1 input on I_1 or I_2. All of the possibilities are represented in the following table.

Present inputs		Output of delay	Output
I_1	I_2	K	O
0	0	0	0
0	0	1	0
0	1	0	0
0	1	1	1
1	0	0	0
1	0	1	1
1	1	0	0
1	1	1	1

This system can be represented by the Boolean equation

$$O = K \, (I_1 \vee I_2)$$

However, neither this equation nor the preceding table adequately express the time relationships which exist. The presence of a 1 output from the delay depends on the previous inputs on I_1 and I_2. The signal K

represents the history of the system. To express this history, we'll form a table which includes the past inputs from I_1 and I_2.

Present inputs		Past inputs		Output
I_1	I_2	I_1	I_2	O
0	0	0	0	0
0	0	0	1	0
0	0	1	0	0
0	0	1	1	0
0	1	0	0	0
0	1	0	1	1
0	1	1	0	1
0	1	1	1	1
1	0	0	0	0
1	0	0	1	1
1	0	1	0	1
1	0	1	1	1
1	1	0	0	0
1	1	0	1	1
1	1	1	0	1
1	1	1	1	1

Letting the superscript n represent a present input, and $n - 1$ the previous input, we have

$$O^n = (I_1^{n-1} \text{ v } I_2^{n-1})(I_1^n \text{ v } I_2^n)$$

This equation says that the emitting of an output at a time n will occur if there is at least one input at time n, along with at least one input in the previous time unit $n - 1$.

Where feedback exists, a network must be expressed by equations which represent the history of the system. Such equations, which use a mathematical language known as *recursive functions*, constitute the algebra of automata. Consider, for example, the circuit of Fig. 7-18.

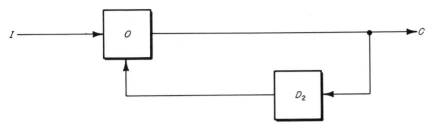

FIGURE 7-18 A sequential circuit with a D_2 delay.

The present output of this network is a function of its present input I^n, and its past output O^{n-2}.

(1) $$O^n = I^n \vee O^{n-2}$$

A general formula for the behavior of a sequential circuit must express its output in terms of all present inputs and memory states. (The information in a delay resulting from previous inputs constitutes a memory state.) Letting the letter S represent the present state of memory, equation (1) becomes

$$O^n = I^n \vee S^n$$

To ascertain whether there will be a present output from the circuit, it is necessary to know the history of the inputs, as well as the initial state of the system.

It is apparent that networks can be devised with very complex interrelations among numerous memory devices. A computer can be conceived as a system of gating and feedback circuits for switching stored information so as to perform arithmetic and logical functions. More generally stated, a computer consists of gating networks which cause a system to go through various required memory state transitions.

THE AUTOMATION OF COMPUTER DESIGN

Thus far, more work has been done in the application of logical algebras to the design of combinatorial circuits than to networks with memories. And even in the case of combinatorial systems, there are many difficulties in making fruitful use of Boolean algebra. For example, the minimum network from a purely logical point of view may not be the simplest from an engineering standpoint. Furthermore, electronic timing requirements may not be properly established by Boolean equations.

Many practical problems in the manufacture and maintenance of data processing machines also complicate the use of logical algebras in design. In producing equipment, the greater the variety of circuits needed, the higher the cost of manufacturing. However, in many instances it is possible to utilize the more complex electronic networks for functions which could be performed by simpler circuits. From a strictly logical standpoint, this is inefficient. Nevertheless, by taking advantage of this fact, it may be possible to use a relatively small number of standard circuits. In this way, manufacturing costs can be reduced.

The same situation exists when it comes to the maintenance of computers. Thousands of electronic circuits exist in machines, and occasionally some of these networks have to be replaced. Computer installations, therefore, keep an inventory of replacement circuits. But it is easier and more economical to stock a small number of general-purpose replacement circuits than to keep available an enormous number of different networks.

Easier maintenance is also possible with standard circuits. Computing equipment is tremendously expensive, and the loss of a few hours of operational time may cost thousands of dollars. Furthermore, many installations work on tight schedules for preparing output reports. Payroll checks, for example, must always be ready promptly. For these reasons, data processing machines cannot be subject to frequent *down time,* periods when the equipment is not working. High reliability is of course demanded of computers; errors cannot be tolerated. One of the methods used for avoiding faulty operation is to devote a small amount of time every day to scheduled maintenance sessions. During these periods the engineers run special tests to find out which parts are in poor condition. To facilitate their efforts, computers must be designed to make marginal components easily recognizable and simple to replace. The use of a small number of standard circuits helps serve this purpose.

The ultimate goal in the use of Boolean algebra is to automatize the design of computers. This would be accomplished by having one machine design another. This could be done if all of the circuits could be expressed in algebraic form. These formulas would then be entered into a computer for processing. We are assuming, of course, the existence of algorithms which could be utilized by the machine for its computations. For example, if minimization procedures were developed which were purely mechanical, requiring no art, then a computer could be instructed to perform these operations. The output of the data processing machine would be formulas expressing the optimum design for some specified new equipment.

The fact of the matter is that the number and complexity of the networks comprising modern computers is so great that the human mind is sometimes unable to grasp all of the logical subtleties which arise. Therefore, it has become necessary to develop automatic methods to assist in the design of equipment.

Automation of design has been attempted in several areas which are closely related to the preparation of minimal circuits. When a development engineer designs a part of a computer, he sketches out the network on paper. Methods have been devised to code this drawing so that it can be entered into a data processing machine. Many pages of such drawings are needed to describe a complete computer. Since all of these segments are interconnected by wires, a cross-referencing system is necessary between the engineering drawings. Once the drawings have been entered into the computer, the machine can provide this necessary index.

The computer also helps to avoid a great deal of the tedious clerical labor involved in making changes in the circuit diagrams. Such changes in network design inevitably occur frequently while a machine is being planned. The introduction of these alterations is not only a large redrafting task, but involves the creation of a new indexing system between pages. Errors tend to occur when this work is done by humans. However, it is possible for all of these procedures to be done by machine. A computer can check for clerical and logical errors, enter changes, and recheck the new circuit diagrams. A machine can even draw the new diagrams, thereby relieving humans of the drafting work.

Part of the procedure for designing computers is the preparation of wiring charts for the new machine. The inside of a computer is a spaghetti-like network of wires stretching in a variety of ways from one end of the machine to another. The minimization of wire lengths, taking into account such factors as electronic interference between wires, is an important problem. This can be solved by machine. Here again, the effect of engineering changes on the wiring arrangements is introduced automatically.

Another aspect of design automation is the preparation of a list of all of the parts necessary to manufacture a new machine. Given a statement of all of the needed circuits, a computer can determine how many electronic components are required for each particular network, and hence for the entire equipment. This list of needed materials enables the manufacturing plant to establish the inventory of parts required for production. In this case also, automation enables a continual updating of production requirements to be made when the engineering details are altered.

The manufacturing of computers has been mechanized to some extent. A striking example is the use of printed circuits. This technique prepares electronic networks by a mechanical printing process. Older methods consisted of the laborious process of actually soldering wires to contact points.

It seems likely that more and more of the design and manufacture of computers will gradually be automated. The ultimate goal, of course, would be to be able to give a data processing machine the specifications for a new computer. The machine would then synthesize the minimal Boolean formulas needed for the circuits, develop all of the required network diagrams and wiring arrangements, and schedule and operate an automatic factory to produce the new computer.

8 THE ELEMENTS OF PROGRAMMING

OVER-ALL SYSTEM ORGANIZATION

Electronic data processing machines solve problems by executing a sequence of operations. To carry out programs, each machine is designed to perform certain instructions. The particular set of commands a computer is able to execute is determined by the applications for which the machine is intended. Some equipment is designed to be as general purpose as possible.

The art of the programmer is to prepare the sequence of instructions required for the solution of problems. These commands are given to the machine in the form of codes stored in its memory. Basically, a program can be construed as a sequence of control signals which routes information through the data processing circuits.

A typical machine (Fig. 8-1) has a central processing unit which contains the memory, data processing circuits, and the control circuits. A magnetic drum or disk file is available for auxiliary storage. Input and output is by punched cards or magnetic tape, and a printer is available for the production of output reports. A supervisory control unit, or *console*, is provided for communication with the machine by engineers, operators, and programmers.

AUTOMATIC SEQUENCING

One of the most remarkable characteristics of computers is that they can operate for a long time without any human intervention. The reason for this is that the instructions governing the machine are stored in its memory. After the computer finishes executing an instruction, it merely has to go to its memory to obtain the code for the next instruction. The machine can keep on going this way, executing thousands of commands, until it reaches an instruction telling it to stop.

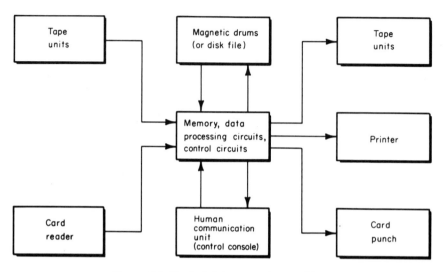

FIGURE 8-1 Typical data processing machine.

To understand how a computer works, let us first consider how an addition is performed on a desk adding machine. The initial step is to obtain one of the numbers to be added. This value is then entered on the keyboard of the machine by pressing the appropriate keys. However, it is not yet available for computation. A further step is required: a button must be pressed to cause the number to be registered internally. Then it is necessary to obtain the second value and enter it, in turn, on the keyboard. To cause addition to occur, the operator presses another button. When the numbers have been added, the sum is shown in some predetermined place—perhaps in a set of dials, or possibly on a paper tape. Usually the operator then writes this result down on a separate sheet of paper.

To the person using the adding machine, this seems like a very simple operation. But it is not quite as simple as it looks. It seems simple because the operator has learned to do a great many things so automatically that he is hardly aware of doing them. If such an operation were to be performed by someone who had no knowledge of figures or adding machines, it would be necessary to break the procedure down into a series of separate steps such as: (1) Obtain a given value; (2) Enter it into the keyboard; (3) Press the appropriate button to get the value stored in the machine; (4) Obtain the second value; (5) Enter it in the keyboard; (6) Press the button causing an addition; (7) Read the result; (8) Write the result in the proper location.

If the clerk had no capacity to remember these steps, it would be necessary to give him an itemized list of them each time he was to perform the operation.

Controlling a computer is similar in many ways. Everything it is to do must be specified exactly, and in the proper sequence. In a typical computer, addition requires a set of instructions very much like the set we have just worked out.

MEMORY ADDRESSES

Unlike a desk calculator, however, a computer has the capacity to store many different items of information at the same time. Consequently, it is not enough merely to give a code specifying an addition, or whatever is desired. It is also necessary to identify the data to be used in the calculation. This leads to a basic principle of computer operation: Data is always identified in a computer by its *location* in the computer, just as data in a ledger can be identified by its position in a column.

Locations are identified in various ways. Usually they are numbered. The number of a location is called its *address*. For example, 10,000 locations may be numbered from 0000 to 9999. (By beginning with 0000 instead of 0001, the ten-thousandth location can be identified with four digits instead of five, a fact that simplifies machine design.)

It is not possible to add two values together unless they can be obtained from their storage location. Therefore, the addresses of the data must be used in the instructions. In many machines, it is first necessary to move a number to a special register, sometimes called an *accumulator*, to perform the addition in that register, and then to move the result to some specified location. To show how this might be done, let us invent a simple computer which uses an accumulator for arithmetic operations.

We will suppose that this machine has a memory consisting of 1000 locations, numbered from 000 to 999. Each location can hold 10 characters. For example, location 800 might contain year-to-date salary, and 801 might contain this week's earnings, as follows:

Location 800 | 0 | 0 | 0 | 0 | 0 | 0 | 7 | 2 | 9 | 0 | (year-to-date salary = $7290)

Location 801 | 0 | 0 | 0 | 0 | 0 | 0 | 0 | 1 | 4 | 5 | (week's earnings = $145)

MACHINE INSTRUCTIONS

Instructions in this machine consist of a one-letter operation code and a three-digit address. An instruction called LOAD is used to move a number from a designated memory location into the accumulator, in so doing erasing whatever information was previously in the accumulator. We will assume that the operation code for LOAD is L. Let the instruction ADD, with code A, be employed to add the number in some specified memory location to whatever is in the accumulator. (See Fig. 8-2.) To move a number from the accumulator into memory, the instruction UNLOAD (code U) is used.

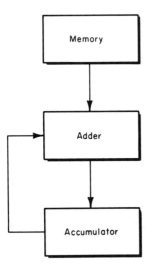

Hence, to add this week's earnings to year-to-date salary, we use the following instruction sequence: (The "explanation" is for the reader's benefit; it is not part of the program.)

FIGURE 8-2 Schematic flow of information in the add order.

Instruction	Explanation
L 800	Year-to-date earnings are placed in accumulator.
A 801	Week's earnings added to year-to-date earnings. Result left in the accumulator.
U 800	Updated year-to-date earnings are placed in location 800, erasing previous number.

This sequence of steps is entirely independent of the actual numbers being added. The computer adds together whatever values it finds in locations 800 and 801.

STORAGE OF INSTRUCTIONS

An important point to remember is that the instructions themselves occupy storage locations in the same way as data. To illustrate, let's assume that the three instructions we have written are placed in locations 100, 101, and 102. This program would therefore be expressed as

Instruction location	Instruction
100	L 800
101	A 801
102	U 800

These instructions would appear in memory in the following fashion:

Location 100	L	0	0	0	0	0	0	8	0	0
Location 101	A	0	0	0	0	0	0	8	0	1
Location 102	U	0	0	0	0	0	0	8	0	0

What would happen if we had made a mistake with the first instruction and had written L 100 instead of L 800? The answer is simple: the computer would load into the accumulator whatever it found in location 100 instead of the contents of location 800. In this case, it would actually load the instruction L 100 into the accumulator. This is an important point. The computer cannot tell the difference between data and instructions when it fetches information from storage. It is up to the programmer to write his program in such a way that the results are sensible. The machine has no occult powers; all it can do is to follow instructions blindly. If the programmer makes a mistake, an improper result will occur.

Actually, as we shall see, the capacity of a computer to operate on an instruction as if it were data turns out to be of very great value. The ability of a machine to *loop* is based upon this characteristic.

Let us now add to our repertoire of machine instructions. Assume that the letter M is the code for MULTIPLICATION. This code causes the computer to multiply the contents of the accumulator by the contents of a designated memory location, and to leave the product in the accumulator. We now can write a program such as:

Instruction location	Instruction
100	L 200
101	M 201
102	U 202

This sequence of instructions loads the contents of location 200 in the accumulator, multiplies this number by whatever is in location 201, then returns the product to location 202.

DECISION MAKING

If all a computer could do was to execute one instruction after another in sequence, it would not be capable of any remarkable feats. The capacity of data processing machines to *branch,* that is, to choose what commands it will carry out next, is what enables computers to take over many human activities.

Branching is based on a computer's ability to compare two numbers. As a consequence of this comparison, the machine either executes the next instruction, or executes a command located somewhere else in memory. In this way, the computer decides which series of instructions it will next carry out.

In our machine, branching requires the use of two commands: the COMPARE (code C) order and the TRANSFER-ON-HIGH (T) instruction.

The COMPARE instruction compares the number in the accumulator with a number in some specified memory location. If the number in the

Instruction location	Instruction	Explanation
120	L 800	Place the contents of memory location 800 in the accumulator.
121	C 801	If the number in the accumulator is higher than the number in address 801, set the trigger on.
122	T 400	If the trigger is on, get next instruction from location 400. If the trigger is off, get the next instruction from location 123.
123 124 . . . 399	instructions in branch A	
400 401 . . .	instructions in branch B	

accumulator is greater than the number in memory, a trigger is set within the control circuits. The TRANSFER-ON-HIGH order examines this trigger. If it is off, the machine executes the next instruction in sequence. If the trigger is on, the computer carries out the command contained in the memory location specified in the TRANSFER-ON-HIGH command.

On page 110 an example of how our computer compares the contents of memory location 800 with the number in 801. On the basis of this comparison the machine either continues to execute instructions in sequence, or else branches to carry out the commands starting at location 400.

By the way, if the trigger is on, it is automatically turned off after the execution of the TRANSFER-ON-HIGH order.

If this were a paycheck computation, the decision might be to find out whether the employee had already paid his maximum social security deduction. The number placed in the accumulator would be $174, the maximum deduction, and the number in location 801 would be year-to-date deductions. If the maximum deduction were higher than the year-to-date deductions, the machine would branch to location 400, where there would be a program to calculate this week's social security deduction. If the maximum deduction were not higher than year-to-date deductions, the computer would not make any social security deductions, but would continue with the paycheck computation, using the instructions starting at location 123.

ADDRESS MODIFICATION

In our simplified machine, the way to bring information into the computer from punched cards is to use the READ (R) instruction. To make things easy, let's assume that each punched card contains only 10 characters. The address in the READ command specifies where in memory the information from the card is to be placed.

Suppose we wished to read in the data from 100 punched cards, stacked one after the other in the card reader. The information is to go consecutively into memory locations 700, 701, 702, . . . , 799. We could accomplish this task by the program shown on page 112.

Such a program would take up 100 memory locations. In practice, this would be very inefficient as there usually aren't enough memory locations available to permit the programmer to use up locations when he doesn't have to do so. In fact, where identical instructions have to be repeated thousands of times, as in many mathematical computations, the technique we just used would be impossible. Indeed, it was just this problem which caused Von Neumann to suggest the idea of the stored program.

To avoid repeating the same instruction again and again, the pro-

Instruction location	Instruction	Explanation
100	R 700	Ten characters from first card go to location 700.
101	R 701	Ten characters from second card go to location 701.
102	R 702	Ten characters from third card go to location 702.
. . .	. . .	
199	R 799	Ten characters from 100th card go to location 799.

grammer takes advantage of the fact that instructions can be operated upon in the same way as data. After the computer has executed R 700, the program will add 1 to 700, thereby producing the command R 701, which is stored back in location 100. After R 701 is executed, the program will add 1 to 701, thereby producing R 702, which is stored back in location 100. The computer will execute the command contained in location 100 again and again. Each time the address into which the punched-card data is read is increased by 1.

We will keep the number 1 stored in location 900. By the way, we will make use of a new instruction here. It is called GO (G), and commands the computer to go to a specified memory location for its next instruction.

Here is the program for reading in 100 punched cards:

Instruction location	Instruction	Explanation
100	R 700	Read a card into the specified address.
101	L 100	The accumulator now contains R000000100.
102	A 900	The accumulator now contains R000000101.
103	U 100	Memory location 100 now contains R000000101.
104	G 100	The computer gets its next command from 100, and repeats the procedure.

When the computer goes to location 100, the original command has been modified. Instead of R 700, this memory location now contains R 701. The machine accordingly reads the next punched-card's data into location 701.

In the second time around, the instruction at 101 causes the computer to LOAD the command R 701 into the accumulator. The machine adds 1 to this instruction, producing R 702, which is UNLOADED back into location 100. The machine returns to location 100. This time it finds R 702 there, and executes this instruction. Each time around, the address of the READ instruction is increased by 1. This procedure is called *address modification*.

TERMINATION OF A LOOP

There is one problem with the program we have just written. These instructions are known as an *endless loop*. The machine will continue going around this loop indefinitely. (In practice, the computer operator would notice what was happening, and would intervene manually.) We want the computer to stop after it has read the information from the 100th card. The instruction to stop is HALT (H). However, the machine has no real understanding of what it is doing. Somehow, the programmer must tell the computer when to complete the loop.

We shall make use of the branching technique to test for the termination of the loop. Let's store the number R000000800 in location 901 for use in this test. We will make the following arrangement: Each time, after the computer has added 1 to the READ order, it will compare the modified command to R000000800. The first 99 times the machine makes this comparison the READ command will be smaller than R000000800. But on the 100th time around the loop, after the computer has executed R 799, the machine will increase this command by 1, making it R 800, which is equal to R000000800. At this point we will arrange for the computer to branch to the HALT order. The revised program appears on page 114.

During its 100th traverse of the loop, the computer increases the command in 100 from R 799 to R 800. For the first time the trigger is not turned on by the comparison. Therefore, the machine does not branch to 100 again, but goes to location 107 for the HALT order.

With the growth of sophisticated programming and design techniques, special *indexing* commands have been made available which tremendously facilitate the problems associated with loops. These methods had their advent in 1949 at the University of Manchester computer in England, and were first utilized in machines designed for scientific computation. Indexing is a mechanism for making it easy to increment addresses and

Instruction location	Instruction	Explanation
100	R 700	Read a card into the specified memory address.
101	L 100	The first time around, the accumulator contains R000000700. The 100th time around, the accumulator contains R000000799.
102	A 900	Add 1 to the instruction now in the accumulator.
103	U 100	Memory location 100 now contains its previous instruction, whose address has been increased by 1.
104	L 901	Place R000000800 in the accumulator.
105	C 100	Compare R000000800 to the contents of location 100. The first 99 times the trigger will be turned on.
106	T 100	If the trigger is on, get next instruction from 100. If trigger is not on, get next instruction from 107.
107	H 000	The computer stops.

to test for the end of a loop. The commands are quite powerful, and are also used by experienced programmers for a number of other purposes.

INTERPRETATION OF INSTRUCTIONS

The control system in a stored program machine includes a control counter which keeps track of where the next instruction is to be found in memory. When the machine is started, the operator enters the address of the first command in this control counter. The control circuitry steps this unit by 1 after each instruction is obtained. This prepares the machine to obtain from memory its next order in sequence.

To carry out a particular instruction, the machine must execute two operational phases: *instruction time,* during which the machine obtains and interprets its next command, and *execution time,* during which the machine actually performs the command. Instruction time is not under the control of the program, but is built into the machine's control system. In our simple machine, these circuits appear as shown in Fig. 8-3.

As soon as the control system emits the *I*-time signal, several operations are initiated. The address in the control counter is routed to the memory address control circuit, which obtains from memory the characters constituting the next instruction. The high-order character in the command contains the operation code. This code is routed to the operation register; the other three characters are sent to the memory address register. The character in the operation register is sent to a decoding network whose output sets a trigger for the specified instruction. This trigger emits the routing and control signals for carrying out the command. At the same time the control counter is stepped by 1, so that it now contains the address of the next instruction.

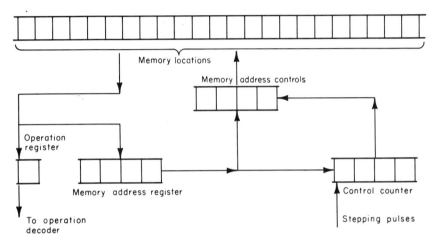

FIGURE 8-3 Schematic instruction time control system.

When instruction time has ended, actual execution of the command occurs. At the conclusion of execution time, a signal is generated to commence the next instruction time. The automatic repetition of this two-stage cycle continues for as long as the machine is in operation.

We now can understand how a GO command is executed. What happens is that the location in the memory address register is routed into the control counter, replacing its previous contents. As a result, during the next instruction time the machine will get its instruction from the address specified by the GO command.

FLOW CHARTING

Problems run on data processing machines usually require thousands of instructions. Before the coding is prepared, a programmer creates a block diagram, or *flow chart*, which outlines the over-all logic of the problem. In fact, flow charting is the most difficult part of programming. Once this diagram is completed, the coding is relatively easy.

In a large problem the flow chart becomes a labyrinthian network of interconnected boxes, each box designating a procedure to be embodied

later in coding for the machine. A complete flow chart may cover numerous large sheets of paper.

To illustrate in a simple way what a flow chart is like, let's consider
an easy problem. Suppose there are four different numbers in memory,
and we wish to find which number is the largest. We'll call these numbers

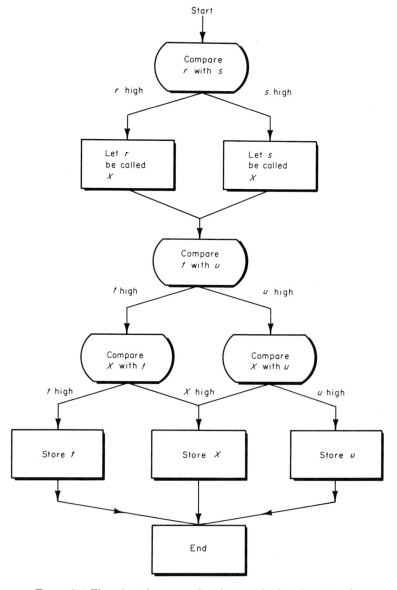

FIGURE 8-4 Flow chart for comparing the magnitudes of r, s, t, and u.

r, s, t, and u. A block diagram for the solution of this problem is shown in Fig. 8-4.

We first compare r with s. Since the numbers are different, the comparison must either find that r is high, or that s is high. To keep in mind the result of this comparison, we attach the label "X" to the number which turned out to be high. Then we compare t with u. Again there are only two possible results; either t is high, or u is high.

As the result of the two comparisons, we have eliminated two numbers. All we have to do now is to compare the two remaining numbers. We take the number designated as "X," and compare it either with t or u. Since we don't know in advance whether t or u is the higher of the two, we provide for both possibilities. If t turns out to be higher, we compare t with X; if u was higher than t, we compare u with X.

Let us suppose that t was higher than u. In this case, we would compare t with X. Now there are two possibilities; either t is higher than X, or X is higher than t. The winner of this comparison is the highest of the four numbers, and is stored in a special memory location. If u was higher than t, a similar procedure is executed.

Since all a computer can do is to follow the instructions which are given to it, the machine must be told what to do in every contingency. The flow chart therefore takes care of all logical possibilities. Thus, regardless of which number is the highest, the computer can handle the situation.

DESK CHECKING

The programmer is by no means finished with his problem when he has completed the writing of the instructions. His next step is to "desk check" the program. This means going over the instructions with some test data. If the program comes up with the correct result after processing these examples, then the programmer is ready to test the program on the machine.

The procedure of desk checking invariably reveals not merely programming errors, but also instances where the sequence of instructions can be simplified. Unnecessary commands are called *redundant*. They slow up machine processing and take up memory space which may be needed for other purposes. In some instances these factors are not significant. For example, if the running time is short and the program will be run only once, these considerations can be ignored. However, in other instances the program may be economically or operationally impossible to run unless it is simplified. Certain programs with large inputs are run frequently, and if they are unnecessarily long, the procedure becomes too expensive and too difficult to schedule. A payroll program usually falls into this category. Apart from these practical implications, however, much of the fascination and challenge of the programming art arises from the effort to "tighten up" a sequence of instructions to the greatest possible extent.

COMMUNICATION WITH COMPUTERS

One of the major values of a modern computer is that, once started upon a task, it will proceed to execute this sequence of actions without human intervention. A stored program constitutes a control system which provides the machine with a required sequence of information transformations. In practice, of course, communication between man and machine is required for getting the computer ready for running a program, and for intervening occasionally during the data processing.

There are a wide variety of input and output devices for exchanging information between a computer and its human masters. The most common of these are magnetic tape units, card readers, and card punches. Direct manual communication between the machine and its operator is via the supervisory control panel (console), which usually includes a typewriter for enabling the computer to send messages to the person in charge.

The supervisory control panel contains a keyboard which enables the operator to enter information into any desired memory locations. The individual at the console can also instruct the machine manually to perform commands not contained in the program. Among the other devices on the panel is the *start* key which, when depressed, causes the machine to commence instruction time, using the number in the control counter as the location of its first instruction. To direct the computer to start at a particular command in memory, the operator manually instructs the machine to perform what we have called a GO order. This has the effect of putting a new number in the control counter. When the start key is now depressed, the machine will take its first command from the address specified in this GO order.

The console also contains sets of neon lights which display the contents of various control registers, and which can be used to display any memory location. When the machine comes to a HALT instruction, the cycle of instruction time and execution time is terminated, and the machine ceases operation. The address of the HALT order is shown, thereby telling the computer operator where the machine has stopped in the course of executing a program. In practice, the HALT command is often used for communication between the machine and its operator. For example, the computer may be programmed to type out the following message on the typewriter, and then to come to a stop:

PLEASE ENTER DATE IN LOCATION 473

The operator enters the date as requested, and then presses the start key, whereupon the machine continues with the program. In this way the computer can be told what date to place on its output reports, or what date to use as the basis for some calculation.

The human at the supervisory control panel has many duties. Reels of tape must be removed or mounted on tape units, decks of cards placed in the card reader, and paper placed in or removed from the printer. At many installations, a number of different programs may be run on the computer every hour, and the person at the console may be responsible for scheduling these problems and for keeping track of the tape reels needed. In many instances these activities become so involved that a special job classification is created for positions of dispatcher and tape librarian. Considerable time may be wasted in setting up a machine for its next program. It takes about 45 seconds to place a tape reel on a tape unit, and there are often as many as 10 tape units used for a run. In addition, there are a number of time-consuming details involved in placing a program into memory. Efforts have long been made to reduce the role of the human operator to a minimum by means of automatic tape-handling, scheduling, and program supervision.

Programmers rarely run their own programs on the machine once they have been completely checked out. However, they are required to prepare write-ups for use by the operator of the equipment. This program documentation informs the operator of manual communications to the machine required at various points during the run. It also states what magnetic tape units are to be used, what reels of data are to be mounted, and what card decks are needed. Information such as the location of the first instruction in the program is also included.

The instructions constituting the program are read into the machine's memory from the card reader or magnetic tape. This procedure is usually initiated by a few commands entered by the operator from the supervisory control panel. The console operator next places the address of the first instruction into the control counter. He then presses the start key, and the machine begins instruction time for the first command in the program. Most instructions are executed in the order of microseconds, so that several thousand commands may be performed before the operator has lifted his finger from the key.

Once the machine is started, the immense speed of execution of commands prevents the onlooker from seeing the neons light up for any one instruction. Only when a program loop is being repeatedly executed a great many times can command executions be discerned by the onlooker.

Prior to running a program on a computer, it is necessary for the operator to clear the memory, special registers, and control circuits of any information which may have remained from the previous program.

If this is not done, errors may result from the presence of data and instructions which are not wanted. Clearing the memory usually means placing 0 bits in all locations. This operation is accomplished by pressing the *clear memory* key on the supervisory control panel.

9 MAGNETIC TAPE OPERATIONS

MAGNETIC TAPE

The use of magnetic tape as a means of storing information is based upon the same principles of magnetization and induction as are utilized in the magnetic drum. The tape is surfaced with a magnetizable material, and is moved past a reading and writing head which obtains or stores binary digits. The tape is wound around a reel (Fig. 9-1). As the reel unwinds, the tape passes the read-write station and is taken up by a second reel, like a roll of film in a camera. The physical ends of the tape are marked by reflective spots. These are sensed by a photoelectric cell near the read-write head. Special procedures are incorporated into programs to take care of the end-of-tape condition. An *erase* head is energized to remove previous information from the tape whenever the machine begins to "write" on the tape.

The rapid acceleration of the tape from a state of rest to full velocity necessitates the presence of loops of tape on each side of the read-write head. When an input or output order is executed, the loop supplies the tape for the next record. Through this technique heavy reels do not have to be continually accelerated and decelerated. A switch in the vacuum column, operating on air pressure indicators, controls the movement of the reels in supplying or taking up tape from the loops.

Information on magnetic tape usually appears as a succession of seven-bit characters, written vertically. Records are demarcated by empty spaces called interrecord gaps.

A typical input order is executed as follows: the computer sends a signal to the tape unit requesting that the next record be read. At this moment the magnetic tape is at rest, with the interrecord gap underneath

121

0	1	1		1	0	0	1	1		0	1	0	1	C
0	0	0		0	1	1	1	1		0	0	1	0	B
0	0	0	Interrecord	1	0	0	1	0	Interrecord	0	0	1	0	A
0	1	0	gap	0	0	0	1	0	gap	0	0	0	1	8
1	0	0		0	0	0	0	1		1	0	0	0	4
0	0	1		1	1	1	0	0		1	1	0	0	2
0	1	1		0	1	1	1	0		1	1	1	1	1

Magnetic tape

4 9 3   S L L I M   7 3 A 9

read-write head

Direction of motion of tape

the read-write head. When the signal is received, the tape is set in motion. No information is received until this gap is passed, i.e., until the actual record is in position to be sensed by the read-write head. Each successive

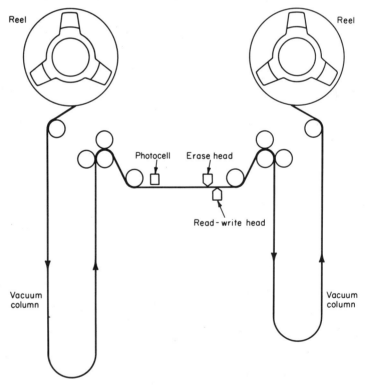

FIGURE 9-1 Magnetic tape unit.

character is now brought into the machine until the next interrecord gap is reached, at which point the instruction is terminated.

When writing on tape, the machine creates an interrecord gap at the end of each new record; information previously on the tape is erased as writing occurs. Additional instructions are available to backspace and to rewind the tape.

How is source data placed on magnetic tape? In most instances the original information is first placed in punched cards. It is then possible, without using the computer itself, to transmit all of the punched-card records to reels of tape. This procedure is called *card-to-tape* conversion. Information on magnetic tape can be brought into a machine much faster than on punched cards. A punched-card reader attached to a computer reads in at the typical rate of 250 cards a minute, or 20,000 characters a minute. On the other hand, magnetic tape, as we have seen, can be brought into an electronic data processing machine at speeds in the order of tens of thousands of characters a second.

SORTING THE INPUT

It is usually necessary to arrange data in some special order before it can be used by an electronic computer. Actually, the notion of an orderly arrangement seems to be basic to any form of intelligent activity, no matter what sphere of human life we deal with. Whether we are concerned with an article in a lady's handbag, a business letter in a desk, or scientific data in a notebook, all of these items must be stored in such a way as to be quickly and efficiently obtained again, when needed. The very conception of counting involves the notion of order; *a*counting is the maintenance of order in the operation of a business.

Both in manual and mechanized information-handling systems, data is almost always organized into arrays we call *files*. The classical manner for storing commercial or governmental information is to use filing cabinets. These files are arranged according to some criterion (often best known to a secretary), and is usually based on some chronological or alphabetic sequence. Duplicates, triplicates, quadruplicates, etc., of source documents may be used in the same office to constitute another file ordered by a different method. Copies of original forms may often be utilized for setting up identical files in other departments of the same concern or in the offices of other companies.

Before data processing can take place, it is usually necessary to search the files to obtain all of the relevant information. A large percentage of the time spent by clerical workers is occupied in storing documents according to some sequence, duplicating source material, transmitting documents to other filing locations, and retrieving information from storage systems when it is needed.

Two of the media used for mechanizing these file-handling activities are decks of punched cards and reels of magnetic tape. The records on these cards or tapes are sorted by some alphabetic or numeric criterion, such as last name or social security number. The information can then be entered into a computer for processing.

The sorting of punched cards is carried out by the sorter and the collator. It is often cheaper to sort cards on this equipment before converting the records to tape. However, the punched-card procedures are far slower and are subject to errors resulting from human card handling.

The alternative is to convert the cards to tape first, then to sort the tape records. The importance of this activity is indicated by the fact that in many commercial data processing installations as much as 25% of the available computer time is spent simply in sorting information on magnetic tapes. Where tens of thousands, or hundreds of thousands of items of data must be placed in order, the development of efficient sorting techniques is of the utmost importance. Although based upon simple ideas, sorting is a complex function which can be carried out in a number of ways.

The sorting of a small number of records on tape can often be accomplished by bringing all of this information into memory, rearranging it by some technique, and writing it out again on tape. Such a procedure, called an *internal sort*, is feasible only with a small number of records, for it is limited by the amount of available memory.

SORTING PLAYING CARDS

Some insight into sorting can be obtained by considering how to order a deck of ordinary playing cards. (See Fig. 9-2.) The method most people tend to use in performing this operation is first to distribute the 52 cards into four "files" of 13 cards each, based on whether the card is a spade, heart, diamond, or club. The next step is to pick up each suit in turn, rearranging the cards while holding them in hand. The final procedure is to merge together the four ordered suits. If carried out by data processing machinery, this type of sort would require three *runs*, or *passes*, of the information through the computer.

This method is possible because of the way in which a deck of playing cards is constituted. Everyday life, however, rarely provides a distribution of information which lends itself to such a sorting procedure. To illustrate this point, let us add some complexities to the problem. Suppose four decks of playing cards are shuffled together, and 52 cards are drawn at

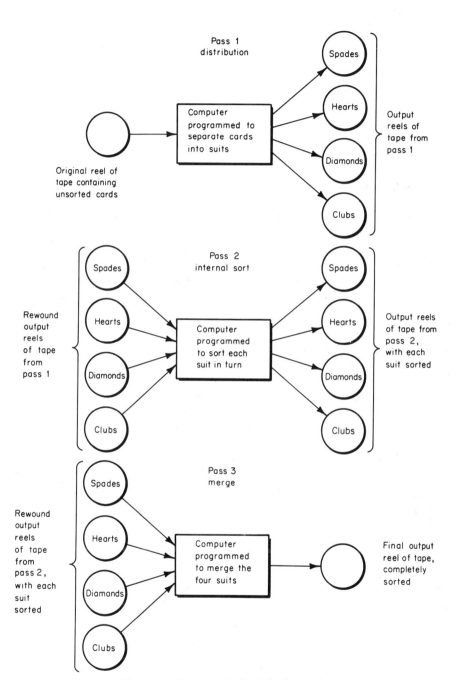

FIGURE 9-2 Sorting a deck of playing cards.

random from this pack. How can we sort these 52 cards, assuming that we can hold only 16 cards in our hand at any given time?

It is hardly possible this time that we would again obtain four suits of exactly 13 cards. Indeed, we might not even obtain four different suits, for one or more suits might not be represented at all. Obviously, the method described above would be difficult either for a human or a computer. The restriction on the number of cards which can be held in the hand for regrouping is analogous to the memory limitation which causes a constraint on how many records can be sorted internally within a computer.

TWO-WAY MERGE

One of the simplest sorting procedures is a two-way merge, using four tapes. This technique consists of interweaving strings of records which are placed in order. In the first pass two items at a time are read into memory from tape 3, the input reel. These are placed in order, and the pair is written out on tape 1. The next ordered pair is written on tape 2. This alternation process is repeated continually. When every item has been read, all reels are rewound and tapes 1 and 2 become the input for the second pass. Now one pair at a time is read in from each tape. Since the two-item strings are already in sequence, it is necessary only to merge the pairs to create a four-item string. After every successive group of four records is written out alternately on tapes 3 and 4, these reels are rewound and become the input to pass three. This process continues, with the strings becoming longer and longer, until on the final pass the two last sequences of items are merged to complete the sort.

Two-way Merge Sort

Tape 3 (original input to be sorted)	First pass outputs	Second pass outputs	Final pass output (completely sorted tape)
75	(tape 1)		
14	14 75	(tape 3)	
92	(tape 2)	14 57 75 92	
57	57 92		(tape 1)
10	(tape 1)		06 10 14 46 57 75 91 92
46	10 46	(tape 4)	
91	(tape 2)	06 10 46 91	
06	06 91		

It is apparent that with a large input many passes would be needed if this method were to be used (2048 items would require 11 passes). Such excessive machine running time can be reduced if the merge is preceded by an internal sort; this has the effect of reducing the number of passes which are necessary.

STRING FORMATION

One of the most common sorting methods consists of forming a maximum number of strings of sequenced items on the first pass, and merging these strings on the following passes until the sort is complete. The following shows how this procedure can be carried out with four tapes.

Input data	Tape 1	Tape 2	Tape 3	Tape 4
	Start of pass 1		Start of pass 2	
03	03	20	03	02
45	45	22	20	21
53	53	71	22	71
20	02	36	45	77
22	21		53	
02	77		36	
21	37		37	
77	65		65	
71	End of pass 1		End of pass 2	
37				
65	Start of pass 3		Start of pass 4	
36	02	36	02	
	03	37	03	
	20	65	20	
	21		21	
	22		22	
	45		36	
	53		37	
	71		45	
	77		53	
	End of pass 3		65	
			71	
			77	
			End of pass 4	

Each successive record from the original file is read into memory, and is written out on tape 1 if it is higher than the previous record. When a *step-down* occurs (i.e., an input record is lower than its predecessor), this record is written on tape 2. The next step-down record is written on tape 1. The tapes are alternated every time a step-down occurs until the input is exhausted, at which point the tapes are rewound. In the second pass, the first pair of strings is read from tapes 1 and 2, merged, and placed on tape 3. If the first record in the second pair of merged strings from tapes 1 and 2 is higher than the last record in the first string, then the second string is also placed on tape 3. If lower, the second string is written on tape 4. This type of procedure is repeated for the remainder of the second pass, and for subsequent passes. The sort is complete when there is no step-down in a given pass, at which point all of the records must necessarily be in sequence.

INPUT-OUTPUT PROBLEMS

After information on magnetic tape has been sorted into the necessary order, it is ready to be brought into the central processing unit. Here the required arithmetic or logical transformations are performed, following which the data are written out on tape or printed.

The printing of output information is a mechanical process, and is therefore relatively slow. For this reason, the usual practice is to write final results on an output tape. This reel of tape is then removed from the tape unit and placed on a separate tape-to-printer unit not connected with the main processor. In this way, printing can be carried out independently of the computer, leaving the data processing equipment free to perform other activities. If this overlapping were not possible, a valuable machine would be tied up while the routine process of printing was going on. This would be equivalent to using an expensive computer as a printing press.

It was recognized early in the development of data processing technology that, even with the use of high-speed tape units, input and output operations tended seriously to decrease the efficiency of the machine. The execution of arithmetic and logical commands within the central computer was faster than the time for reading and writing on magnetic tapes. As a result, most of the time required for solving a problem was spent in tape input and output operations. The actual computational facilities were often idle, waiting for information to come in from the tape, or waiting for the completion of an output operation. This difficulty was particularly significant in commercial data processing.

One way to reduce input-output time is to group the records on tape. Most of the time spent in tape operations consists in accelerating and decelerating the tape. This must be done every time a record is read from or written on tape. However, if a number of items are united into one group, a great deal of time is saved. For example, if there are 20 different records on tape, there must be 20 acceleration and deceleration periods. But if these 20 records are grouped into one large record, then only one acceleration and one deceleration of the tape is required to bring the information into the machine.

Another technique is to provide for simultaneous read-write operations. The computer can be designed so that it can carry on input and output operations at the same time. Such commands tend to cut input-output time in half, thereby effecting great economies.

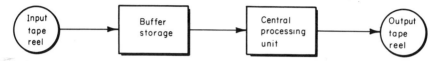

FIGURE 9-3 Buffering system for overlapping input operations with computation.

Buffering methods (Fig. 9-3) were used in commercially manufactured computers as far back as UNIVAC I. A buffer is essentially a device for overlapping an input or output operation with internal computation. This unit is a high-speed memory which receives data from input or output equipment, and which holds this information for use by the central processing unit. This enables arithmetic and logical commands to proceed at the same time as tape operations.

The buffer storage is first filled with a tape record, by means of an instruction in the program. The next command orders the buffer to transmit its information into the main memory in the central processing unit and to commence reading in from tape again. The moving of data from buffer to central storage is very fast, as it is performed at electronic speeds. When this operation is terminated, the central processing unit is free to continue with further instructions in the program while the buffer is slowly being filled up again from tape. Usually there is ample time for the necessary computing to be completed during this filling of the buffer. By placing a buffer between all input-output devices and the main processor, it is possible to compute simultaneously with the execution of reading and writing operations.

A technique used in recent machines for overlapping input-output operations with internal processing is as follows: Several input characters at a time are brought from tape to a small internal register. Every time this register is full, the regular program is interrupted long enough to permit the new information to enter memory. When this has been accomplished, the arithmetic and logical commands are allowed to continue. It is to be emphasized that once information is read from tape, the time required to transmit it into memory from the special register occurs at internal processing speeds. In this way, very little computing time is used for bringing information into the machine. A similar technique is used for output operations.

Considerable effort has been made by manufacturers to reduce the imbalance between input-output time and actual data processing time by increasing the speed at which data can be transmitted between tape units and the central memory. Some recent machine systems have tape speeds which enable hundreds of thousands of characters to be read or written in one second. Tape equipment is under development which will read and write information at the rate of 1,500,000 characters per second. The reels to be used with these tape units will store in the order of 60 billion characters, or the equivalent of a library of about 150,000 volumes.

PRINTING THE OUTPUT REPORTS

Whenever a data processing machine prepares an output for printing, some "editing" of this information is required to place it into the desired form. For example, for a payroll check the data must be arranged on tape so that it will appear in the specified lines and positions on the checks. Often a preprinted continuous form is inserted into the printer. As each item is read from the tape, it is placed in the appropriate position on the check form. When the computer prepares the tape, special *carriage control characters* are placed with each item to control the skipping of lines by the printer. The positions of characters in each line are adjusted by placing the information appropriately in a line of blank characters. When the line is printed, the blanks do not appear and the data fields are printed as specified.

Another method for positioning information on output reports is to have a plugboard on the printer for rearranging output information from tape. The editing of output data is very time-consuming, and is a relatively simple operation. It is wasteful for the powerful logical and computational capacities of an expensive machine to be used for this purpose. It is desirable to provide a small, inexpensive auxiliary computer in some installations to edit output information.

The continuous preprinted forms used for documents and reports are not usually produced by the computer manufacturers. They are purchased from large companies which specialize in preparing paper for the output of data processing equipment. The vast outputs of many commercial installations are often produced in duplicate, triplicate, or multiple copies. Business forms are, therefore, a significant expense in the operation of an installation. Since a great many of the output reports prepared by computers are for internal reference within a company, it is often suggested that such documents be placed on microfilm. Special magnetic tape-to-microfilm printers are being marketed for this purpose. Microfilming greatly reduces the space required to store outputs. Through the years these sheets often come to occupy large amounts of warehouse space. In many instances these outputs are rarely if ever needed.

The relatively slow process of printing information from output tapes has often proved to be a bottleneck in data processing installations. The speed of this equipment has therefore been continually increased by manufacturers. One frequently used printer produces 1000 120-character lines per minute. However, the volume of output at some installations is so great that more than one of these machines is needed.

A number of operations other than printing are sometimes involved in preparing output reports. For example, thousands of bills may be printed on one continuous roll of paper. These documents must be mailed individually. Therefore, they must be separated from the roll. This requires a pass on a *bursting* machine. A number of these paper-handling procedures, such as folding, stuffing, collating sheets, and mailing may be required at an installation. Equipment for these purposes is manufactured by several companies.

10 PROGRAMMING TECHNIQUES

One of the most common procedures in data processing is the search for particular items in a file, and the adjustment of these records. The following is an illustration of an inventory control program in which this operation is required.

Suppose a retail store keeps an inventory of 100 different items, each of which is assigned one of the two-digit codes 00, 01, . . . , 99. Whenever a sale occurs a clerk prepares a sales slip containing the code of the item and the number of units bought. Similar source documents are prepared when purchases of new merchandise increase the inventory.

The source documents are keypunched into cards with the following format:

Columns	Information
1-2	Item code
3-4	Number of units sold or purchased
5	Transaction code

A 1 is punched in column 5 to designate a sale; a 2 for an addition to inventory. The cards are then converted to 80-character records on magnetic tape. This tape is used to update a master inventory tape file consisting of 100 10-digit records, each containing the number of units in stock for a particular item. At the beginning of the program, the entire 1000 digits comprising this stock record are read into memory, where they appear as follows:

Location 200 ⬚⬚⬚⬚⬚⬚⬚⬚⬚⬚ Inventory for item 00

Location 201 ⬚⬚⬚⬚⬚⬚⬚⬚⬚⬚ Inventory for item 01

Location 299 ⬚⬚⬚⬚⬚⬚⬚⬚⬚⬚ Inventory for item 99

The program reads in each record from the transaction tape. New merchandise is added to the number of units on hand for each item type. Sales are subtracted from the stock record. The basic procedure is to retrieve the master inventory record for each item type, perform an addition or subtraction, and place the adjusted record back in the master file. If the stock record is ever reduced to zero, a notice is printed out by the machine. Assume that a sale can never produce a negative stock balance. We'll use a TRANSFER-ON-ZERO instruction to test for the presence of a zero balance in a record. This command causes the machine to branch if the contents of the accumulator are zero. If the accumulator is not zero, the equipment takes the next instruction in sequence.

How does the machine find a stock record which needs to be updated? It would obviously be inefficient to search the entire list each time. One of the programming techniques used in such cases is to base the memory address of each stock record on its item code. In this instance we have

$$\text{item code} + 200 = \text{memory address}$$

To find where an item is located, we add 200 to the item code. This provides the location of the record.

Let's try an example. Suppose a transaction record indicates that seven units of item 02 have been sold. The machine must get the stock record for this item. It performs the calculation

$$02 + 200 = 202$$

The computer subtracts seven from this record, and replaces the former inventory record by the updated record. The flow chart for the entire procedure is given in Fig. 10-1.

In practice, this program would include a test for the last record on the transaction tape. This test would be necessary to enable the machine

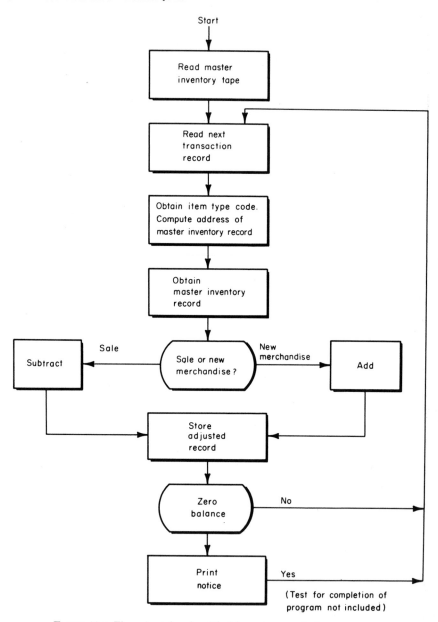

FIGURE 10-1 Flow chart for simplified inventory control program.

to know when the procedure was at an end. The computer would thereupon write out the updated master file on tape. This new master file would be used the next time transactions were to be processed. We have not included these operations in order to make our illustration as simple as possible.

Skill is also required in avoiding inefficiencies in the manner of recording source data. In this case, only five columns in the punched card are used. The result is that 75 blank columns are handled unnecessarily by the equipment. One method for averting this wasteful expenditure of time would have been to place more than one transaction record on each punched card.

STORING THE PROGRAM

A program is stored in memory in the same way as data. It is read in either from punched cards or tape. But if memory is clear of all commands originally, how can anything be brought into the machine? This procedure is carried out by a loading program, which is used along with certain instructions initiated manually from the console.

Let's consider a simplified version of how a program is read into memory from the card reader. The instructions are punched into cards. Assume that each card contains 10 commands, along with the memory location where the first of these instructions is to be stored.

After the first 10 instructions in the program have been punched in the first card, a second card is used, following the same format. As many additional cards are punched as are necessary. An entire deck of punched cards is usually needed.

The loading program commences by reading in the first card. Its basic object is to move the 10 commands to the specified memory locations. The program reads in the second card after the first has been processed. The procedure continues in a loop until the entire deck has been loaded.

The last card in the deck of program cards contains the address of the first instruction in the program. What is needed now is a transfer of control order to get the machine started at this command. This operation is carried out by the loading program.

We still haven't explained how the loading program itself gets into the computer. This is done manually. The loading program is itself on a card. The operator instructs the machine from the console to read this card into memory. Then he commands the computer to start operation at the first instruction in the loading program. From this point on everything occurs automatically. The program is read in and executed without any human intervention.

Suppose a program is so large that it won't fit into memory? This is a common occurrence. One solution to the problem is to make use of the fact that many of the instructions in any program are no longer needed after they have been executed. Hence, additional instructions can be read into memory where such commands are located. As we know, the original information is erased automatically whenever the machine reads new material into its memory.

PROGRAM TESTING

The loader is one of a class of programs known as *utility programs.* These are standard programs which all machine installations require for everyday operation. Among this group are such programs as the memory print, which lists the contents of memory after a program has come to a halt, and the tracer, which follows transfer orders during the running of a program. These are used for the testing of programs.

It is very rare for a program to be free from errors when it is first prepared. A mistake causes either a faulty output or an unexpected halt in the program. Errors can be categorized roughly as either logical or clerical. Logical errors stem mainly from errors made in the preparation of the flow chart. Since flow charts often are extraordinarily complicated structures of interrelated loops and decisions, it is very difficult to foretell the results of all possible instruction sequences. Another type of logical mistake results from the improper use of the machine's instructions. Many of the commands tend to possess special characteristics when used under unusual conditions, and it is necessary for the programmer to be aware of these idiosyncracies.

Certain concatenations of instructions may also produce errors or unusual results. Mistakes of this type are often the result of very subtle factors. Indeed, some errors arise from unanticipated consequences of the logical design of the equipment. When a new machine is first programmed, a number of such idiosyncracies may be discovered and publicized among users of the computer. Some of these unusual characteristics of machines, by the way, are deliberately utilized in "trick" programming to produce ingenious results.

Clerical errors are usually blunders of a petty nature, such as using incorrect storage addresses or transferring control to the wrong location. On a more elementary level, there often occur mistakes such as failing to comply with certain minor conventions required in preparing the instruction cards.

DEBUGGING

Data processing machines operate in a strictly robot-like fashion. They perform precisely as they are commanded, and can exercise no judgment. They have no understanding of the intentions of the programmer. Even the best programmers frequently make logical and clerical errors, and such mistakes necessitate an analysis, often very detailed and laborious, to ascertain the source of the difficulty. A single error may take days to uncover.

The removal of mistakes by test runs on the machine is popularly called *debugging* a program. Errors made by programmers are, of course, to be distinguished from faulty operation of the machine resulting from engineering factors such as the deterioration of vacuum tubes. Dr. Grace Hopper, a pioneer programmer, tells of a lengthy testing session at the Harvard Computation Laboratory in which an apparently erroneous program was checked and rechecked repeatedly, without the difficulty being located. Ultimately the root of the difficulty was found; a fly was stuck in one of the relays! The insect had been caught in the relay when it closed at some previous time, and was now interfering with the logic of the machine by preventing an electrical contact. Miss Ellen Kerksieck, IBM programming standards manager, has suggested that it was this occurrence which gave rise to the term "debugging" a program, but this etymology (or entomology) is dubious.

It is common for programmers, particularly beginners, to feel strongly that their work is correct, and that the computer is at fault when an error occurs. This feeling is rarely justified for the programmer usually ultimately finds some subtle error in his instructions or logic. In the anecdote related above, it seems that neither the programmers nor the engineers were responsible for the malfunctioning of the machine. The writer can recall a personal instance of a similar nature. While testing a program, static electricity accumulating on his shoes caused the card reader to operate whenever he touched this unit. This caused the erroneous reading of cards into the computer's memory.

SUBROUTINES

The programming for a data processing installation requires the efforts of a large and experienced staff working over a long period of time. Considerable research and development has therefore been undertaken in the attempt to reduce these costs. One of the earliest methods used for easing the task of programming was to make use of subroutines.

A subroutine is usually a portion of an entire program which performs some subordinate function within that program. Subroutines vary in size, ranging from about 15 instructions to several hundred. They obtain certain information from the main program, operate upon this data, and then make the processed information available to the main program.

A frequent characteristic of a subroutine is that it often can be written as a separate job assignment by a programmer not acquainted with the main program. Certain subroutines tend to be present in a large variety of programs, and are therefore kept in a *library* where they can be made available for all users. The use of standard subroutines is particularly common in scientific programming where the computation of mathematical functions is required.

Professional organizations of users of computing machinery have been formed to gather and disseminate programs gathered by member installations. Different computing groups can in this way share their efforts. The pooling of programs is not confined simply to subroutines, but is often extended to large programs which are needed at many scientific computing installations.

The use of library subroutines and the sharing of programs is less valuable among commercial data processing organizations, for the reason that business problems are rarely uniform in nature. For example, the payroll procedures of two different corporations are rarely the same, even in the same industry. Therefore, it is usually necessary for both companies to prepare their own specialized programs. The calculation of a square root may differ in mathematical method and in the degree of accuracy obtained, but in all other respects it is the same computation. In commercial work, however, subroutines are much less likely to be standardized enough to be worth sharing.

ASSEMBLY PROGRAMS

It is often necessary for one program to control another program. An example of this technique is seen in the *supervisory* or *executive* program. A good illustration is the transfer tracing program used in debugging. This program follows every transfer of control which is executed during the running of a program, and prints out a record of all such transfers. Sources of error within a long sequence of instructions can often be uncovered in this way.

The transfer tracing program is placed in memory along with the running program. The supervisory program at all times retains control over the sequence and execution of all instructions in the actual program being run on the machine. The transfer tracing program monitors the instructions in the object program, and determines whether these are transfer-of-control commands. If so, the supervisory program prepares an output message.

The fact that supervisory programs can control and modify other programs suggests that executive programs be used to assist in the preparation of programs to be run on computers. Such techniques are called *automatic programming*. The ultimate goal would be to build sufficient intelligence into a supervisory program so that, given a data processing problem, the executive program could produce the sequence of instructions needed to solve the problem. One of the first steps taken toward automatic programming was the development of *assembly* programs.

After a program has been written, it is checked for errors. At this time it is common for instructions to be inserted or deleted from the sequence. This causes a number of problems of a clerical nature. For example, when an instruction is inserted, it must be fitted into the sequence. To provide a location for the new command, all of the instructions following it are assigned memory locations one higher than those they occupied previously. One of the ensuing difficulties is that many of the transfer-of-control instructions in the program now have the wrong address. It is necessary for the programmer to adjust all of the addresses which have been affected by the insertion of the new command. The programmer tends to make additional errors in the course of this laborious and uninteresting task.

Another clerical problem in programming arises from the fact that many constants and data fields are used by most programs. The programmer must keep track of where this information is located in memory so as to assign the proper addresses to the commands. In practice, this is a dull and time-consuming activity.

The purpose of assembly programs is to help eliminate these burdensome details and the clerical errors stemming from them. The essential feature of the assembly program is that it enables the programmer to use symbolic addresses in his coding, rather than actual memory locations. For example, suppose weekly wages were stored in location 842. Instead of writing the code

ADD 842

the programmer could code

ADD WAGES

Elsewhere in the program, the programmer would indicate that some memory location is to be reserved for the item WAGES. The exact memory location need not be specified.

In a similar manner, the programmer doesn't have to specify in his program the exact locations where his instructions are located in memory. Here again he can use a symbolic address, so that the code might look like:

Instruction location	Instruction	Explanation
BEGIN	ADD WAGES	The computer adds the number in the location specified by WAGES to the contents of the accumulator.

After such a program is coded, it is punched into cards. The deck of cards is read into a computer, where it is processed by an assembly program. This program assigns a memory location to each instruction. Then it assigns a memory location to each item such as WAGES. Finally, the assembly program inserts the address of WAGES in the instruction.

The output of the assembly program is a deck of cards (or records on tape) containing this program with the proper addresses substituted for all symbolic addresses. The above symbolic instruction might now appear as

Instruction location	Instruction	Explanation
133	ADD 914	The computer adds the number in location 914 to the contents of the accumulator.

The original program is called a *source* program. After it is converted into a real program by the assembly program, it is called an *object* program.

It is very simple for the programmer to insert or delete instructions from the source program since no memory locations are specified. Among other functions performed by the assembly program is to convert the operation codes stated in English (such as ADD) into the codes which are used inside of the computer.

PROGRAMMING LANGUAGES

Another early automatic programming method was the use of supervisory programs called *interpreters*. This technique permitted the programmer to employ certain "pseudo-instructions" in his program. A pseudo-instruction is a command which is not in the machine's repertoire of orders. A program was placed on cards and read into the computer by the interpreter, which monitored the program. When the interpreter recognized a pseudo-instruction, it would call upon an appropriate subroutine to perform the indicated processing. Of course, the interpreter was devised to handle only a specified group of pseudo-instructions.

To make programming easier, programs called *compilers* were devised on the basis of early experience in the writing of assembly programs and interpreter programs. Source programs became more and more divorced from the actual codes (called *machine language*) which the computer uses to carry out instructions. Soon the programmer could employ expressions such as

LOOP 30

Such a statement would be converted by the compiler into machine instructions for repeating a specified set of commands 30 times.

One of the most well-known programming languages is FORTRAN (FORmula TRANslation), developed by John Backus of IBM. This language enables programmers to specify complicated mathematical functions by using simple abbreviations. For example, the programmer can employ the code SQRT to obtain the square root of some number. The compiler converts SQRT into a sequence of machine instructions.

Such techniques enable a programmer to state his problem in a language closer to English. They permit the programmer to express his thoughts in a more familiar way, relying upon the compiler to translate the programmer's statements into machine codes. Of course, the programmer must adhere rigidly to the rules of the programming language, otherwise the compiler does not properly interpret his statements.

It should be emphasized that a program written in a programming language is a source program. It must be punched into cards, and processed by a compiler program in the computer. The compiler then prepares an object program which now is placed in the computer and executed.

The use of compilers to ease the preparation of programs has become almost universal. Programming languages have become increasingly more sophisticated. They are used for preparing mathematical calculations and for stating complex ideas for translation into machine code.

The practical objective of automatic programming is to enable programs to be prepared quickly, efficiently, and with a minimum of effort, by individuals who are not trained programmers.

The expense of programming is an important factor in purchasing or leasing a computer, and is weighed carefully along with the operating advantages of a particular machine. One authority has estimated that the average cost of each instruction in a user's program is between $4 and $5. Tens of thousands of instructions are required for the many different programs needed in computer installations. To lighten this burden, manufacturers usually provide a compiler for each machine they sell or rent to their customers. Since extensive experience is not needed to prepare a program with the aid of a programming language, the cost of training and maintaining a large staff of professional programmers is thereby reduced. The more elaborate compilers are very complicated programs which not only assist in preparing object programs, but also handle many of the arduous details involved in debugging.

Considerable effort has been under way for many years to prepare programming languages to ease the programming of business problems. This problem is more difficult than the writing of compilers for scientific programs. Where mathematical work has to be done, the carefully defined syntax of arithmetic and algebra can be used as a programming language. No such logical formalism exists for commercial problems.

The main problem in developing a programming language for business applications is to devise a symbolism of sufficient power and generality to enable commercial problems to be stated with a minimum of difficulty. COBOL (COmmon Business Oriented Language) is a prominent example of such a language.

An even broader problem exists when the enormously complicated accounting systems of businesses are automated. Years of study by a large staff of methods analysts are often needed to attain a complete understanding of how all of the procedures function and interact. When these procedures are placed in an electronic data processing machine, the programmer must base his work on numerous reports prepared by the methods men. Simply to understand all of these intricacies is a large undertaking for the programmer. To convert this information into efficient machine language programs is, therefore, a difficult task. What is needed is a type of compiler which can take as input a large number of interrelated facts, expressed in a language close to English, and produce a set of programs which will carry out the required procedures. The achievement of this goal would also be of great value in engineering and scientific applications, where the problems can be equally complex.

The development of automatic programming techniques is also being spurred by the fact that faster and better machines are continually being placed on the market. To take advantage of these technological advances, an equipment user would of course have to replace his present machine with a more advanced computer. But in so doing he may render all of his existing programs obsolete. It would be very difficult to prepare a program which could translate programs written for machine A into programs which could run on machine B.

One possible solution to this problem is a universal programming language which all equipment users would employ for the preparation of their source programs. A compiler would be written for each different machine. Every compiler would be able to accept source programs in the universal language, and would have the ability to convert this information into a sequence of instructions for its particular computer. By saving the original source programs, it would be possible for any installation to obtain, whenever necessary, the same program compiled for a different machine.

COMPUTATIONAL TECHNIQUES

Much of the skill involved in programming comes to the fore not in writing the instructions themselves, but in the planning of the over-all solution of the problem.

Consider, for example, the computation of the function

$$y = x^4 + 3x^3 + x^2 + 2x + 4$$

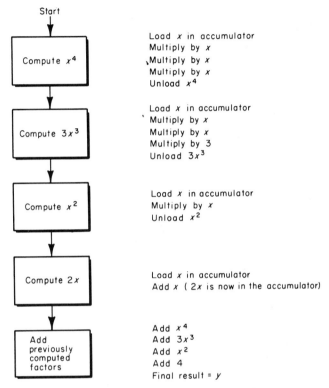

FIGURE 10-2 Computation of the function

$$y = x^4 + 3x^3 + x^2 + 2x + 4$$

without using the nesting technique.

The problem could be solved as indicated in Fig. 10-2. This method requires 19 instructions:

Multiply	7 commands	
Unload	3 commands	
Load	4 commands	
Add	5 commands	
Total........	19 commands	

An elementary technique called *nesting* enables this computation to be carried out with nine instructions as listed on the next page.

Instruction	Factor used in operation	Resulting number in accumulator
LOAD	x	x
ADD	3	$x + 3$
MULTIPLY	x	$x(x + 3) = x^2 + 3x$
ADD	1	$x^2 + 3x + 1$
MULTIPLY	x	$x(x^2 + 3x + 1) = x^3 + 3x^2 + x$
ADD	2	$x^3 + 3x^2 + x + 2$
MULTIPLY	x	$x(x^3 + 3x^2 + x + 2) = x^4 + 3x^3 + x^2 + 2x$
ADD	4	$x^4 + 3x^3 + x^2 + 2x + 4 = y$

COMPUTATIONAL ERRORS

The solution of scientific problems on a computer requires a careful study of the best equations to use for obtaining maximum accuracy in evaluating mathematical functions. This involves an analysis of the various types of errors which may arise as a result of the computational method used.

Bertrand Russell once remarked that the more exact a man says he is, the more reason one has for regarding him as inexact. In accounting applications, results of processing are almost always completely precise. A minor imprecision may stem from rounding off to the nearest cent. For example, if an employee works 42.4 hours at a rate of $3.24 per hour, his salary is $137.376, which is rounded to $137.38, thereby causing an inaccuracy. In scientific computation, however, invalid results stem from different sources. Experimental data are subject to errors resulting from the inaccuracy of measuring instruments. In addition, instruments can make measurements only to a limited degree of accuracy. Obviously, when computations are made on the basis of approximate observations, there is the possibility of compounding these errors through long sequences of calculations. Contrary to popular belief, the number of decimal places to which an observational datum is carried does not necessarily mean that it is more accurate than a measurement with less decimal places. The real determining factor is the relative error. A measurement of a short copper tube to the nearest thousandth of an inch is less accurate than a measurement of a mile of a highway to the nearest foot. Another type of error arises from the use of mathematical constants which have no exact value, such as π or $\sqrt{2}$. Such quantities can be carried to any number of decimal places without reaching an end. If the value of π is taken as 3.14, an inaccuracy exists because 3.14159 is more precise. But the value of π can always be extended to more decimal places, so that complete accuracy is impossible.

Computational errors resulting from experimental approximations or from inexact constants can be analyzed mathematically. This enables the problem to be computed so that the error in the answer is contained within any desired set of bounds.

Consider the conventional procedure of rounding a number by adding 1 if its last digit is a 5. That is,

13.425 is rounded to 13.43
147.5 is rounded to 148.

Such a method leads to the growth of inaccuracies, for the addition of several numbers rounded in this fashion results in an excessively large sum. It would be better to add 1 in only one-half of these instances, for the errors would then tend to cancel each other out. This can be achieved by adding 1 only to odd numbers, and leaving even numbers unaltered. The assumption here is that odd and even numbers are encountered an equal number of times. Following this rule in the above two cases, we would have:

13.425 rounded to 13.42
147.5 rounded to 148.

One of the most serious problems in any long sequence of arithmetic operations occurs as the result of the loss of significant figures in subtraction. For example,

92.487   is correct to five digits
$-$91.835   is correct to five digits
0.652   is correct to three digits

Suppose, as part of the same problem, the number 0.597 is obtained through a similar subtraction, and is then subtracted from 0.652

0.652
$-$0.597
0.055

Now multiply this result by some number, say 131.42. It is apparent that in the course of this computation, a loss of accuracy occurs. This type of error can be avoided by increasing, if possible, the number of significant digits in the original data. Sometimes it is possible to transform the equations to be computed into formulas which can be calculated without giving rise to these problems.

Another class of invalid results arises from the fact that often the only way, or the easiest way, of computing a function is by a method which contains inherent inaccuracies. For example, the trigonometric function *cosine* can be calculated by a Taylor expansion, which is an infinite series.

$$\text{cosine } x = 1 - \frac{x^2}{2} + \frac{x^4}{4} - \frac{x^8}{8} + \dots$$

Since it is impossible to calculate an infinite number of terms, some error in the computation must occur for there will always be terms remaining to be calculated.

Computational errors necessarily arise in matrix manipulations, one of the most common types of operations encountered in computing. Consider the simultaneous equations

$$3x + 2y + 5z = 11$$
$$6x + 4y + 3z = 8$$
$$2x + 3y + 2z = 1$$

This problem can be solved in a few minutes by elementary algebra. However, when the coefficients are more than simple integers, the arithmetic operations become quite laborious. How would you like to be asked to solve this set of equations manually?

$$0.5824x + 3.9842y - 8.5329z = 85.7312$$
$$9.8741x - 4.3211y - 0.3641z = 11.8279$$
$$4.6673x + 7.6883y + 1.1872z = 43.9876$$

The physical labor and time required for the solution of these equations is obviously extensive. In practice, a system of simultaneous equations may involve as many as several hundred unknowns. The number of arithmetic operations in a complex problem may therefore run into the millions. Indeed, it is for this reason that scientists and engineers use large-scale computers costing hundreds of thousands of dollars a year.

DESIGN TECHNIQUES

Programming abounds with opportunities for fashioning elegant solutions to problems. The organization and design of computational equipment offer similar intellectual challenges.

Most machines are organized so that only a fixed number of characters can be handled by an instruction. Information is stored in memory in specified blocks of locations, called *words,* and any one command can operate upon only a single word at a time. Instead of addressing a variable-length field, an instruction in a fixed-word-length machine addresses an entire word.

One advantage of the fixed, as opposed to the variable word-length, is that the programmer does not have to be concerned about the demarcation of fields in memory. There are numerous pros and cons as to which mode of machine organization is preferable. Certain machines represent a compromise between the two viewpoints. The flexible field length feature is very useful in commercial applications. However, in mathematical computation, fixed words are desirable for several reasons. One major consideration is the fact that where huge amounts of calculation are necessary, it is important to perform all arithmetic operations at a maximum speed. For this purpose the adder must be as fast as possible. It is obviously quicker to perform an addition by adding all of the digits in a number at the same time. This is called *parallel addition.* Circuits can be built to perform this function, but they require fixed-word-length fields to operate upon. In designing a fixed-word-length computer, it is difficult to choose the proper number of characters to comprise a word. If the word is too large, a good deal of adder hardware is frequently unused. On the other hand, if the word is too small, special programming techniques must be resorted to in order to produce answers of the desired precision.

One undesirable characteristic of fixed-word machines is that it often becomes necessary to "pack" information in words in order not to waste memory positions. Thus, if a large number of 4-digit fields and 5-digit fields must be stored in memory, it would be inefficient to use entire 10-digit words for these fields. Instead, both fields are placed within the same word, and the programmer keeps track of where they are located. For example, suppose we wished to store the 4-digit *rate* field and the 5-digit *item number* field in a 10-digit word. This might be done as follows:

$$
\left.\begin{array}{ll}
\text{Rate} & 1500 \\
\text{Item number} & \text{7B253}
\end{array}\right\} \text{Data to be stored}
$$

1	2	3	4	5	6	7	8	9	10	
1	5	0	0	7	B	2	5	3	b	Packed word

$$\underbrace{}_{\text{Rate}}\quad\underbrace{}_{\text{Item number}}$$

The packing of information into words causes other problems, however. It would obviously be meaningless to perform an operation such as addition upon a word which contains more than one stored field. Hence, it is necessary to "extract" out each field whenever it is needed. Special commands are available for this purpose in fixed-word-length machines. At best, packing and unpacking are clumsy procedures. They require additional clerical work on the part of the programmer, and entail extra running time on the computer. After information has been packed, unpacked, and processed, it is often necessary to repack the data.

INSTRUCTION FORMAT

Another way in which design technique varies is in the choice of *instruction format*. This term refers to the manner in which commands are stored and interpreted by the machine. For example, it is possible to place two instructions in the same word:

1	2	3	4	5	6	7	8	9	10
R	0	5	5	3	A	0	7	8	2

Left-hand   Right-hand
instruction   instruction

In such a case, the control system would be designed to execute the left-hand instruction first, then the right-hand instruction. The machine would still continue to obtain its commands from consecutive memory locations. This method of logical design results in considerable savings of memory space but causes additional programming complexity and more complicated control circuitry.

Another design technique is to place two addresses with each instruction. A machine organized in this way might have a command of the type

ADD   0553   0782

which might request the machine to add the contents of word 0553 to the contents of word 0782, and to place the sum in the accumulator. This two-address instruction accomplishes in one command what would otherwise require two instructions. It is also possible to design a machine with three address commands.

Another technique is to let the second address in an instruction specify the location of the next command to be executed. The sequence of instructions in such a machine is not determined by the stepping of the control counter, but is determined by this auxiliary address present with each command.

As has been stated, computers are built with certain types of applications in mind. These uses require somewhat different data processing methods. The organization of a machine is based upon the characteristic operations it is designed to carry out. The instruction set built into the equipment is a means for executing these operations. Certain types of instructions are more or less forced upon the designers. For example, the use of tape units as input-output devices necessitates the presence of instructions to perform such functions as rewinding the reel, backspacing the tape, and sensing the end of the reel.

11 THE SYMBOLS OF HUMAN STRIVING

THE EMOTIONAL SIGNIFICANCE OF DATA

In his occupational life, man has become increasingly a manipulator of symbols rather than a producer of goods. In 1900 one worker in forty was a clerical employee; today one out of every six individuals is busied with paper work. Record keeping is one of the largest industries in the United States. The familiar scene of an entire office floor filled with row on row of desks and files is duplicated innumerable times in all of the huge buildings comprising the skylines of our big cities. Here a large percentage of our population, working as typists, clerks, bookkeepers, and accountants, spend their work life in the processing of information.

These office procedures are often tedious and dull, and not the least of the contributions of automatic data processing is that it has released many individuals from uninspiring jobs. No doubt this trend will continue, with the invention of more and more devices for the handling of information by machines. There is a tendency, however, both for the person immersed in an office routine, and for the professional programmer absorbed in a complicated application, to lose sight of the broader significance of their activities. The little spots of magnetized material on a reel of tape or the pencil marks on a piece of paper are not lifeless symbols. On the contrary, these records are a representation of the emotional relations among individuals, and reflect many of their deepest hopes and anxieties. The setup of a file in the machine system of a life insurance company, along with the program for handling the record, are challenging technical tasks for those in the data processing profession. But to an insured family this record, on tape or cards, is the difference between security or despair. Similarly, the symbols processed by a pension trust, whether represented by typewritten sheets in a cardboard folder, a group of punched cards, or by bits on magnetic tape, are not simply information, but are the signs of the confidence and trust of large numbers of people.

Stand on the gallery of the New York Stock Exchange, and look down on the mass of hurrying, scurrying individuals bidding, offering, buying, and selling. Little scraps of paper with special symbols record the consummation of transactions. A complex information-handling system interprets, summarizes, and analyzes these activities, communicating data all over the country within a short time. Steps are now under way to automate the intricacies of the stock exchange.

Several of the large brokerage firms have long since mechanized many of their procedures. Such problems as the preparation of monthly statements for customers, the mailing of confirmations of orders and transactions, and the scanning of margin accounts are some of the operations now being handled by electronic data processing equipment. Here again, amidst the fascinating technicalities involved in the data handling, there is a tendency to forget that each transaction is an event of extreme emotional significance to the individuals involved. Each scrap of paper produced by a sale on the floor of the New York Stock Exchange is a symbol of the ambitions and dreads of many people, and may radically change the lives of large numbers of individuals.

The processing of commercial data is thus not simply an interesting problem in systems engineering, but is a method for symbolizing a continually changing structure of human rights and obligations which deeply affect the hearts and minds of everyone in the country. The institution of money, the very basis for our economic, sociological, and psychological security, has undergone a tremendous transformation in the last several decades. Over 90% of all commercial transactions in the United States are now consummated by checks, 11 billion of which are written every year. No gold, silver, or paper currency changes hands. There is simply a pair of entries, one in the file of the person who drew the check, and one in the file of the individual receiving the payment.

FIXED-ASSET ACCOUNTING

There is a growing tendency among economists to conceive of money as simply a "unit of account." According to this point of view, money is mainly a device for measuring and keeping track of economic interrelations. Wealth is not constituted by a hoard of precious metals. It is based on factories, raw materials, and the ability to make good use of these resources.

In any conceivable form of social organization, certain basic resources must be kept available and in satisfactory condition, whether these economic goods be pottery and spears, or jet airplanes and nuclear reactors. In a large company these basic resources, or capital, consist largely of plant and equipment, and an extensive accounting system is needed to keep track of the acquisition, location, depreciation, obsolescence, and replacement of these fixed assets.

The wearing out of capital goods is not only an expense which has an important influence upon the taxes a company must pay to the state, but is also a depletion of resources which affects the amount of insurance which must be carried. Financial planning for the replacement of worn-out capital resources, and the control and reporting of the company's assets are among the other many needs of management which are served by plant and equipment accounting. We will now illustrate, in a simplified way, how this processing is carried out in a punched-card machine installation.

Whenever any new asset is acquired, such as land, buildings, or machinery, various types of basic data, in the form of source documents, are created. This information consists of the details of the purchase or manufacture of the item. A serial number is given to the asset, and is used on all records pertaining to that capital good. This code may be stamped or painted on the item, or may be impressed on a metal plate attached to the asset.

Punched cards prepared from the source documents contain such data as item number, code for geographical location, the date the asset was acquired, the date the item will probably be scrapped, the cost of the item, and the amount by which the asset is to be depreciated, in accordance with some formula. The cards are verified for accuracy, and interpreted to facilitate human handling. These cards are kept together in one deck as assets are acquired by the company. At the conclusion of every accounting period the cards are sorted by item number and acquisition date. The deck of cards is now listed and summarized, to provide a historical record of the acquisition of fixed assets.

The master property record file, which contains a record of all of the plant and equipment owned by the company, must be up-dated by the entry of the new acquisitions. This master file consists of punched cards representing all of the corporation's fixed assets and is, for convenience, kept in order by item number and geographical code. To enter the new acquisition cards into the master file, the new acquisition cards must, therefore, be sorted again, after which they are merged with the master file by means of the collator.

The above procedures require a series of passes of decks of punched cards through several machines. This is illustrated in Fig. 11-1.

As time goes by, each asset usually is lessened in value. This decrease in worth is part of the expense of running a business, and a corresponding amount of money is put in a reserve fund for the replacement of this loss of capital. Accordingly, the entire master file must be processed at regular intervals to determine the additional depreciation accrued during the preceding period. Contained on each card in the master file is infor-

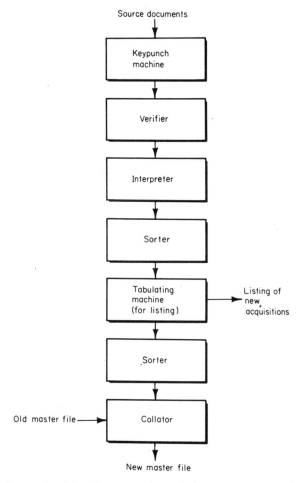

FIGURE 11-1 Machine system for updating a property record file.

mation enabling the machine to compute the current depreciation amount, as well as the present reserve for depreciation. The old master file is the input to the depreciation run. The accounting machine computes the new reserve amount for each item, and punches out another deck of cards which become the new master file. This file is now listed, with totals taken at various levels of asset grouping, to provide a report on the present value of the company's property. The file can be sorted mechanically in any number of ways to produce tabulations for any desired purpose. For example, the cards might be sorted by year of anticipated salvage, in order to schedule a budget for replacements. Or a listing by operating departments can be scheduled for cost accounting purposes.

When a capital resource is moved from one location in the company to another, this change must be reflected in the organization's records by changing the location codes in the master file. The old card for a trans-

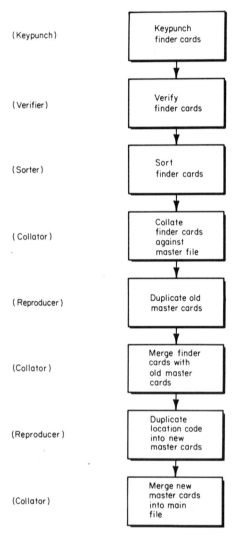

FIGURE 11-2 Flow chart for making new master record cards from finder cards.

ferred item, therefore, must be reproduced into a new card with a changed location code. When there is a continual movement of equipment within a company, the record keeping for these occurrences may become a large clerical activity. With a small number of transfers, old cards can simply be picked out of the main file manually, and all columns, other than location code, reproduced into a new card. The new location can then be keypunched into the card, which is at this point manually replaced into the file.

Mechanization is required when a large volume of equipment transfer occurs. Whenever any asset is moved, its serial number and new location are punched in a *finder* card. These cards are kept together in a deck, and at appropriate intervals are sorted by serial number. They are then collated against the master file, the collator selecting from the master file all cards which match. The master cards are then duplicated (except for location code) into new master cards, which are then merged with the finder cards. By suitable wiring of the reproducer, the location code in the finder card is now reproduced into the new master card. The finder cards and the old master cards are now dispensed with; the new master cards, now complete, are merged back into the main file.

Each of the boxes in the flow chart of Fig. 11-2 represents the pass of one or more decks of cards through some punched-card machine. If the same plugboard machine is used more than once, a different control panel is usually required. There are often a number of different ways of setting up a problem for processing by a system of punched-card machines. Beyond the data processing techniques, of course, loom the broader problems of the goals and policies of management which are served by the generation, analysis, and summarization of business information. The procedures used for a given application are often dictated by the equipment which happens to be installed or available. The rental or purchase of additional equipment may exceed budgetary limitations. It may, therefore, be necessary to frame a problem solution in terms of the available machines, despite the fact that speed and efficiency advantages might be possible by ordering other equipment.

TAPE PROCESSING FOR INSURANCE

Data processing on punched-card equipment requires a series of passes of decks of cards through a number of different special-purpose machines. Because of their much greater flexibility and memory capacity, stored-program machines are general purpose in nature. By an appropriate sequence of commands, the central processing unit can be instructed to perform any desired function. What is more, the use of the stored-program concept lends tremendous additional capabilities to data processing machinery, so that they are capable of far more complex applications than was possible previously.

Speed alone, however, makes this equipment invaluable in many large applications. This is particularly evident in the case of corporations which sell some product or service to consumers. The huge life insurance companies, for example, must keep records for millions of customers. Apart from actuarial computations and numerous accounting functions, premium notices must be sent out periodically, based on the various complexities of the outstanding policies. The core of such insurance applications is a master tape file comprised of records containing data related to number of policy, name of policy holder, address of policy holder, amount of insurance, gross premium, current dividend, dividend interest rate, loan principal, loan interest rate, agents' codes, commission payments for each agent, date of issue of policy, and date of premium anniversary. This file usually includes all policies which are in force, paid up, or which have lapsed for one year.

A data processing application with modern equipment usually consists of a series of *runs* or *passes*. These terms mean the reading in of one or more tapes as inputs, and the writing out of one or more tapes as outputs. Sometimes a computer is programmed to put its results out directly on a printer. In most cases, however, the output is placed on a reel of tape which is later printed out in an auxiliary operation.

This application consists of six runs. The first five passes (Fig. 11-3) are concerned largely with the preparation of data for the main run. It is in this sixth pass (Fig. 11-4) that the actual work is done. Here the machine produces the premium notices which are mailed out to the policy holders. This billing run is primarily a pass which updates the master file with new information, prepares a new master file, and writes out tape records for printing on the premium notice forms. Before this main run can occur, however, several preliminary passes are necessary to place the new information in a form suitable for use in updating the master file. The new information records include such items as address changes, name changes (when a woman is married), the addition of new policy holders, changes in existing policies, data affecting loans, modifications of interest rates, and other accounting data. Each record contains a code which identifies the type of new information being entered into the system.

The preliminary passes on the new information records are frequently called *pre-edit* runs. The first four runs in this application are of this nature. They involve such procedures as validity tests, which make certain that the source information is not in error. Also performed are accounting checks which ascertain whether all of the data has been entered correctly. The tape records are grouped to reduce tape time in

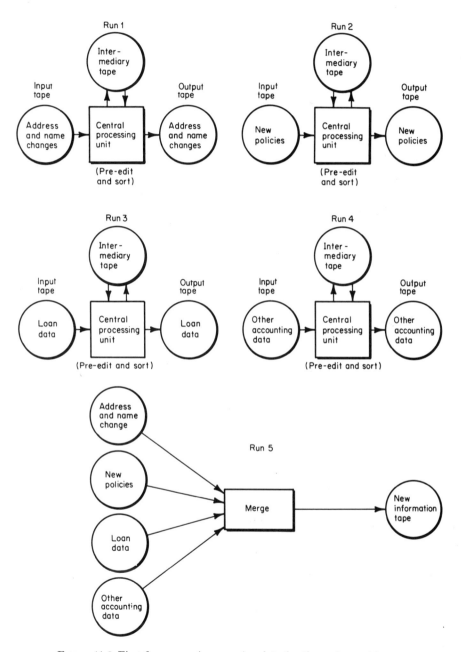

FIGURE 11-3 First five passes in preparing data for the main machine run.

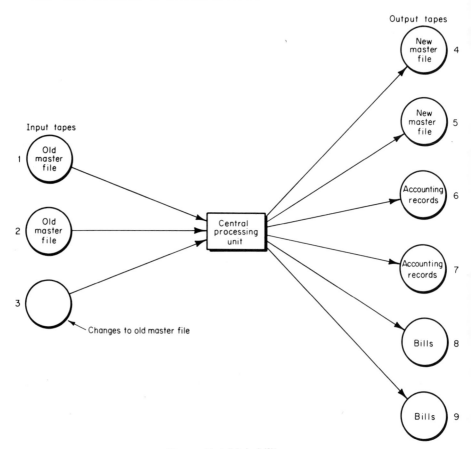

FIGURE 11-4 Main billing run.

the main run, and the fields are condensed and reshuffled into more convenient forms. Another activity carried out in the pre-edit runs is to
sort the new information into the same order as the master file. In run 5
all of these tape records are collated into one tape file.

Run 6, the main billing pass, consists of five major procedures:

1. The matching of new information records against the master file,
   and the entering of the new data into the old master records.
2. The making of tests and decisions based on the large number of
   possible combinations of events and conditions encountered in
   various life insurance contracts.
3. The preparation of a new master file as an output.
4. The preparation of output tape records to be used for the printing
   of premium notices.

5. The preparation of various accounting records associated with the policies.

There are innumerable programming and systems technicalities in data processing applications. We can attempt here only to convey a feeling for the many types of problems which are present.

Since the master file may consist of dozens, if not scores, of reels of tape, a great deal of expensive time would be wasted if the machine had to remain idle while reels were being mounted and dismounted from tape units.* To avoid this inefficiency, two input tape units are specified for the old master file in the main run. During the running of the program, the computer begins by reading from tape unit 1. When all of the information on this reel has been used, the machine starts to read from tape unit 2. At this point the first reel is taken off tape unit 1, and the third reel mounted in its place. When the second reel is exhausted, the computer obtains its information from tape unit 1, and the fourth reel is mounted on tape unit 2. This alternation is continued until the entire master file has been read. This technique gives the machine operator the opportunity to change reels while the computer is reading from the other tape unit. The same method is used for writing on output tapes. In run 6, two tape units are made available for this purpose for the new master file, the accounting records, and the bills.

Before any of the premium or accounting calculations can be performed for a particular policy record on the master file, the machine must ascertain whether any change to that policy has occurred. Both the master file and the changes tape are in policy number order.

The first step performed by the computer is to read in a policy record from the master file. Then, the machine reads in the next record on the changes tape. The policy numbers of the two records are compared. Three possibilities now exist:

1. If the two policy numbers are equal, the data in the master record is updated or modified by the information in the changes record. A code in the changes record instructs the machine what type of alteration of the master is required. After these modifications are made, another change record is read in and the process is repeated if it matches the master. More than one change to a particular policy in the main file is possible. When all changes to the given master record have been processed, the altered master record is written out as part of the new master file, and the next input master record is read in.

---

* However, new equipment is now available which makes it possible to load two reels on a tape unit at the same time.

2. If the master is higher than the changes record, then the changes record constitutes a new policy to be entered into the file. A new policy record is created and is written out on the new master file. The next change record is now read in from the input reel.

3. If the master is lower than the changes record, then no alterations are needed and the old master record is written out unchanged on the new master file. The next input master record is now read in.

These procedures are characteristic of almost all applications where master files must be updated and processed. The reading in of the old master file and the changes tape continues, of course, until both files are exhausted.

Before writing out records on the new master file, the machine processes the policies. Each policy must be checked to determine whether it is an active or an inactive account. Lapsed accounts contain a date at which they are to be purged from the file. The program checks such lapsed accounts against the purge date, and if this date has been reached, the policy is not written out on the new master file. Instead, a record stating that this policy has been eliminated is placed on a special output tape. If the purge date has not been reached, the record is retained in the new master file. Other inactive accounts reflect instances in which advance payments have been made or in which billing has for some reason been suspended.

The billing run occurs every month and, accordingly, the program must determine if the premium is due at the time when the run is performed. The premium notice is adjusted if a loan on the policy is outstanding, and special accounting records are prepared if this is the case.

A large part of the processing consists of numerous tests and calculations to determine the dollar amount of premiums now due on policies. Because of the different types of policies sold to the public, many varying possibilities have to be checked. For example, certain "Modified 5" policies specify that after five years the amount of the premium is to increase. The machine recognizes whether a given policy belongs in this category by examining a code contained in the record. If the policy is of the Modified 5 type, the program compares the present date with the date when the specified five-year period is to terminate. If this date has been reached, the amount of the bill to be sent to the policyholder is computed in accordance with the increased rate.

Similar testing and processing is required for other types of policies. The program must decide whether a policy is term insurance. The holders of such policies have the privilege of converting to a regular policy, providing this right is exercised within a specified time.

The machine also ascertains when a particular policy has reached the end of the premium-paying period. When this occurs, accounting notices are written out for use in adjusting the agent's records. The master record is adjusted, usually by placing a code somewhere in the record to indicate that premium notices no longer should be prepared.

The dividend to which the policyholder is entitled is also ascertained. If this dividend is to be applied toward the premium, its amount must be reflected in the premium notice. The dividend may also be accumulated within the policyholder's account, or may be applied to reduce a loan. The computation of the agent's commission is based upon the various factors present in the policy contract. In some instances, more than one agent is involved, and the information in the policy record enables the program to determine how the commissions are to be divided. Various commission plans may be employed by the insurance company, and the sequence of instructions must be able to handle all cases. Accounting statements are prepared during the billing run to enable the company to pay the proper commissions to its agents.

SUBSCRIPTION FULFILLMENT

Another example of a large file-maintenance application is the subscription-handling procedures of large magazines. These companies have millions of customers who subscribe to the publication for a period of one or more years. Accounting information must be kept for each customer, and name and address labels must be printed for mailing out the copies.

When a subscription lapses, magazines usually send out promotional material in the attempt to induce the customer to mail in a renewal form. Often this advertising is mailed as much as three months before the expiration date, with further material each month thereafter. If the subscription is not renewed, the publication continues its promotion for a number of additional months. When a subscription is renewed, the magazine must enter this information into its files. A new subscription requires the formation of a new file record and the instituting of a procedure for mailing the publication to this customer.

In addition to carrying out these procedures, the company has to perform a great many accounting functions, such as billing subscribers and keeping track of their payments. There are a large number of address changes which must be entered promptly into the files to prevent customers from not receiving copies of the publication. Cancellations must also be processed. Finally, a considerable volume of complaints is often received from subscribers who claim that they have not been sent their copies of current or past issues. These queries from customers must be carefully answered after an investigation of the files and associated records of mailings.

The following is a tabulation of the data processing statistics of an actual publishing firm. Certain facts have been altered somewhat to preserve the identity of the company. This concern publishes three magazines: a semimonthly, a monthly, and a bimonthly.

	Magazine A	Magazine B	Magazine C
When published	(twice a month)	(once a month)	(every two months)
Volumes per year	6,000,000	4,800,000	420,000
Volumes per issue	250,000	400,000	70,000
New subscriptions per year	120,000	240,000	24,000
New subscriptions per issue	5,000	20,000	4,000
Renewals per year	96,000	72,000	24,000
Renewals per issue	4,000	6,000	4,000
Changes of address per year	48,000	48,000	6,000
Changes of address per issue	2,000	4,000	1,000
Cancellations per year	4,800	6,000	600
Cancellations per issue	200	500	100
Complaints per year	48,000	36,000	6,000
Complaints per issue	2,000	3,000	1,000

A code is assigned to each subscriber. The name and address file is placed on magnetic tape, along with amounts owed on subscriptions, expiration dates, and miscellaneous other information. Each subscription period, changes cards pertaining to new subscriptions, renewals, payments, address changes, etc., are keypunched from letters from subscribers and subscription forms. If these source documents do not contain a subscriber code, the code is entered from an alphabetic listing of subscribers. New customers are assigned a code. The changes cards are converted to magnetic tape.

The inputs into the system are the changes tape, the old master file, and the old city file (see Fig. 11-5). The data handling for each magazine is executed separately. Each publication has its own master files and changes tape. In each case five runs are required for all of the necessary processing. (See Figs. 11-5, -6, -7, -8.)

The first run is needed for the updating of a city master file. Since there are 720,000 subscribers, it follows that in preparing the mailing labels the computer must print out 720,000 city names. To keep all of this information in the master file itself would involve retaining millions

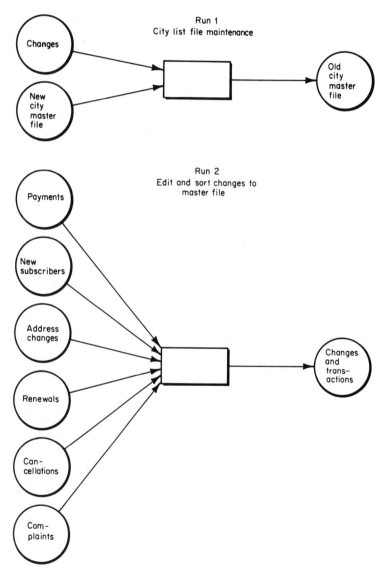

FIGURE 11-5 Subscription fulfillment Run 1 and Run 2 (simplified).

of characters on the reels of magnetic tape. In turn, the greater length of these files would considerably extend the time required for reading and writing these tapes. A statistical sampling indicates that large blocks of subscribers live in the populous cities. If the city address of each subscriber were kept with his individual record, as described above, there

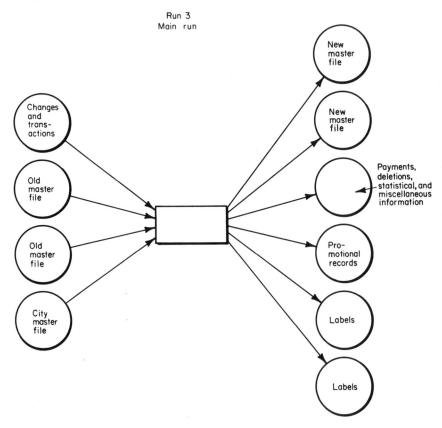

FIGURE 11-6 Subscription fulfillment Run 3 (simplified).

would be a tremendous repetition of city names in the files. The name of a large city might be repeated tens of thousands of times.

Since there are only about 20,000 cities on this subscription list, this duplication can be avoided by keeping a city master file. Each city is assigned a code which is placed both with the city name in the city master file and with the subscriber name in the master file. Both files are sorted into state, city, and subscriber code order. During the main run, when the mailing labels are prepared, both of these files are brought into the computer. The city name for any subscriber can be obtained by matching the city code in the subscriber's record against the codes in the city master file.

Since new cities must occasionally be entered into the city master file, and unneeded city names deleted, run 1 is necessary for the updating of this file.

The decision to keep a separate city master file is a problem in the design of the over-all data processing system. The tape time saved in the reading and writing of the master file by excluding the city names

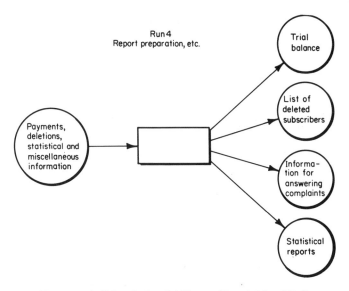

FIGURE 11-7 Subscription fulfillment Run 4 (simplified).

must be balanced against the time for updating the city master file in a preliminary run. Actually, run 1 is of negligible duration, most of the time being consumed in mounting the reels of tape. Furthermore, this preliminary run might often be dispensed with since there might often be long periods of time when no new cities would appear on the subscription list. By keeping the names of states on the city master file, an additional saving of space on the master file is achieved.

Run 2 is a pre-editing pass. During this run, the changes records are sorted into the same order as the master tapes so that the two files can later be collated. A number of checks on the validity of this input data are also performed at this time to prevent incorrect or inadequate information from being entered later into the master file. Since each record is coded to designate the type of change it contains, it is possible to check the item to make sure that it contains all of the necessary and proper information. For example, a record coded as an address change should contain the subscriber's new address, along with his city and state code. The money shown on a payment record should be in definite amounts or within certain limits.

The main run has as its inputs, the old city master file, the old master file, and the changes tape. These three files are collated together.

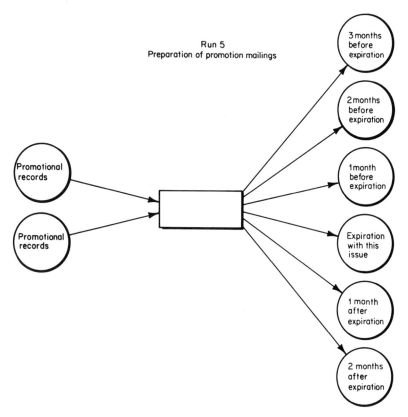

FIGURE 11-8 Subscription fulfillment Run 5 (simplified).

During this pass, the computer prepares reels of labels for all subscribers who are to receive the publication. The machine also produces labels for subscribers who are due for promotional material. The program decides when subscriptions have expired and which subscriptions will expire shortly. The type of promotional material sent out depends upon the expiration date of the subscription.

The updating of the master file follows the same lines as in life insurance premium billing. Changes are collated against the subscriber records. When a match occurs, the change record is examined to ascertain what type of transaction is present. Since a large percentage of the subscriptions are on credit (the subscribers send in order blanks asking to be billed later), there are a large number of payments on the changes tape which must be entered into the master file. Address changes and renewals require alterations of the master records. Occasionally, a reader may request the cancellation of his subscription, in which case his record is dropped from the new master file. Complaints from readers are processed manually. The machine prints out its information on the discontented subscriber for perusal by the clerical staff. Deletions are made when customers do not renew their subscriptions.

A list of deleted records is "outputted" for reference purposes. Various statistical reports are produced to provide information for circulation audits and management control. Among these reports is a tabulation of the unpaid subscriptions. In some instances this report is "aged," to show how long each account has been delinquent.

In the main run, a number of outputs are placed on one tape (payments, deletions, complaints, etc.) since not enough tape units are available for each report separately. This procedure takes the following form: As information is obtained during the main run for any of these reports, it is written out on the same tape. The records are thus intermixed on the output reel. In run 4, all of these records are de-merged, each being placed on its appropriate tape. During this process the machine accumulates totals and analyzes the information in the specified ways. The final output tapes are printed in a separate operation. All of the different promotional records are likewise placed on one tape. These records are separated into categories in run 5.

THE BANKING SYSTEM

Perhaps the most graphic illustration of the emotional significance of data processing is the manipulation of the symbols comprising our bank balance.

The processing of billions of checks involves a highly intricate, nationwide system of data handling. One study indicates that the average check deposited or cashed in a given bank takes $2\frac{1}{3}$ days to be collected from the bank on which it is drawn. About 40% of all checks are presented at the same bank at which they are payable, about 20% are drawn on banks in the same city, and approximately 40% are payable at out of town banks.

What happens when a depositor draws a check upon his account? The payee deposits this check in his own bank. If the payee's bank is different from the original depositor's bank, the check is sorted out by the payee's bank and sent to a regional clearing house. Here all checks in this category are sorted and sent to the banks on which they were drawn.

All of the checks drawn on each particular bank must now be sorted by that bank into account number order, subtracted from the current balance in depositors' accounts, and summarized and analyzed for various banking records. At the end of the month all of the cancelled checks drawn against a given account must be collected together, and returned to that depositor along with his statement.

It is apparent that a tremendous job of sorting and distributing checks is continually going on in the clearing houses and banks. Within each particular bank there are a number of difficult processing problems. Before a withdrawal can occur, a bank must ascertain whether the amount can be covered by the balance in the account, and must in addition find out whether a stop order has been entered. Checks must be posted (entered) rapidly into each account so as to maintain an up-to-date record of the money in that account, and numerous credit inquiries must be answered within a short time. The total value of the checks drawn every year has been estimated to be in excess of $2 trillion, and it takes about 500,000 bank employees to handle these transactions. Numerous accounting controls are necessary to make sure that no defalcations are occurring, and to achieve this purpose all accounts and transactions must be in balance at the end of every day. Furthermore, at each step in the accounting procedures there must be proof procedures to prevent errors and thefts.

An illustrative banking installation has a central data processor with a paper tape reader, eight magnetic tape units, and a high-speed printer for handling 80,000 checking accounts and an average of 90,000 check transactions every day. A trial balance is produced at the end of every day, in account number order, including the date of the last transaction, name of the account, messages concerning stops and overdrafts, and present balance. In addition, there is a daily register of all activity, comprised of both deposits and withdrawals. Statements are mailed once a month to all depositors. To facilitate this procedure, 5% of the statements are handled by the machine every day, the processor computing the activity in the account and the resulting service charges. The over-all system takes the form shown in Fig. 11-9.

The source documents—daily deposits and checks drawn on the bank —are converted to punched paper tape by clerical personnel. Batch totals are taken to establish auditing controls. The first computer run verifies these batch controls. If a batch total does not match with the computer's total of the records in the batch, the entire group of records is placed on an output tape for manual perusal. The output of run 1 is an intermediary magnetic tape. This becomes the input into run 2, where the input records are sorted into account number sequence. Summaries of the day's transactions are also produced at this time.

In run 3 additional input, comprised of miscellaneous information such as address changes and corrected batches of transactions, is converted to paper tape, sorted into account number order, and merged with the main input. The main run is a file maintenance pass on the master records containing depositors' accounts. In addition to creating a new master file, run 4 also outputs a trial balance. In the final run the daily group of statements are produced, along with records of service charge computations, a listing of the day's transactions, and various reports for the bank management.

While this system enables the postings to be made automatically to depositors' accounts, it does not handle the problem of collecting the physical checks for mailing back to the depositor at the end of the monthly period. Since there are 90,000 checks to be handled each day, it is obvious that there is an enormous paper handling problem which is not solved by this installation.

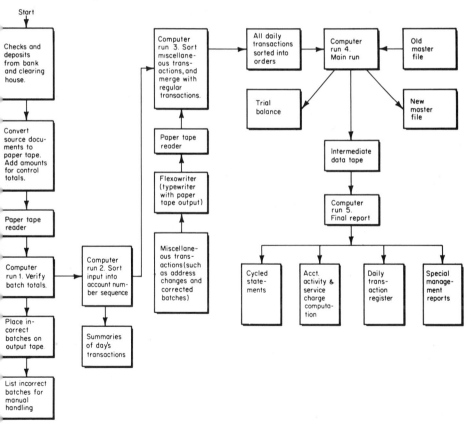

FIGURE 11-9 Daily run—banking.

Several methods have been proposed for mechanizing the physical processing of checks. To be handled mechanically, the checks must contain information in a form which can be read by a machine, and which is clear enough to enable the equipment to produce reliable results. Even if this problem is solved, there remains the task of getting the checks into an input device which will be able to read the information in a uniform way. The checks must be of uniform size, and the symbols must be placed on the document so that the sensing unit can obtain its data from the same part of every check. Punched-card checks and checks imprinted with magnetic ink, now in common use, fulfill such requirements.

The standardization of check formats has been a formidable problem, since there are a wide variety of physical types of checks traditionally used by the nation's banks. In addition, the type fonts used for the characters on the checks are highly variable, and there is a wide variety of ways in which banks put this information on their checks. Some institutions place pictorial material and special gimmicks on their checks, and this has the effect of making these documents incapable of conforming to any established standard.

One of the machines devised for reading checks is the character-sensing machine, a device which can recognize printed letters and numbers. This equipment usually operates on either a matching or analysis principle. In the former method, the machine optically senses the character to be recognized, and compares this letter or number with a set of characters stored within the machine. The equipment "recognizes" a character by accepting that letter or number which best fits the inner character set.

Character sensing by means of the analysis of the sensed information involves more built-in intelligence on the part of the machine. All letters and numbers to be read are categorized beforehand by the designers of the equipment. For example, only certain letters contain a vertical bar at the left of the character, namely, B, D, E, F, H, K, L, M, N, P, and R. Within this group of characters, a vertical bar on the right is possessed only by H, M, and N. These three letters can be isolated by means of criteria pertaining to crossbars and connecting lines.

Character-sensing equipment is now being used for the processing of Travelers' Checks. Actually, the significance of equipment of this type extends far beyond banking, and has a tremendous potential for the entire field of information handling. One of the main bottlenecks in data processing, both from the standpoint of time and cost, is the transcribing of source documents into machine-readable forms such as paper tape, magnetic tape, and punched cards. Research has been under way for many years on methods for the optical reading of handwriting, but it is apparent that this entails great difficulties.

Another method for processing checks is exemplified by ERMA (*E*lectronic *R*ecording *M*ethod of *A*ccounting), a machine manufactured by the General Electric Company. This automatic system, installed at the Bank of America in Los Angeles, performs the bookkeeping for over 200,000 checking accounts. The equipment reads and sorts checks, and posts transactions to 550 accounts each minute. An experienced clerk can carry out the same procedure at the rate of about four accounts per minute.

The ERMA system consists of a document reader, a central processor, a control console, tape units, a printer, and other peripheral equipment. The printer is under computer control and prepares statements for each customer and for each branch bank at 900 lines a minute, an average of about 50 statements per minute.

The checks used by the Bank of America have numbers imprinted in magnetic ink across their lower edge. These characters represent such information as the number of the issuing bank, the number of the bank branch, and the depositor's account number. The customer must use these documents for his checks. When these checks are presented at the bank, a clerk imprints their dollar value on the check in magnetic ink. The checks are fed into a document-handling device which reads the magnetic characters and transmits the information into the central computer. The machine can process checks which have been overstamped, folded, or otherwise mutilated.

The central computer, upon receiving the records from the checks, sorts these data into account number sequence at the rate of about 30,000 decimal digits per second. The data processing machine then looks up the depositor's account in its files, records the transaction, and calculates the new balance. In posting to accounts, the computer ascertains whether stop payment orders have been entered or whether certified checks are outstanding against the account. In such instances, the machine produces a message indicating that this account must be given special handling The machine produces a customer statement upon request, or at periodical intervals. Service charges are computed automatically and applied to accounts.

The sorting of the physical checks is performed separately by a special device not unlike a conventional punched-card sorter in principle. These canceled checks are placed in the depositor's file, and are sent to the customer along with his regular statement.

One procedure which has been suggested for the sorting of the actual checks provides a way of dispensing with this vast paper-handling job.

In addition to reading the information from the check, the device which senses this data would also take a photograph of the document. Both the pictorial image of the check and the binary digits representing its information content could now be placed on magnetic tape. The entire record would now be sorted by conventional methods. In the course of posting to the depositors' accounts, the machine would include an image of the canceled checks. At the end of the month, therefore, instead of sending back the checks themselves, the bank would return photographs of these documents.

While the processing of checks is perhaps the most interesting of all of the banking applications, there are actually more than 90 different types of services which these institutions perform. These include personal trusts, installment loans, commercial loans, mortgages, factoring accounts, corporate trusts, payrolls, and savings accounts. Each of these operations involves accounting for tens of thousands, if not hundreds of thousands of records. Programs have been planned for these applications, and it seems likely that ultimately all of these services will be handled by electronic computers. When the nation's 15,000 banks complete the automation of all of these operations, the symbol of money will be almost completely transformed from a tangible article of value stored in vaults or exchanged in trade. It will have become a pattern of social information defining the reciprocal claims and responsibilities of all members of the community.

ELECTRONIC ACCOUNTING

The entire economic system will probably be represented ultimately in the electronic files of the corporations comprising the industrial capacity of the United States. A large percentage of the economic goods and services which are produced and exchanged now constitute the accounts receivable and accounts payable records kept by the country's enterprises. These applications, in turn, tie in closely with most of the standard accounting procedures whereby companies keep track of the manufacturing and distribution of their products. Most of these procedures have already been mechanized, either by means of punched-card systems or by electronic data processing equipment.

Industrial data processing may be conceived as originating in the sales order, a handwritten or preprinted document indicating that a sale has been made. Where goods are sold over the counter, the record is often produced in the form of a sales slip (with multiple copies) which is then converted to punched cards. Another common method for entering this information into a mechanized system is the affixing of pre-punched tags to the articles offered for sale. When a purchase is consummated, part of the tag is torn off by the clerk, and is then entered into a specially designed reading device. The volume of face-to-face sales is indicated by a recent estimate that in the United States there is one cash register for every 25 men and women. Numerous procedures have been suggested for avoiding the laborious keypunching of all of these transactions. Magnetic ink may well provide a frequent solution to this large transcription problem in retailing, just as it has in banking.

The billing of retail customers has in recent years been deeply affected by the institution of the credit card, which will probably still further reduce the use of cash in the economic life of the country. The number of cards now issued runs into many millions. If we assume that each individual makes 10 purchases a month with his credit card, we can predict that this institution will, in the future, account for hundreds of millions of retail transactions a month.

Machine-readable documents must also be produced from sales orders sent in by salesmen or customers. These inputs initiate the shipment of merchandise and the payment of commissions to salesmen. From this data the company is also able to analyze which products are selling best, in which price ranges, in what geographical localities, and in what categories of customers. Forecasting of future sales, determination of profitable discounts, adjustments of salesmen's incentives, control over advertising and sales aids, and the ascertaining of desirable territorial coverage are some of the economic functions rendered possible by the processing of this information. Analysis of profit by territory, salesman, type of industry, and other categories are other important byproducts of these procedures.

Products available for sale constitute another major asset of business organizations, and a large part of most companies' financial capital is invested in such goods. The number and type of the items in inventory are changing continually because of sales and additions to stock, and their value fluctuates with changes in demand. The proper management of the huge funds invested in inventory hence requires extensive record keeping, analysis, reporting, and decision making. The objectives of inventory accounting are to provide accurate information on what is in stock and what is on order, and to assist a company's officials in ascertaining at what levels the inventory should be kept at any given time.

The handling of sales orders obviously is closely related to inventory control. The volume of present sales and the forecast of future business determines when a company must begin to replenish its stock of merchandise. As we have seen, the inventory records in the master file are diminished by sales. The analysis of this information affects the scheduling of shipments of products from warehouses. Sales orders furnish the basic information for billing. They are used for setting up the accounts receivable, a record of money owed by customers. This file is updated periodically with incoming checks, credit allowances, special and regular discounts, records of returned merchandise, bad debt memos, and numerous other types of information.

In manufacturing companies, sales orders determine the scheduling of production and, in turn, give rise to the problems of material accounting. In planning production, an "inventory explosion" is necessary to determine in complete detail all of the raw materials and parts which will be required for the manufacture of every item. Starting with the volume of production planned, a series of successive expansions of material requirements is carried out. Assemblies are broken down into subassemblies, subassemblies into parts, etc., until every nut and bolt needed in the manufacturing process is ascertained. The resulting bill of materials is a complete list of every item required. This list is compared with existing inventories, and where raw materials, parts, or subassemblies must be procured, purchase requisitions and orders are initiated. This brings into existence the accounts payable, a file of amounts owed to other firms. The General Motors Corporation, to cite one example, is reported to rely on more than 27,500 businesses to supply its enormous needs.

The receipt and issuing of material for plant purposes generates an extensive internal flow of documents within a manufacturing company. The maintenance of this large and varied inventory likewise involves a large data processing job. By assigning each item a code number, it is possible to mechanize most of these procedures. (See Fig. 11-10.)

Material accounting furnishes one of the main inputs into the cost accounting procedures. This processing ascertains the actual cost involved in the manufacture of every item. Cost accounting enables a company to establish its sales prices so as to attain the desired profit margin. Without some conception of how much each product costs, the company may unintentionally lose money. Cost accounting also enables management to compare the operating costs of each department with standard costs, to ascertain whether these departments are operating in an efficient manner. Materials used in production, along with the wages paid to those individuals directly concerned in the manufacturing process, are often called *prime costs*.

The other main factor in production expense is overhead, which consists of a long list of indirect costs, such as heat, power and light, insurance, taxes, repairs, supervision, timekeeping, depreciation, maintenance, general supplies, and factory clerical wages. Since overhead applies to the entire plant, some formula is devised to allocate these costs to each particular department and product. In addition to manufacturing costs, there are also administrative expenses (such as are involved in the company's central offices) and selling expenses. The cost of each product may include a nationwide sales organization consisting of branch offices, salesmen, sales assistants, advertising campaigns, and all of the diverse clerical and administrative costs associated with these activities.

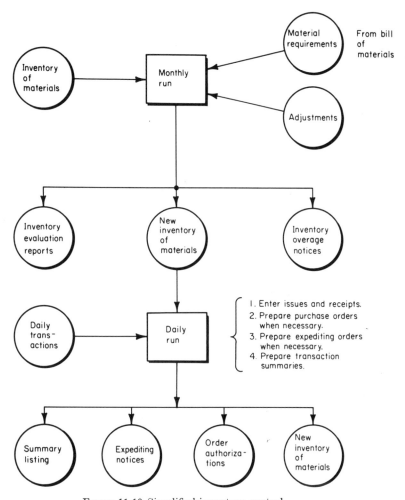

FIGURE 11-10 Simplified inventory control.

Payroll procedures feed into all of these classes of expenses. These procedures themselves may be highly complex. Some of the inputs are: deductions authorized by the employee, such as bonds, union dues, and hospitalization insurance; personnel changes, such as new hires, transfers, and releases; time cards made out by the employees covering their hours at work in possibly differing departments; withholding for federal, state,

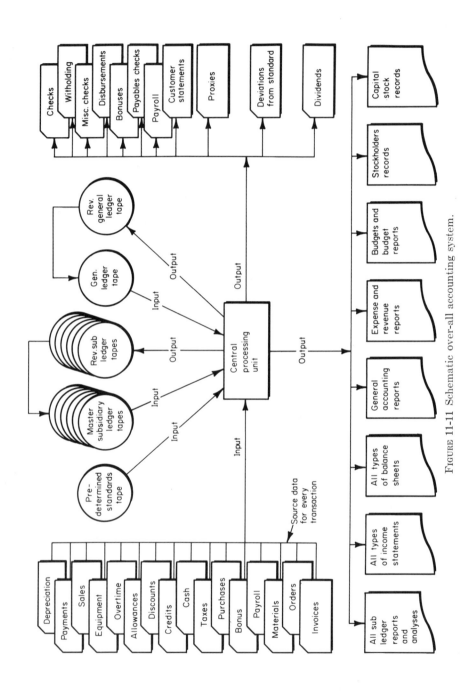

FIGURE 11-11 Schematic over-all accounting system.

176

and local taxes; sick pay; and leaves of absence. Numerous employee benefits must be calculated, along with a variety of reports for public agencies and the company management. The production of the payroll checks has as a necessary consequence procedures for reconciling these checks after they are cashed or deposited by the employees.

Financial planning and budgetary control are economic functions which interact with all of these processes of buying, selling, producing, and distributing. Material acquisition for the plants, payroll, overhead expenses, and capital improvements must be paid through the treasurer's office, which must make the funds available from anticipated revenues. Budgets must be submitted by department managers, approved in terms of over-all company planning, and periodically controlled and adjusted. The profit and loss statement must be prepared from operating data, and the balance sheet from ledgers containing records of the firm's assets and liabilities. Stockholder information, such as proxies, must be processed, and dividends computed for shareholders. (See Fig. 11-11.)

PLANNING A BUSINESS SYSTEM

To describe in detail the large number of interconnected accounting procedures which express the economic life of a modern corporation would require several volumes. Each procedure usually is a large undertaking in itself. The tracing of the flow of accounting information through a big company is a tortuous, exhausting task, often so complicated that no one person can understand all of the ramifications. In many instances information-handling systems in large enterprises have not been planned for in advance, but have grown through the years, through patches, accretions, augmentation, and the meeting of individual needs as they arose. Unnecessary reports and duplicated effort may exist in various parts of the labyrinth, and outworn useless practices, like a vermiform appendix, may persist as vestiges of earlier stages in the system's complex evolution.

While the programming of a machine run requires skill, an equal if not greater degree of ingenuity and hard work is needed for the definition of a problem and the setting up of its over-all solution. Any particular application usually involves a large number of different computer runs. Most of the inputs and outputs are to some degree interconnected, and considerable ability is required to plan these passes so as to minimize the time and equipment needed to accomplish the desired results. Often there are a number of different ways in which the computer runs can be set up and programmed. Files can be duplicated, consolidated, or sorted differently, information can be entered into the system at different points, output reports can be combined, enlarged, or simplified, redundant information eliminated, and clever memory allocation methods can be devised to handle special problems. Given a set of inputs and output reports, there are almost always several over-all alternative procedures for carrying out processing.

The evaluation of a proposed procedure involves a consideration of the feasibility of the method: Is it possible to prepare the programs in the manner indicated? Would the proposed procedure require excessively complicated programs? Next there is the problem of whether the system as planned would enable the installation to meet its schedules: Would all of the inputs be ready at the proper times? Would there be ample time for the printing of reports and statements before the deadline? Finally, time estimates are made to determine whether the proposed procedure would be economical: Would extra machinery be needed if this method is adopted? Would extra shifts of computer operating time be required? Is this procedure faster or slower than other proposed solutions?

There is as yet no theoretical approach to designing a series of computer runs to accomplish a desired purpose. The planning of data processing systems is still an art based on experience, training, and ingenuity. The problem is complicated by the fact that business procedures are often exceedingly difficult to define. Many of the procedures are usually not documented. A staff must spend protracted periods of time, often months, to understand each portion of an entire information-processing system. In most instances, innumerable little exceptions and requirements have grown into the procedures over the years.

The installation of electronic data processing necessitates a careful study of the existing accounting procedures. In some instances this study alone has resulted in such a widespread overhauling of current methods that enormous benefits have accrued even without the introduction of the high-speed stored program machines. It is perhaps apropos here to mention in passing a method cited by C. Northcote Parkinson for the elimination of paper work. This student of the wonders of bureaucracy reported in *The New York Times* that a large British retailing chain with over 237 branches decided one day that it could be assumed that the managers could trust the supervisors, and the supervisors could trust the clerks. By coming to this conclusion, the firm was able to dispense with time cards, file cards, complaint forms, and stockroom documents, thereby doing away with 22,000,000 pieces of paper weighing 105 tons.

Actually, what is needed is a method for mechanizing the description and analysis of information-handling systems, along with a procedure for optimizing their design. An automatic method for minimizing time, equipment, and cost would be of immense value throughout the data processing industry.

The enormity of the mass of economic symbols which are daily processed in the United States is indicated by a glimpse into some rough business statistics.

There are on the order of 65,000,000 nongovernmental employees for whom payrolls and personnel records must be processed. Some $500,000,-000,000 of life insurance premiums are in existence, and inventory for trade and manufacturing purposes is in the vicinity of $90,000,000,000. Sales from manufacturing and trading run well above $50,000,000,000 and consumer credit over $40,000,000,000. The number of shares of stock outstanding exceeds 6,000,000,000, and the value of bonds in existence is over $100,000,000,000. The total income of all individuals is on the order of $400,000,000,000 a year.

The story of business data processing does not end with the standard accounting procedures described in the last few pages. There are innumerable other economic activities in which huge volumes of information must be handled. Virtually every movement we make involves the cooperation of large numbers of people whose activities generate a large variety of data. Taxicab companies use computational equipment to handle their revenue accounting and to prepare driver operating statistics, as well as to process payroll and maintenance records. Transit organizations such as subways and bus lines have similar problems. The collection of tolls on thousands of miles of turnpikes is a major application, as is railroad ticketing and the handling of airline reservations. The mere supplying of food for big cities likewise involves numerous types of transportation record keeping. The recording of railroad freight shipments and the accounting for the nationwide system of tracks, yards, and terminals are large data processing problems. The movement of freight by truck is an entire industry with its own problems in information handling. The wholesalers who serve as intermediaries in the distribution of consumer goods often require data processing machines to assist with their accounting.

COMPUTERS IN THE GOVERNMENT

Nearly every aspect of our lives is reflected to some degree in the billions of punched cards used yearly in the multifarious automatic information-handling systems of American business enterprises. Schools and hospitals have long made use of data processing equipment for their record keeping, as have local and state governments. New York City employs a computer for payroll and retirement accounting. One recent application has been the installation of punched-card machines to select individuals for jury duty. Electronic computers are also being used to check the arithmetic in income tax returns.

The Federal Government employs electronic equipment extensively. UNIVAC I, was obtained by the Census Bureau in 1951. Since then the number of installations of stored program machines has increased continually. At the present time nearly all departments in the Government with large record-keeping activities have had their paper work reduced by electronic equipment.

In the Department of Defense electronic computers are being used for logistical purposes, as well as for personnel accounting, financial accounting, and statistical studies. The catalog of material carried in stock by the numerous supply and logistic systems of the Government comprises over 3 million different items. This file, along with a number of other related files, contains information concerning the technical characteristics of the items, availability of stock, requirements data, etc. Hundreds of millions of transactions must be processed every year in the maintenance and analysis of this cataloging system.

Military commands are increasingly using electronic computers for the efficient selection of personnel. When a particular position has to be filled, a request is sent to the installation. Here magnetic tape master files are maintained for every member of the armed force and its civilian employees. Each record contains data on the individual's job preferences, personnel history, training, and other skills. The files are updated daily with new material. When requests arrive, a program searches the tape for possible candidates, and prints out information on each person selected. A human board of review makes the final evaluation of these individuals.

In the civil branches of the Federal Government some of the major applications have been in such areas as the Social Security Administration wage record processing, Treasury check-handling procedures, Department of Agriculture commodity stabilization computations, and Bureau of the Census statistical reporting. The Treasury Department, for example, handles hundreds of millions of checks a year, and the reconciliation of these checks is a major data processing job. The Bureau of Public Debt in the Treasury Department may daily issue or redeem 750,000 savings bonds. The Post Office Department processes more than 300,000,000 money orders every year, and the Veterans Administration handles millions of records for veterans. There are, of course, several million civilian and military Government employees for whom payrolls must be prepared, and for whom records must be kept. According to the second Hoover Commission, all Government operations lumped together involve the creation and processing of more than 25,000,000,000 pieces of paper. In many instances these records are handled a number of times, and a colossal number of transactions are transcribed from these source documents and subjected to additional processing.

The Bureau of the Census has come a long way from the punched-card machines invented by Hollerith for the 1890 census. This organization does far more than the mere counting of population information; it turns out a large number of monthly, quarterly, and annual reports, such as Foreign Trade Statistics, Current Business Surveys, Current Population Survey, and the Annual Survey of Manufacturers.

As in commercial data processing, one of the main problems besetting the Bureau of the Census has been the conversion of source documents (the Census questionnaires) into a machine-readable form. In 1950 over 14 months and $6,000,000 was spent in keypunching source data. At peak periods almost 2000 keypunch operators were required for this operation. To solve this problem, the Bureau of Standards designed and built FOSDIC (Film Optical Sensing Device for Input to Computers). This unit works on the following principle: Source documents are prepared in the field by the checking of carefully positioned boxes on standard forms. These documents are then microfilmed. The microfilm is scanned electronically, after which the information is placed on magnetic tape. Improved models of FOSDIC have been developed continually. The present FOSDIC III can convert microfilmed census data to magnetic tape at about 20,000 characters per minute. All source documents are sent to Jeffersonville, Indiana, where about 20 cameras are in full-time operation converting the forms to microfilm reels. These reels are sent to Washington, D.C., where five FOSDIC III units work continuously on the conversion of these data to magnetic tape. About 14,000 reels of magnetic tape comprise the input to the census procedures. As in much business information handling, the preliminary runs are largely concerned with pre-editing the data to eliminate inconsistent and inadequate information from the tapes, and the printing out of this data for review and correction by clerical personnel.

One of the most spectacular governmental data processing operations is that carried out by the Social Security Administration. Using three large computers, this agency keeps a file for about 120,000,000 individuals. Each record in this file contains a person's total earnings subject to social security, along with other data needed to calculate his retirement benefits or to furnish earnings information upon request. This master tape must be updated by the periodic social security payments sent in for about 65,000,000 people. This task is complicated by the fact that approximately 9,000,000 of the quarterly payments sent in contain improper names or account numbers. The magnitude of these errors is so great that programs have been prepared to examine this incorrect data, and to correct the names and account numbers automatically. Corrections can be made in 90% of the cases, thereby saving the Government about $1 million a year. The basic function of the installation is, of course, the calculation of benefits for some 2,500,000 annual claimants for retirement and survivor payments. The Social Security Administration is perhaps the best example of a sociological information pattern whose symbols, maintained and processed electronically, represent to a large degree the economic and psychological security of masses of people.

12　THE CONQUEST OF THE PHYSICAL UNIVERSE

SPACE COMPUTING

The development of space technology has been made possible with the aid of trillions of calculations on electronic computers. An installation in Washington, D.C., was the earliest orbital tracking center in the country. It was here that around-the-clock computational facilities were first maintained for the prediction, from radio observations, of the paths of all launched satellites. The initial programming effort for the computations, headed by D. A. Quarles, Jr., included over 80 different programs containing more than 25,000 machine instructions. These programs have since been improved and enlarged in scope. Later, the center utilized two IBM type 7090 computers. (See Fig. 12-1.)

Contrary to a frequently held popular opinion, the position of satellites orbiting around the earth is not directly ascertained by the antennas at tracking stations. Actually, these special radio receivers merely obtain data relating to the angular position of the space vehicles. Computers smooth and edit this information, and process it using sophisticated orbital techniques to determine the spatial locations and motions of the satellites. It is of interest that one of the complexities of orbital calculations stems from the nonuniform gravitational field of the earth. This lack of uniformity of the force of gravity results from a number of factors. These include the bulge at the equator and other deviations from sphericity, and variations in the distribution of the mass of the earth.

The determination of trajectories is one of the main computational efforts required in this new technology of satellites, re-entry systems, and space probes. The calculations include finding the optimum time for firing, and ascertaining the correct combination of burnout, azimuth, velocity, and angle of flight. The spatial orientation of the axis of the various stages of the vehicle must be considered, and geographical position must be proper for the firing of retrorockets. A large and diverse number of engineering problems are involved, spanning the fields of propulsion, aerodynamics, structures, and controls.

FIGURE 12-1 IBM 7090 data processing system. (Photograph courtesy of IBM)

After a space vehicle has been launched, a complex surveillance system is necessary to track the object in flight. At Cape Kennedy numerous ships along the range assist in tracking and retrieving missiles. For activities such as a lunar probe, ground stations operate from many parts of the planet. Special radio receiving units and radio telescopes are among the devices used for tracking. Where adjustment rockets or retrorockets must be fired, a rapid and accurate interlinked system of communications and computing is necessary. A National Space Surveillance Control Center is located at Hanscom Air Force Base, where information is received from 125 major tracking stations after each new American or foreign launching. The data, sent via telephone lines cleared to prevent interruption, enables the center to collect information on the space vehicles and to compute their position and velocity.

The scientific value of space exploration is derived to a large extent from the receiving of telemetered information from the vehicles. Instrumentation aboard the vehicles records the extra-terrestrial data, and radios this information back to the home planet. Pioneer V, for example, carried a 150-watt transmitter and a 5-watt transmitter. The telemetry package weighed 11 pounds, and was 286 cubic inches in volume. The instrument made observations on radiation, temperature, and other conditions within the vehicle, and edited the data before transmission. The data were sent out in digital form, i.e., as a stream of coded numbers. If a digital device were not present, the information would have to be transmitted as a continuous function, such as an oscillogram, requiring conversion before it could be used as an input to digital computers.

Upon receiving signals, the Earth stations record the data and make the information available to computation centers for processing. From these observations, material of great value for physics, astronomy, and biology is derived. For example, data concerning the origin, development, constituency, spatial distribution, and behavior of the atmospheres surrounding the planets, Sun, and Moon, is being collected. Information pertaining to the Earth's atmosphere is of great importance in weather studies, and enables scientists to evaluate the effect of the atmosphere on instrumented and manned space flights. Regions surrounding other stellar bodies are being studied to obtain data on ionized gases, energetic particles such as cosmic rays, and electric, magnetic, and gravitational fields.

Space Technology Laboratories has been responsible for the research, development, and operation of the Air Force intercontinental and intermediate range ballistic missile programs. The Computation Center in Los Angeles is the heart of the organization's data processing activities. In addition to two large-scale scientific computers, the center contains data-reduction equipment for the conversion of observational data into information which can be handled by the digital processing equipment. The staff includes physical scientists, engineers, mathematicians, and computer specialists. The mathematical analysis department constructs mathematical models and works on the numerical analysis necessary for the trajectory computations. The programming group prepares programs such as are used for tracking vehicles in flight. Evaluation of launchings is performed by comparing the observed flight data with a simulated trajectory. The data collected by ground stations from the vehicle's telemetry system is reduced and analyzed to enable engineers to calculate the characteristics of the missile's performance and possible malfunctionings.

The orbit of TIROS I (Television Infra-Red Observation Satellite) was computed by an IBM type 709 in Washington, D.C. This vehicle contained television equipment to take pictures of Earth under remote control. In addition to determining the orbit of the space craft, a specially developed machine program enabled scientists for the first time to ascertain the satellite's angle with respect to the Earth's surface. With the aid of this data, the command centers instructed the television equipment to operate only when the area being traversed was in the light of the sun. The TIROS I experiment, which obtained much data of meteorological value, was sponsored by the National Aeronautics and Space Administration (NASA). One of the main contractors was the Astro-Electronic Products Division of the Radio Corporation of America. The principal ground stations, built by RCA, were at Fort Monmouth, New Jersey, and at Kaena Point, Hawaii.

When a space vehicle is launched, electronic computers decide within 30 seconds whether the proper trajectory has been attained and if the velocity reached is sufficient for the capsule to stay in orbit. If the computers decide that the launching is successful, burnout occurs within 3 minutes. Burnout is the termination of rocket propulsion, either as the result of the using up of the fuel or by the deliberate shutting off of the rockets.

Should any malfunctioning occur immediately after launching, a water landing off Cape Kennedy would take place. In the event that it proves necessary to bring the capsule down shortly thereafter, the firing of retrorockets under ground control would cause the vehicle to fall somewhere between the launching site and northwest Africa. A computer located in Bermuda has the main responsibility for calculating the trajectory of descent in the case of such an abort.

The tracking and ground instrumentation systems continuously predict the location of the capsule from the time of launching to the landing of the vehicle, and the communications and computing network perform the necessary control functions. The location of the capsule upon landing is transmitted to recovery units as soon as the vehicle returns to Earth. Telemeter reception from the capsule is provided, as well as voice communication with the astronaut.

The computer programs written for the Mercury project perform a number of functions. They check for unreasonable data and transmission errors in the input, and remove spurious information. Programs carry out the numerical integration of the six current components of the orbital parameters, taking into account the Earth's gravitational field, atmospheric drag, and the spatial orientations of the capsule. The point on the surface of the Earth underneath the satellite is calculated, and information is provided to the network of tracking and instrumentation stations. The programs compute the correct time to fire retrorockets for landing in the recovery area. The place where the vehicle will land is computed by programs which handle such problems as interpolation, drag, rocket thrust, trajectory, and rate of parachute descent under the influence of crosswinds and other meteorological conditions.

INTERPLANETARY FLIGHT

The sending of space vehicles to other planets requires navigational and guidance equipment far more advanced than that now being used in operations close to Earth. The present need for smaller and more compact electronic computers for space vehicles will therefore increase with the advent of interplanetary flight. Such computers will be of high speed, light weight, small size, and great reliability. They will have low power consumption, and will be capable of withstanding difficult environmental conditions. The speed of computation required in this equipment will depend upon the nature of the vehicle and on the accuracy which is needed. The stored intelligence represented by microminiaturized computers aboard space craft will, of course, be accompanied by "effector organs" such as side rockets, axis orientation control systems, and retro-rockets. There will also be communication systems for sending information to Earth and receiving commands from the home planet.

The launching of interplanetary vehicles requires intensive trajectory computations. Every planet is in continual motion around the sun, and the relative positions of these bodies keeps changing. Each state of the solar system exerts a different set of astrophysical influences upon a space vehicle launched from Earth. Since any given state of the solar system is never repeated, a separate trajectory must be computed for every planned flight. As in the case of satellites in orbit around Earth, an extensive tracking system is needed to monitor the position of vehicles launched to other planets.

The radio signals sent out from space ships must be able to penetrate through the spheres of ionized gases surrounding Earth, and must be above 100 megacycles in frequency. Since the vehicles cannot contain sources of high power, large antenna dishes or equivalent equipment are needed on Earth to receive information from the space probes. It is obvious that this problem becomes increasingly difficult as our explorations of space take rockets farther and farther away from their home planet.

COMMUNICATION WITH OTHER WORLDS

The development of techniques for receiving and analyzing information from outer space has led to the establishment of Project Ozma, the systematic search for intelligent life in other parts of the universe. The project, named after the story-book land of Oz, was formed by nine universities in cooperation with the National Science Foundation, and uses the National Radio Observatory at Green Bank, West Virginia, as its cosmic listening post.

This observatory has a radio telescope with a special amplifying device. The receiver is a saucer-shaped antenna 85 feet in diameter, and will be used 6 hours a day by Project Ozma. The device is first being aimed at the stars Tau Ceti and Epsilon Eridani, which are 70 trillion miles away. According to one estimate which has been made, about 10%

of the stars in our galaxy could have solar systems capable of supporting life. Since there are 200 billion stars in the Milky Way, it follows that there could be 20 billion stars which might have planets on which living beings could exist.

The assumption which has been made is that intelligent organisms or machines existing elsewhere in the universe would use a repeated code of some type, such as a series of numbers, simple sums, or prime numbers, in attempting to communicate with other living beings. These signals would constitute uniformly patterned pulses mixed in with random noise received by our Earth observatory. Scientists on Project Ozma began their initial observations by monitoring extra-terrestial bodies at a radio frequency of 1420 megacycles. This is the frequency at which hydrogen emits such energy in outer space. It therefore is a universal constant which could be used by any intelligent living beings who had reached our level of technology.

OTHER SCIENTIFIC AND ENGINEERING APPLICATIONS

Almost every branch of science and engineering has benefited from the development of electronic computers. Aeronautical engineering, biology, chemical engineering, chemistry, highway engineering, soils engineering, electrical engineering, hydraulics, marine engineering, mechanical engineering, metallurgy, meteorology, military engineering, naval engineering, nuclear engineering, and physics are among the diverse branches of technology where applications have been made of high-speed, stored-program machines. Within each of these domains of human knowledge numerous uses of computers have been made. For example, the magazine *Computers and Automation* listed the following applications in the field of marine engineering: compartment pressures in emergency situations, compartment ventilation calculations, force analysis of space structures, form calculations, fuel rate analysis, gyroscopic compasses sea-test, hydrostatic functions, large ship maneuvering, plate and angle combinations, ship displacement calculations, ship models, ship waterline characteristics, shock isolators, turbine reduction gear systems, and ullage tables.

NUCLEAR COMPUTING

Among the first uses made of electronic computers was the application of this equipment to the extensive calculations needed in nuclear engineering. The Atomic Energy Commission has been, and remains one of the major customers for computational equipment. At present, this equipment is being widely utilized for the design of nuclear reactors. With the introduction of such instruments as control rods, this equipment is becoming more complex, thereby requiring greater accuracy in the solution of neutron diffusion equations.

The design of reactors is essentially a simulation problem, engendered by the fact that it is too expensive and time consuming to design these units by building experimental models. By simulating the design of reactors, it is possible to evaluate a large range of values of the significant design parameters. This would be impossible with direct experimentation with real models. The planning of nuclear reactors involves a large number of interrelated factors. The paths followed by neutrons within the complex pattern of fuel, moderator, and structural elements can only be calculated by digital computers. The use of computational equipment is, therefore, necessary for the design of civilian power reactors, commercial ship reactors, army package power reactors, and navy and aircraft propulsion. Among the problems solved are calculations of the rate of generation and decay of neutron-absorbing poisons, heat transfer, the effectiveness of control rods, stress analysis, the computation of experimentally undetermined cross sections, the design of shielding, reactor control, and system transient responses.

The input data for the machine computations involved in nuclear reactor design consist of measurements of probabilities of nuclear occurrences such as fission and absorption. Also entered into the computer are the dimensions, structural material, and operating temperatures of the reactor. The program sets up a mathematical model of the reactor within the machine. The activities of the neutrons are then simulated and traced at certain points within the model by the iterative solution of a neutron diffusion equation. The output shows the distribution of neutrons, and indicates what the power of the reactor will be. With the aid of this information, scientists can predict what fuel and protective shielding requirements are necessary to maintain the desired power level in the reactor.

Electronic computers are also being used to interpret the measurements obtained from underground nuclear explosion tests. The blasts are typically carried out in a 216 cubic foot chamber bored into a mountainside in the test reservation north of Las Vegas. The total energy release from a nuclear bomb with the power of 20,000 tons of TNT takes place in less than 1 microsecond. Computations indicate that during this moment the pressure leaps to 7 million times normal sea-level pressure, and the temperatures goes up to about 1,800,000°F. The solid rock chamber expands in a few hundredths of a second to a sphere about 125 feet in diameter.

PHYSICS

Another important task performed by computers has been the accurate solution of Schroedinger's equation for understanding the physics and chemistry of substances. Schroedinger's partial differential equations enable physicists to calculate the electric and magnetic fields within atoms, as well as the energy and other characteristics of these systems. In the field of hydrodynamics, the theory of the motion of fluids, many complex computations have been made by computers. The thermal histories of the Earth and moon have been studied by the numerical solution of the heat transfer formulas in a solid in which heat is partially transmitted by radiation.

Research in solid-state physics often requires highly complicated mathematical equations to formulate the behavior of millions of particles. Studies of neutron diffusion in lead have been carried out by the computation of the neutron flow in a lead shield with a defined neutron source at numerous varying levels of energy. The solution of this problem is iterative, since each study of an energy level depends on the residue of neutrons resulting from the prior energy level studies. The output of the program consists of counts of the neutrons passing through or being absorbed by the shield, thereby describing the shielding capacity of the lead. Computers have been used to describe the electrical activities of transistors under the influence of electrical fields. The results of such computations show the ways in which the bearers of electric energy in a transistor can lose energy or deviate from their path of motion.

WEATHER PREDICTION

Numerical weather forecasting, first attempted in 1922, was unsuccessful at that time, partly because meteorology and the mathematics of numerical analysis were not sufficiently developed, and partly because high-speed computers were not yet available. It was estimated by L. F. Richardson, who pioneered in the field, that the immediate calculation of the weather for the entire planet from data made available at a given time would require the efforts of 64,000 people. During the last decade, however, significant advances have been made in the science of weather prediction. One current research project has set up a system of partial differential equations which express atmospheric conditions all over the globe. The sphere is mapped to a plane by stereographic projections, and difference equations relate the values of the variables at various mesh points located from 100 to 200 miles apart. The grid is three dimensional, several layers being taken in the vertical direction to correspond to different pressure levels.

OPTICS

The designing of lens systems for optical manufacturers has been greatly facilitated by electronic computers. These lens systems, which are used for products ranging from eyeglasses to bombsights, process light rays emanating from some object, and produce an image whose quality is dependent upon three variables—shape, composition, and location of the lenses in the system. The design of a specific lens system consists of shifting these three factors until the desired image is produced. Each change of value of a variable necessitates a series of long, repetitive calculations which can be carried out rapidly with the aid of electronic computers.

THE GAS INDUSTRY

Nearly every area of the gas industry has benefited from the use of data processing equipment, which has provided such services as pipe line design, compressor burner efficiency of synthetic gas, reservoir phase behavior studies, pipe line simulation, gas availability studies, and line pack calculations. One of the most interesting applications of electronic computers to the problems of gas utility companies is the analysis of a gas distribution network. This analysis is necessary when the company is considering the changing or enlarging of its distribution systems, or when the placing of an increased load on the pipe system is being discussed. Existing computer programs enable non-high-pressure systems with as many as 750 pipes to be evaluated. More extensive systems can be analyzed with slight modifications of the programs.

The problem resulting from increasing the load on a distribution system is the possibility of adverse effects as the result of this change. If an increased load does result in excessive pressures within the system, various proposed modifications to the system must be evaluated from both an engineering and economic standpoint. Computers enable gas line distribution systems to be studied to find out if potential trouble areas are present, and facilitate the analysis of changes and additions to an existing system. The inputs to the program are the diameter and length of each pipe (or its resistance factor), the assumed flow and direction of flow in each pipe, and data representing the arrangement of the pipes in the system. The output furnishes the necessary information on pressure drops within all of the pipes in the system.

ROAD BUILDING

Computers play an important role in the Federal Aid Highway Act of 1956, which committed the United States to spend over $100,000,000,000 in the following 10 or 15 years in the construction of highways. The modern roads must meet very strict engineering standards in order to bear the tremendous traffic loads anticipated. Moreover, these super-highways cannot simply follow the terrain as did roads in the past. They must be straighter, wider, and more level. For this reason, there are more bridges than were previously necessary. To minimize the costs of construction, cut and fill computations are made. Stress analyses are carried out to make sure that bridges meet their specifications at the lowest possible cost. A bill of material is prepared for every item used in the construction of each bridge. It is necessary to ascertain how many beams are needed, their dimensions, and their precise place in the planned structure.

The analysis of proposed highway designs and locations is not difficult from a mathematical standpoint, but does involve large amounts of tedious, repetitious computation. Programs have been written which will determine profile grades, select slopes, locate the slope stakes, compute volumes of cut and fill, make adjustments for shrinkage, and accumulate net volumes. Shrinkage parameters can be modified if different materials are encountered, and other proposed designs can be analyzed by simple adjustments to the input data. Such programs, although prepared for use in highway design, are also adaptable to other civil engineering problems, as for example, the computation of the capacity of reservoirs, the volume of material needed in dams, required quantities of dredging, the amount of borrow pit material, and the quantities of foundation excavation.

The use of electronic computers enables highway engineers to consider a large number of detailed proposals, thereby assisting them in optimizing locations and grades. Planners are freed from calculating drudgery, and have more time to spend in the creative aspects of highway design. Among their other contributions is the preparation of more accurate estimates of excavation costs in preliminary design work.

MECHANICAL ENGINEERING

Illustrative of the uses which are made of electronic data processing equipment in mechanical engineering is a program employed to compute the harmonic content of the angular velocity of crankshafts in internal combustion engines. The results of these computations enable the sources of disturbing forces to be traced and corrected. This program reduces hours of manual calculations to minutes of machine time, and provides a higher degree of accuracy. It can handle any type of crankshaft, and enables proposed modifications of design to be analyzed by varying the input parameters. Programs have also been written to study the design of cams. These devices are used in machines which execute complex motions. The design of these units involves more extensive computation than most other mechanical components. Lengthy, repetitive calculations are required to evaluate polynomial forms and displacement curves, triangulation, and the determination of pressure angle and radius of curvature.

PETROLEUM

The design of distillation equipment for the petroleum industry has for some time been a fruitful field for the application of automatic computers. The separation of crude oil into various components is achieved by means of tall fractionating towers which handle tens of thousands of gallons every day, and a slight discrepancy in the design of such a tower can cause large quantities of valuable components to be lost. The towers are comprised of a number of plates or stages through which the crude oil passes in the process of being separated into such materials as gasoline, kerosene, and lubricating oil. Newly developed programs will enable designers of this equipment to determine how many of these stages are necessary to produce yields of the desired specifications. Computational equipment will also determine what products can be obtained with the use of an existing tower, given a particular input to the distillation process.

ELECTRIC POWER

Public utilities providing electric power have applied data processing equipment to a large number of their engineering problems, including short circuit studies, loss formula, economic dispatch, transient stability, economic conductor size, transformer load management, turbine heat rates and efficiencies, economic fuel purchasing, capacitor bank placement, and sag and tension calculations. The planning of electrical systems, the evaluation of their layout, and the study of equipment uses require the analysis of system load flow. Computers can be used to calculate complete input and voltage information at the terminals and power flow in every branch of the system.

THEORETICAL SCIENCE

Although they have been used extensively for the solution of problems which have an immediate practical significance for science and engineering, electronic computers are also being widely employed for basic research on the frontiers of the man's theoretical conceptions of the universe. Illustrative of such projects is work under way to test some of the unexplored consequences of Einstein's general theory of relativity with the aid of new computer techniques. It is hoped that these modern computational methods will provide new understanding of the geometric structure of space, the nature of mass, and the behavior of gravitation and radiation.

The basic problem in theoretical physics today is the structure of matter and energy. Physicists have been unable to apply various parts of quantum theory because the internal structure of these elementary particles is not understood. Many scientists feel that if quantum theory were based upon Einstein's conception of empty closed space, many new insights into the nature of subatomic entities would be forthcoming. This computer project, it is believed, will help to synthesize these two great physical theories. In solving Einstein's gravitational field equations, mathematicians are transforming a system of partial differential equations into difference equations. The latter will probably be the most complex system of equations ever to be attacked numerically, and the solutions will require weeks of machine time on the most powerful existing computers.

MEDICAL DATA PROCESSING

Within the next few decades we may expect far-reaching applications of electronic computers in the field of medicine. In addition to handling the accounting for hospitals, institutions, and the private practice of physicians, these machines will be utilized extensively in the processing of data obtained from patients' case histories, in the abstracting of medical information to aid in diagnosis, and in the summary and analysis of research information. Workers in the field look forward to the establishment of large computational facilities in every population center. Each installation will be in communication with the others, and will exchange information to assist the practicing physician, to gather and process data for medical research, and to summarize information for public health purposes.

The Systems Development Corporation reported a study in cardiovascular disease which was carried out by means of automatic computers.

This project consisted of research on bacterial endocarditis based upon case histories of patients gathered over 10 years at a Veterans Administration Center. The data were transcribed into punched cards, and bivariate distributions were obtained. Computer programs were prepared to test causal relationships among the variables and to assist researchers in developing hypotheses concerning the interplay of factors. In this disease, which causes about 4% of all heart fatalities, a variety of bacteria, such as streptococcus, may infect the heart valves. The result of the infection depends upon numerous variables, including the nature of the malignant organism, the heart valve attacked, the length of the infection, the patient's age, and the manner in which antibiotics are administered. The determination of the influences of these factors may involve complex statistical techniques.

Another experiment studies the causal relation between diet and coronary artery disease. Two groups of subjects are used for the project, one set serving as a control, and the other as an experimental group having a different type of fat present in its food. The individuals in the two groups are measured periodically in terms of bodily health, deaths, and occurrence of heart attacks, using electrocardiographic data, and laboratory tests such as serum cholesterol.

One of the main problems in medical data processing is the keeping of patients' records. It is becoming increasingly rare for any individual to be attended by the same physician throughout his life. The citizens of the United States are continually moving, and thereby changing their doctors and hospitals. For this reason, no complete history of an individual's symptoms and illnesses is maintained. One solution to this problem would be a central file from which every physician in the country could obtain medical data on his patients. This would imply the establishment of a standard source document for the recording of information by every doctor in the nation. Only in this way could all of the data be systematically collated. Perhaps some form similar to that used by FOSDIC at the Census Bureau could be devised for this purpose.

Such a standardization would involve many problems. There are a variety of complex illnesses for which patients are treated, many of which cannot be easily categorized. In addition, the reporting of medical data on a rigidly constructed document ignores the factor of insight and "feel" which plays a large part in the diagnosis and treatment of patients. Nevertheless, tremendous advantages would accrue if such standard source records were to be adopted. Private physicians would be benefited, as well as medical researchers. The summarization and analysis of public health information would also be greatly facilitated.

The use of computers to aid in the diagnosis of illnesses and the selection of therapies has often been suggested. What is envisaged is the storage of information concerning disease patterns, relations among symptoms, and types of therapies for various classes of health problems. Upon the request of a medical doctor, a data processing machine could look up data in these files, and prepare reports for assisting the physician in the treatment of his patient. The computer could prepare lists of possible diagnoses based upon data received from the physician. It could indicate additional tests to further pinpoint these diagnoses, print out suggested methods of therapy for the diseases, compile information pertaining to the case history, and analyze quantitative data obtained from the patient.

The conversion of electrocardiographic and electroencephalographic data into digital form for processing by computers are obvious computer applications in the medical field. It is apparent that a number of other interrelated physiological variables such as respiration, systolic and diastolic blood pressure, and bodily temperature, can be studied in this manner. Considerable work has been done in the development of electronic instrumentation, such as mechanical hearts and physiological monitors for post-operative care. Such devices have made biological measurements more accurate and more easily obtainable. They have also greatly enlarged the scope of research, due to their speed, versatility, and precision. These techniques seem destined to result in important biophysical discoveries in the future, and will play a vital part in the medical aspects of human travel into extra-terrestial space.

13   ADVANCED DATA PROCESSING

REAL-TIME COMPUTING

The living organism, in adjusting to its environment and in fulfilling its potentialities, continually modifies its spatial orientation and manipulates objects in the surroundings by means of its sensory-motor apparatus, guided by its intelligence. According to Paul Schilder, the individual develops a cortical image of the representation of his body in space and time, new *gestalten* being continually formed by incoming impressions. These images coordinate the innervations of a person's musculature with the sensations received by his organs of perception, thereby enabling him to execute rapid decisions in complex environmental situations.

Although organic life possesses a capacity for creativity and emotion inherently lacking in machines as we know them, there are nevertheless large areas of similarity between organisms and automata. A fruitful cross-fertilization between biologists and data processing theorists is to be expected during the second half of the twentieth century. Very likely a new science of determined systems will emerge as a result of future philosophical syntheses. Certainly, the computing machines which will be built and placed in use during the next decade will increasingly resemble, in functional operation, the characteristics of organisms.

The data processing applications we have thus far considered have taken the following form: A mass of data gathered from scientific observations or commercial transactions is transcribed to cards, paper tape, or magnetic tape. This information is then entered into the computer, which processes the input in the desired way, outputting pages of printed material, cards, or tape for further processing. There are three salient characteristics of such applications:

1. The data is processed serially. Information is ordered, one item after another, and entered into the machine in this fashion. The machine is programmed to receive the data in this sequence, and instructed to prepare outputs in a preordained way.
2. The data is not entered into the machine system immediately after having been created. Several hours, days, weeks, or even months may pass before the information is transcribed into an input form and processed by the machine.
3. The decisions which result from the computation are not put into effect until some time after the original data have come into existence.

This type of application, often called *batch processing*, has required programming techniques and procedures to solve the problems which arise in this form of data handling. This is particularly evident in file-maintenance activities where, as we have seen, both the master file and the changes file are first sorted into the same order, then collated against one another. This method of record keeping has a number of important disadvantages: It often occurs that very few of the master records are affected by the changes records. Yet a large amount of time must be expended in passing the entire master file into the computer just to get to this small number of needed records. Additional machine time is used for the preparation and writing out of the new master file. Another disadvantage of the batch processing method is that in many instances it is necessary at random times to obtain, process, and return information from the files. It is obviously impractical to mount a reel of tape on a computer to search for one particular record every time an item of data is called for. Such a procedure would be a wasteful use of the machine's capacities. It also would tend to tie up the computer for major amounts of time, simply to make these searches of the tapes at random intervals.

During the first decade of electronic data handling, almost all of the machine systems which were manufactured and used were based upon the batch processing principle. Many problems in commercial, military, and government organizations could therefore not be handled efficiently by existing equipment. Banking operations, for example, require frequent references to depositors' accounts to ascertain whether checks will clear and to answer credit inquiries. Numerous companies which deal with consumer goods or services, such as public utilities, must be able to answer immediately telephone requests for information. Brokerage houses have for some time utilized tens of thousands of miles of high-speed telegraph networks to link Wall Street order rooms with their branches in hundreds of cities scattered over the country.

If a machine is to perform the same procedures as a human, it must be capable of receiving and transmitting input and output data at any required time. It must be able to obtain immediately from its memory whatever information is needed to handle any problem. In computer terminology this is called operating in *real time*, with a *random access* memory. These capacities, along with a stored program, enable machines to function, to an increasing degree, in the same manner as organisms.

RANDOM ACCESS MEMORIES

Any information storage unit from which information can be obtained immediately without going through a serial search procedure is a random access memory. The conventional magnetic core memories are in this category. These core units, however, are usually of small capacity, say from 20,000 to 120,000 characters. They are used mainly for storing instructions, constants, and intermediate results of computations. The

FIGURE 13-1 IBM 1301 disk storage. (Photograph courtesy of IBM)

conception of random access usually has reference to a large auxiliary memory unit which is devised to store files of information running into millions of characters, and which can be interrogated by humans from specially designed terminal units.

Two of the first efforts in random access applications, the ERA Speed Tally, used for inventory control, and the Teleregister Reservisor, used for airline reservations, employed magnetic drums as memories. The amount of storage on drums usually is in the order of hundreds of thousands of characters. Of course, several of these units can be part of the same machine system. The development of disk memories makes available storage capacities up into the tens of millions. (See Fig. 13-1.) These large auxiliary units can be connected with a variety of machine systems. It is possible to combine a disk memory with relatively simple punched-card, input-output equipment, or with a large-scale, powerful, tape processing machines.

The IBM 305 RAMAC is a random access accounting machine which includes any desired number of disk storage units, each holding 5 million alphabetic or numeric characters. An inquiry station is present to enable humans to enter information and to interrogate the file at any time. The automatic processing of data occurs through a combination of a plugboard and a stored program. Input and output is by means of punched cards and a printer. (See Fig. 13-2.)

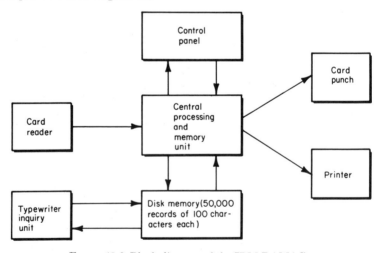

FIGURE 13-2 Block diagram of the IBM RAMAC.

Fifty memory disks are mounted on a vertical shaft (Fig. 13-3) which turns at a speed of 1200 revolutions per minute. Access arms along the outside of the unit are able to move up and down, so as to locate information in any desired disk. Every disk contains 100 tracks, on each of which there is stored ten 100-character items of data. Records are addressed by the instruction SEEK, which causes the access arm to move vertically to the proper disk, then horizontally across the disk to reach the desired track. A read-write head on the access arm senses or records the required information in accordance with the instruction READ or WRITE in the program.

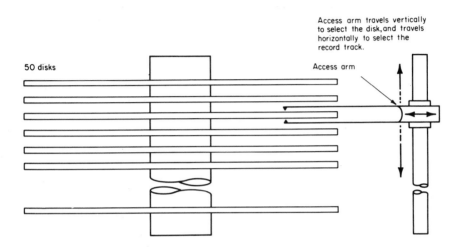

FIGURE 13-3 Access mechanism in the IBM RAMAC.

Newer equipment, the IBM 1301, uses a "comb" of access arms, one for each disk surface. This does away with the need for vertical motion of the access arms.

A DISK APPLICATION

A typical application of RAMAC is in order processing and billing where it is necessary to handle customers' orders immediately and to keep a tight control over inventory. The disk memory enables all transactions to be posted immediately into the proper accounts. At the same time the machine prints out invoices or work orders, decreases inventory balances, prints stock reorder notices if necessary, and checks on the customer's credit.

A large supply company which uses a 305 RAMAC for these purposes has 28,000 items in stock. Each of these items is represented by a record in the disk file, containing such data as its price, stock status, and description. Customers' orders are received over the telephone, and the resulting source documents are carried by conveyor belts to the machine room, where clerks place code numbers on the order. Keypunchers then prepare and verify punched cards from the documents. At this time clerks pull cards containing customer data from a master file, and duplicate them. The reproduced customer cards, along with the order cards, are now entered in the card reader. The machine now initiates SEEK orders to obtain information from the disks. The quantity of the item ordered is subtracted from the amount in stock, and the updated record is sent back to the disk memory. Data pertaining to the item and the customer are printed out on a work order instructing the warehouse to ship the merchandise. At the same time, the machine prepares cards from which the invoices will be printed. Pneumatic tubes carry the orders to the warehouse where the merchandise is immediately picked, assembled, and packed. Copies of the work orders are now returned to the office, at which location the bills are prepared. Through these procedures, the company is able to handle all customers' orders immediately, and to send out their bills the following day.

In addition to punching out work orders and invoicing information, the 305 RAMAC produces a reorder card whenever an order reduces the inventory level below a previously determined minimum point. This information enables the concern's buying agents to initiate purchase orders immediately to restore the inventory back to the desired level. When the warehouse receives shipments of new items, a report is sent at once to the machine room where receipt cards are entered into the equipment for updating the records on the disks. Questions concerning stock availability are answered within seconds by means of the inquiry stations. The operator keys the query into the machine, thereby initiating a SEEK of the appropriate disk. The answer is written out on an electric typewriter.

The 305 RAMAC not only provides faster service to customers, but enables the concern to order stock more rapidly and effectively from its own suppliers. The inventory can be evaluated quickly at any time as to low turnover items, thereby giving the management the opportunity to convert these items into working capital or into faster turnover merchandise.

BANKING

Random access accounting is often called *in-line* processing, because it enables all transactions to be handled immediately by the machine. This principle is particularly useful in industries such as banking. An installation might consist of a disk memory coupled with a medium-sized computer. One bank with about 70,000 special checking accounts in some

40 branches uses this equipment to process as many as 40,000 deposits and withdrawals every day. The bank estimates that telephone credit inquiries are answered in one-third the time required previously, through interrogation of the disks from the inquiry station. Hold amounts are entered into the system in a similar way.

This data processing system is based upon prepunched cards issued to the customers for use as deposit slips and checks. When these documents are received at the main office or a branch, the handwritten amount is punched into the card, which is then entered into the in-line system. The machine initiates the appropriate SEEK to the depositor's account, and updates the record. If an overdraft occurs, a notice is punched out on a special output card and a message is written out on the inquiry station typewriter. After the cards have been processed by the machine, they are sorted to account sequence on punched-card equipment, and filed for returning to the customer with his monthly statement.

In-line equipment is needed wherever a situation demands the immediate processing of information and the answering of random inquiries to a large file. One large area where such machine systems will probably be increasingly utilized is local government accounting. Here it is important to maintain a constant audit of the availability of funds, to enter information into the public records immediately, and to make file inquiries at any desired time. Although no disks are necessary, the Mercury manned-satellite project also exemplifies an instance where input information must be processed immediately by the machine, in order to make decisions which may involve the life or death of the astronaut. This equipment must be ready at all times to accept data sent in from stations in various parts of the globe, to rapidly evaluate this information, and to send out messages to the operation control centers.

COMMUNICATION-BASED COMPUTERS

There are a great many applications in which data is generated at a large number of different locations, and where this information must be transmitted to a central computing unit for processing and decision-making. Equipment is available which can reproduce punched cards over telephone lines to distant locations at the rate of ten 80-column cards per minute. Magnetic tape terminals can transmit characters to another tape unit over long-distance communication facilities. While this equipment does not provide for real-time processing, it is useful when a home office computer is at the hub of a network of small, distant data processing installations in branch offices, factories, and warehouses. The long lines communication facilities provide a continual interchange of information among all of the computing centers. This rapid data handling system is

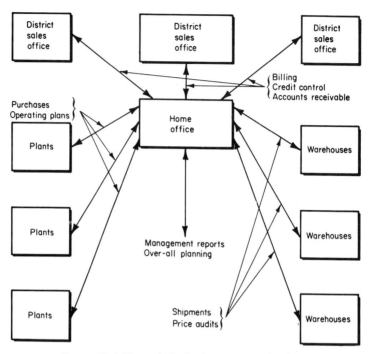

FIGURE 13-4 Network for business communications.

often of great economic value in inventory control, marketing, and production scheduling. The flow of information between a home office and a number of distant district offices, manufacturing plants, and distribution centers might take the form shown in Fig. 13-4.

SAGE

The SAGE system (Semi-Automatic Ground Environment) is a real-time, multiple, input-output data processing network built for the air defense of the United States.

The basic input into this far-reaching system is provided by units which make air observations, and which process and transmit this data to direction centers. (See Fig. 13-5.) These centers, consisting of computational facilities, maintain an image of the tactical air situation at all times, based on a continual inflow of information on all existing air traffic, flight plans, weather data, and the disposition of defensive weapons. From this image, the direction centers ascertain the existence and nature of an air threat, determine the optimum assignment of weapons, and produce orders for the firing and guidance of defensive weapons from combat centers.

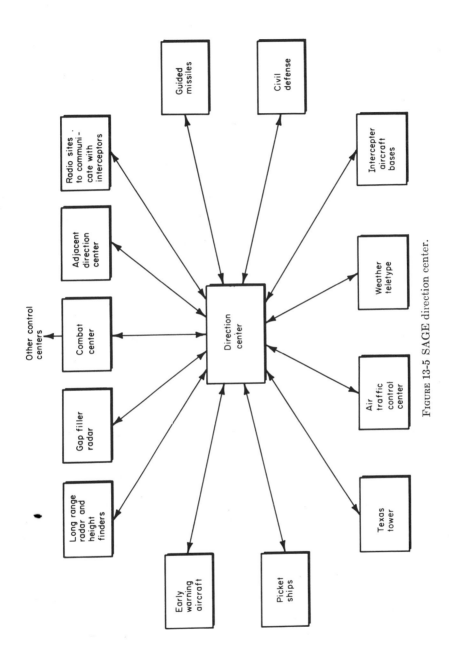

Figure 13-5 SAGE direction center.

The SAGE system extends over the entire continent, which is divided into intercommunicating sectors, each of which contains a direction center at the hub of a network of observation units and weapons installations.

The SAGE system is designed to enable each sector to control a number of BOMARC missiles in the simultaneous interception of enemy aircraft. The first step in the operation of the system is the detection of a signal by a radar unit which indicates the possible approach of a hostile aircraft. The radar unit, in conjunction with a small computer, determines the position and velocity of the object. This information is transmitted over telephone lines to a SAGE computer, which stores this data in its memory. Up to this point nothing is known about the significance of the signal. Let us suppose that a few moments later a second radar signal is picked up and transmitted back to the computer. The central processing unit now ascertains whether the two signals are correlated. If the computer decides that these signals represent the track of an aircraft, it evaluates this flight in terms of its image of the air situation at that time. The object in the air may represent a scheduled airline flight, or may be a friendly plane. The track of the moving object is displayed on a scope for cognizance by a human·operator.

If the airplane being monitored is identified as hostile, the computer tracks its course by continuously predicting its future position and velocity. Humans now decide whether to activate a missile or a manned interceptor. The SAGE system then proceeds to activate a BOMARC missile to intercept the enemy aircraft. This weapon is a rocket which is launched from the ground, and which can be guided at supersonic speeds at hostile airplanes over a range of about 200 miles. The BOMARC can reach an altitude of over 70,000 feet. Launching sites are situated at strategic geographical locations in the United States.

When the operator at the SAGE computer presses the fire button, the BOMARC missile, which may be located thousands of miles away from the computer, is placed in fire-up status. Certain prelaunch computations are made and transmitted to the missile. A second or so after the fire button has been pressed, the BOMARC enters a vertical climb powered by a rocket motor. The computer now tracks both the enemy aircraft and the interceptor missile, continuously correcting the course of the BOMARC in terms of the strategic movements of the enemy aircraft. When the missile is within striking distance of the hostile plane, the SAGE computer tips the rocket into a steep decline, and gives control to the computer within the BOMARC itself. The missile now latches itself on to its target and homes in to the kill.

AIRLINE RESERVATION SYSTEMS

One of the first commercial applications of real-time data processing is the SABRE system, built by IBM for American Airlines. This information-handling system is planned to receive data pertaining to airplane passenger reservations on a real-time basis from the company's agents throughout the country. It will process immediately the information, sending a virtually instantaneous output back to the agents. The "central nervous system" of this "organism," located in a suburb of New York City, includes two type IBM 9090 machines. Its "sensory-motor organs" will consist ultimately of over a thousand terminal sets for agents. Linking these far-flung peripheral units to the main data processor will be thousands of miles of telephone lines.

While the making of an airline reservation may seem on the surface to be a simple accounting activity, the great volume of these requests and the complexity of the bookkeeping combine to create a data processing problem of enormous expense and prolixity. The SABRE system is planned to handle tens of thousands of phone calls every day, together with requests for prices of flights, passenger reservations, inquiries regarding seat availability to and from other airlines, and sales of tickets.

The main function of this data processing system is to provide fast and accurate service to the customers of American Airlines located throughout the country. The main product of this company is airplane flights, and its inventory consists of seats on these trips. The purchase of tickets by consumers is carried out through agents located in various parts of the United States. It is vital for these agents to be able to ascertain rapidly whether or not seats are available for any particular flight, and to be able to confirm reservations quickly and without mistakes. Since thousands of reservations and cancellations are made every hour, it is necessary for the inventory to be updated immediately whenever any such transaction takes place; otherwise there would be a tendency either to oversell or undersell a flight because of inadequate information. To fulfill these conditions, a real-time, random access system with communication links to the entire country is required.

The agent's set (Fig. 13-6) consists of equipment which enables the agent to communicate immediately with the central computer. When a customer calls on the telephone, the agent transmits the inquiry concerning the availability of a flight at the specified time to the machine. This data is stored in IBM 1301 disk memories. A response is sent back to the terminal set almost instantaneously. The agent recommends those flights which seem most suitable. When the passenger selects a flight, the agent presses a *sell* button, and the computer immediately records the

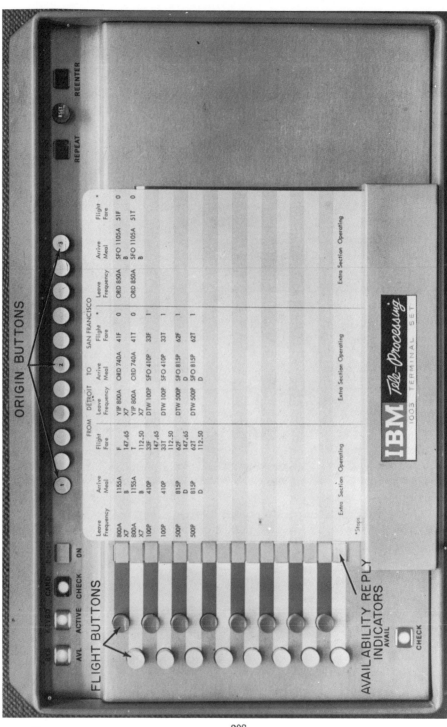

FIGURE 13-6 Air information device on terminal set. (Photograph courtesy of IBM)

fact that a reservation has been made, subtracting a seat from the inventory of available seats on the particular flight.

If the passenger wishes to make a return reservation, this procedure is repeated. Finally, the agent obtains the name, address, and telephone number of the customer, and keys this information into the terminal set. This data is now transmitted to the computer, and entered into its disk files. Whenever the passenger calls again, the information is immediately accessible to the agent, even though he may be located thousands of miles away from the data processing center near New York. On certain days American Airlines has on the order of 600,000 passenger records in its files. The processing of a reservation through SABRE will take about 3 seconds, compared with an average of 45 minutes under the present system.

Among other actions which can be performed by the agent are the obtaining of arrival and departure times for current flights. When changes in the flight schedules occur, the central computer will remind agents to notify their affected passengers. The machine could handle special arrangements, such as passenger requests for car rentals, hotel reservations, or seats on connecting flights. A wait list for customers who desire seats on completely filled flights will be maintained. If space becomes available, the computer will select the next passenger in the queue, and will notify the appropriate agent that this seat is now open to the customer. In retrieving information from its files, the machine will employ a special subroutine to handle problems resulting from the misspelling of the customer's name.

Apart from enabling American Airlines to improve its service to customers, the SABRE system will increase the profitability of the company's operations. Closer control of the inventory will permit the airline to improve its passenger load factor, and will enable the management to obtain up-to-the-minute operating statistics. The machine will prepare timely statistics on time, place of departure, and destination of passengers, thereby facilitating the scheduling of traffic and the formulation of future plans.

The "organismic" concepts embodied in the coming generation of machines are the ability to respond immediately to environmental stimuli, to make rapid decisions in complex situations on the basis of present perceptions and past experience, and to initiate actions whenever necessary. These concepts give rise to a great many new problems in logical design and programming.

REAL-TIME ERRORS

One practical consideration of great importance in real-time systems (Fig. 13-7) is the possibility that parts of the equipment may at some time be out of order. The failure of an in-line data processing machine might well create a chaotic situation of serious dimensions. In a military system such as SAGE, the national defense would be imperiled, and in a business application the entire commercial operation would be thrown into confusion. This problem is not so urgent in batch processing ma-

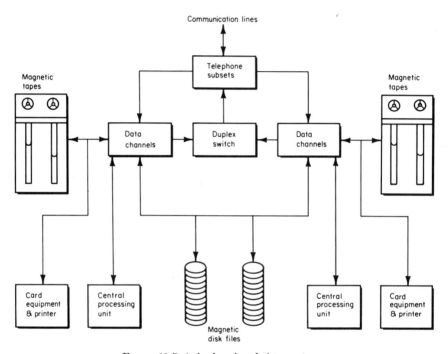

FIGURE 13-7 A duplexed real-time system.

chines, where instantaneous information handling is not required. In the latter situation, the schedule for producing reports may be delayed, and if the application is sufficiently important (as in the case of payroll checks) the problem can be run on a similar machine at another installation. It generally takes, at most, a matter of hours to diagnose and replace faulty components in electronic data processing machines. Such a delay is intolerable in real-time systems, and it is obviously impossible to resort to other users' equipment at such times. This problem is solved in SABRE and SAGE by having two identical computers at the central installation. In the event of the malfunctioning of one of the machines, a duplex switch is thrown, causing the other computer to take over all of the processing functions immediately.

The SABRE system is designed in such a way that failure of local telephone lines or communication units will not interfere with the operations of the remainder of the system. All of the electronic equipment will be transistorized and contain magnetic cores, both of which provide very high reliability. Numerous checks will be used to detect and correct random transmission and processing errors. The inputs are edited for the omission of data. If an agent fails to enter all of the information required for each passenger, the machine notifies him immediately to supply this data.

CONGESTIONS IN INFORMATION TRAFFIC

One of the main problems in the design and operation of in-line machine systems arises from the fact that all of the inputs which are continually pouring into the central processor cannot be handled immediately by the equipment. Each incoming transaction must wait a short time, perhaps in the magnitude of milliseconds, until the preceding inputs have been processed. This situation is analogous to the movement of automobiles through toll stations on a busy thoroughfare. Even though the payment of the toll can be consummated rapidly by each car, the volume of traffic may be so large that queues of automobiles tend to form at each toll booth. Similar waiting lines of inputs come into being in real-time data processing systems. The machine must have the facility to store these transactions temporarily, until it has the opportunity to handle this information. The formation of queues also occurs at various other points within the computer. In toll roads the analogous occurrences are traffic tie-ups caused by bottlenecks along the highways.

Consider the simplified example of a real-time system consisting of three units: an Arithmetic and Logical Unit (ALU), a disk memory, and a printer at a terminal set (Fig. 13-8). Let us suppose that every

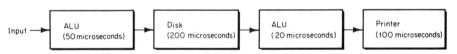

FIGURE 13-8 Path taken by input transactions.

incoming transaction must first of all be processed for 50 microseconds in the arithmetic and logical unit, after which 200 microseconds are required for a SEEK to the disk. Following these operations, an additional 20 microseconds are spent in the arithmetic and logical unit, terminating with 100 microseconds of printer time.

Let us now envisage two transactions (Fig. 13-9), T_1 and T_2, which are entered into the system from terminal sets 10 microseconds apart in time. We shall regard T_1 as entering at time 0, and T_2 at time 10.

Upon entering the machine, transaction T_1 goes immediately to the arithmetic and logical unit, where it is processed for 50 microseconds. After 10 microseconds have passed, transaction T_2 enters the computer, but must be placed on a waiting list for 40 microseconds owing to the fact that the ALU is in use. At time 50, transaction T_1 begins to use the disk, thereby releasing the ALU for T_2. However, the SEEK time is so long, comparatively speaking, that T_2 must again be placed in a queue after it has been processed for 50 microseconds in the ALU. The disk is available to T_2 only after a waiting period of 150 microseconds.

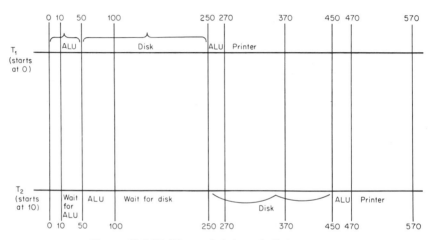

FIGURE 13-9 Waiting periods in an in-line processor.

Note that transaction T_2 is delayed for a total of 190 microseconds. While this queuing time may seem trivial, the effect may be substantial in an actual situation in which thousands of complicated and varied transactions are streaming continually into the system. There are two obvious ways of ameliorating this condition: speeding up the operation time of the units by using faster electronic components, or adding additional units. It may well prove desirable, for example, for future data processing machines to contain two or more adders. This would enable more than one transaction to be processed simultaneously, thereby eliminating some of the internal delays.

Another possibility would be to design a central processing unit for a real-time system in which two intercommunicating computers operate in parallel. Both machines might share the input-output burdens, maintaining access to the same disk files, tapes, drums, and other associated equipment. This type of computational facility, in which two independent sequences of instructions would be executed simultaneously, would represent in a certain respect a departure from the principles established by Von Neumann.

It will be recalled that in the original ENIAC there were a number of different processing units which could operate at the same time. Von Neumann's basic contribution was to bring all of the routing signals controlling these circuits to a central point where these signals were placed under the control of the operation codes representing instructions. This alteration converted ENIAC into a stored-program machine, but it sacrificed the capacity of this equipment to perform a number of arithmetic or logical operations simultaneously. The electronic data processing equipment of the future will, of course, retain the stored-program concept, but may well be designed to enable several stored programs to operate in parallel.

PROGRAM INTERRUPTION

In any event, the control circuitry of computers now being planned is growing in complexity. One reason for this added intricacy is the necessity of enabling certain types of real-time inputs to interrupt the current program, and to demand immediate processing. Just as fire engines are entitled to a clear road to get to a fire without interference, so certain transactions must have first priority no matter what other transactions are being processed or are waiting in queues. This capacity to seize control from the running sequence of instructions involves a number of problems which must be solved either through special features in the logical design of computers or through the introduction of new programming techniques. The latter methods are based upon monitoring programs which retain control over the machine at all times and which have the ability to interrupt a given subroutine at any point, returning to this sequence of instructions after the interrupting transaction has been processed.

Another use of the interrupt feature in real-time systems stems from the fact that the input load on the machine can be expected to vary at different times of the day. For example, if the daily transactions on the New York Stock Exchange were handled by an in-line data processing system, with terminal sets at brokers' offices for entering orders and requests from customers, the volume of input transactions would fluctuate with the state of the market. At peak points the machine would be operating at maximum capacity, whereas when trading was dull, the computer would be operating far below its capacity. To avoid under-utilization of the machine in applications of this type, it is envisaged that such a computer would be occupied during slack periods with conventional batch type problems, such as payroll and billing. When real-time transactions entered the system while the machine was busy with such applications, they would be permitted to interrupt the normal procedures. After these inputs were processed, the computer would return to its steady work.

Closely associated with problems of this type is the probable necessity of scheduling input transactions so as to optimize the flow of information through the system. Reverting again to the analogy of the automobile turnpike, let us suppose that there are a number of toll booths located at the entrance to the highway. One way of reducing this bottleneck would be to add additional collection booths. Another method, however, would be to have a traffic policeman placed some distance prior to the toll stations. The officer would direct the incoming cars to the collection booths in such a way as to equalize the queues of automobiles waiting to get through. Let us further assume that certain trucks require special handling which slows up their payment of tolls. In such instances the policeman might direct these vehicles to special booths. He might also hold up these trucks for brief periods so as to facilitate the handling of momentary peak loads of normal cars at the collection stations. In a similar way, the traffic of input transactions entering an in-line data processing system might be examined by a monitor program, which would then schedule the passage of these transactions through the machine. Analysis reveals that it is not always desirable for the first transaction in a group to be processed before its successors. Anyone who has ever been stuck in a line of cars behind a slow, lumbering truck on a winding country road will appreciate the profundity of this observation. It is often more efficient to let a number of short transactions be processed ahead of a long and complicated input request.

Optimization problems also exist in the connecting of a large number of terminal sets to a central processing unit. It is obviously impractical to connect every terminal directly to the main computational facility, particularly when expensive long-line telephone communications are to be used. The employment of trunk lines is an answer to this problem. At the end of every trunk line is a *multiplexor* unit connected to each of the terminals. When an agent enters information into his set, the data goes into a buffer. The multiplexor is a switching device which regularly scans all of the terminals to which it is connected. When a buffer contains information, the multiplexor immediately switches this data through the trunk line into the central computer, after which it examines the next agent's set. A similar multiplexing system is used to send output information to the terminals.

REAL-TIME RESPONSES

The main objective underlying all of these techniques and problems is to enable the user of the equipment to receive a response to all of his requests within a prescribed length of time. The tolerable time is, of course, dependent upon the nature of the application. When an enemy aircraft is approaching New York at supersonic speeds, or when a customer is awaiting a reply over the telephone, it is apparent that the system must be capable of supplying an answer very rapidly. The fact that the communication-based machine may sometimes operate under peak conditions must be taken into account, for under such circumstances the response time is slower. Economic factors must, of course, be balanced against the meeting of operating standards. It is possible to overdesign equipment, so that it can operate faster than is necessary; it may therefore be too expensive. On the other hand, if costs are reduced, the system may not provide responses at the required speed.

The design of real-time systems is complicated by the fact that, due to the formation of queues, it is difficult to evaluate the operating rapidity of such machines. When conventional batch processing equipment is planned, it is possible to determine with a fair degree of accuracy how fast the machine will handle various applications. This is accomplished by programming these applications in advance for the proposed equipment, and computing the time needed to execute these instructions. In real-time systems this is not possible because of the waiting lines.

Although extensive work has been done on the mathematics of queuing theory, the evaluation of real-time data processing machines is at this point still being carried out by techniques which are basically experimental. A logical model of the proposed system is developed, and is programmed to run on some computer. This model is then tested by applying various sequences of transactions, and by having the computer prepare reports on the simulation. The components and speeds of the proposed machine are adjusted until the simulation program indicates that the planned equipment, in its present form, will meet the required response specifications.

THE AUTOMATION OF MENTAL FUNCTIONS

The need for in-line, random access machines is perhaps indicated by the fact that the United States is covered by a network of 230 million miles of telephone and telegraph wires and cables, enough wire to reach from the Earth to the sun and back, leaving about 40 million miles left over for other purposes. The use of such equipment, however, is not confined to situations in which information must be transmitted over long distances. In many instances a business occupying one large building could greatly benefit from the presence of central files connected to terminal sets on the desks of the clerical staff. Inquiries would be answered on a random access basis, records updated immediately, and statistical reports would be available at any time without anyone stirring from their seats. Moreover, the use of electronic equipment for the storage of information would not be limited to linguistic material. Blueprints, design sketches, signatures, and photographs would be handled by special memories, and would be available immediately at viewers throughout the system. It seems likely that a large part of the innumerable clerical services such as typing, mimeographing, and duplicating will ultimately be taken over by high-speed data processing machines.

Many of these applications will probably involve information retrieval techniques—methods for storing large amounts of data for future reference. One of the most remarkable characteristics of the human brain is its capacity to memorize and recall on a random basis untold millions of items of information. The organismic computers of the future will likewise have the ability to classify and order environmental data. As we have remarked previously, without some way of organizing the world about us, our surroundings would seem chaotic, and we would be unable to engage in effective actions. One is reminded in this connection of tales of Tokyo, Japan, where the streets have no names, and houses are numbered according to the order in which they are built. Even local residents tend to become hopelessly confused when seeking to locate a dwelling amidst the vast maze of nameless streets and alleys which constitute this sprawling city.

While the use of systematic addresses for our dwelling places may seem to indicate an unwholesome trend toward the mechanization of life, such systems appear to be a necessary aspect of the growth of large urban centers. The addresses of New York City buildings, based as they are upon a system of Cartesian coordinates, is unquestionably to be preferred to a completely haphazard arrangement which is permitted to evolve through the years. It is worthy of remark that street numbers tend to acquire in time a romance of their own, as in the case of Forty-Second Street or Fifth Avenue.

A similar systematization of human activities exists in the listing of our telephone numbers. Here again, the method used is very simple: it suffices for a person to know the order of the English alphabet to ascertain what another individual's telephone number is. A more difficult situation exists in the case of the classified directory, where we may have to look under several different headings before we locate the type of business concern we are interested in. As a matter of fact, the Yellow Pages furnishes a typical example of the problems of information retrieval: Given a large number of advertisers, what is the best way to categorize them so as to enable them to be located easily by prospective customers? The advertiser must be placed in a classification where the public is likely to look for him, and the name of the category must be familiar to the users of the directory. It is apparent that a referencing system for a tremendous variety of often recondite business activities is necessary to enable the reader to find the type of product he is seeking. The person interested in Berets will find himself referred to Millinery, and the individual who wants to buy a Lunch Kit-Insulated is sent to Insulated Containers and Carriers.

Whatever may be the method used in preparing the directories, these volumes obviously represent a data handling problem of great magnitude. A volume of the Yellow Pages for one large city alone contains over 330,000 names of businesses and professional people. These are organized under 4000 classifications, plus numerous cross-reference headings.

The problem of cataloging information in an easy, inexpensive way so that it can be recalled again in a different context is the central problem of data retrieval. Almost every field of endeavor, particularly the learned professions, is being increasingly confronted by the difficulty of locating necessary information among vast sources of stored material. The search for precedents among the large libraries of legal reports of various jurisdictions, the investigation of disclosures at the Patent Office, the quest for relevant technical papers among scientific publications, and the finding of articles in newspaper morgues are some of the varied spheres of human activity where men are more and more getting lost among vast, overgrown, inadequately charted jungles of information.

The extent of these problems is indicated by the fact that in the year 1959, in the physical and life sciences alone, there were published 55,000 journals containing 1,200,000 articles. There are now 42,000 specialized occupations and professions in the United States, each of which generates some technical literature. The rapid advance of science and scholarship adds to the problems of this proliferation of information, for the development of new fields, new concepts, and new names causes the old indexes and volumes of abstracts to become obsolete from a nomenclatural and conceptual standpoint. Apart from the problem of obsolescence, however, the sheer volume of published material is sometimes so large that it is at times cheaper for some concerns engaged in research to run the risk of duplicating an experiment rather than to search the literature for a previous report.

INFORMATION RETRIEVAL PROBLEMS

For a number of years, work has been under way to utilize the tremendous speeds of electronic data processing machines to facilitate the tasks of indexing, abstracting, and categorizing information. Certain types of applications, we have seen, lend themselves easily to such treatment. For example, given as input every transaction consummated in a day on the New York Stock Exchange, it is a large, but technically simple task for an automatic computer to prepare the daily stock listings which are printed in the newspapers, including the opening, closing, high, and low sales. This information can be sorted in any number of ways, collated with previous information, and analyzed according to many criteria.

The real problems of information retrieval, however, require a more complex type of intelligence than is employed in such an application. What is needed is the ability in some way to understand nonquantitative concepts. The use of Boolean logical connectives such as *and* and *or* has often been suggested for literature searching. A machine could certainly search for the conjunctions and disjunctions of various classes of information. This method is basically a sorting or matching precedure, and presupposes that the information was stored originally in accordance with an appropriate set of categories. For example, a scholar engaged in research on cabbalistic writings might request from the electronic equipment a print-out of all titles listed jointly under the headings of Mathematics, Magic, and Ancient Near Eastern Literature.

One of the major functions of a mechanized information retrieval system would be to reduce the amount of effort required to create an index of a constantly growing library of publications. This work is now performed by the bibliographers who set up catalog cards in libraries. A high degree of skill and a fair knowledge of each field is needed to classify a publication and to cross-index the information so as to guide researchers to relevant books or periodicals. An automatic system would also perform the occasional revisions of the cataloging system necessary to reflect the changing needs and purposes of the users.

One proposal which has been made is to develop for each scholarly field a list of key words, sometimes called *descriptors*. These words, used singly or in groups, would enable every document to be characterized. Every publication and its list of descriptors would then be entered into a computer's memory. An individual wishing to form a bibliography on a given subject would first decide upon those combinations of descriptors which best described his field of interest. This information would then be given to the machine, which would then search the entire library for documents related to these categories.

This type of technique would be helpful in searching for relevant information in collections of documents. However, there would still remain the problems of devising an appropriate list of descriptors for characterizing the material and some easy way of encoding each publication under the proper heading.

One project along these lines consists of a computer program which prepares a journal of chemical titles. This publication covers about 550 journals of pure and applied chemistry containing approximately 5000 technical papers a month. The purpose of the journal is to list the titles of research papers so as to enable scientists to maintain an awareness of the work which is being done in their particular area. The program produces two long lists. The first is an alphabetical index of authors of technical papers, along with the title of their articles. The second part of the publication is an alphabetical listing of the articles by keywords obtained from the title of the paper. Each title appears in the list as often as it contains a keyword. Along with each keyword, enough of the remainder of the title is included so that a reader can obtain a clue as to the context in which the keyword occurs. A code referring the reader to the actual article is also included. Research workers keep abreast with progress in their branch of chemistry by scanning the list of keywords which interest them. When the contextual words indicate that a given article is significant, the reader turns to the title of the document in the alphabetical author index. The selection of the keywords is carried out automatically by the computer, which is programmed to ignore certain words such as *the, study,* and *of* in the preparation of the list of keywords.

One of the first applications of automatic machinery to the formation of analytical indexes has been the production of a punched-card concordance of the *Summa Theologica* of St. Thomas Aquinas. It has been estimated that it would take 2000 man-years for scholars to index manually the 13,000,000 words comprising the complete works of this theologian. Punched-card machines would require research workers to spend about 40 man-years. With large-scale data processing machines, such indexing takes about 10 man-years.

A concordance is an alphabetical listing of each appearance of every word in a book, along with the passage in which the word occurs. Two of the many uses of concordances are to investigate the common origins of different languages, and to analyze the frequently used patterns of words and ideas in the works of various authors. A concordance enables scholars to examine the contexts in which words are used, and thereby to study the meaning of important concepts in a literature. In theology, for example, words such as *grace* could be compared as to their usage in the Old and New Testament.

The Dead Sea Scrolls have been indexed by computer, the information first being transcribed to punched cards, then converted to magnetic tape. These analytical indexes will play an important role in the textual criticism of these documents. They will enable scholars to interpolate missing words, to study unknown dialects, to study the Aramaic dialect, to examine similarities between Essene and Christian writings, and to compare various versions of Old Testament writings.

At the present time, machines are able to contribute to the problems of information retrieval mainly because of their large random access memories and their capacity to carry out large operations automatically and at great speed. The equipment does not in any sense "understand" the terms which it manipulates. Nevertheless, the information-handling problems confronting modern civilization are so great that the contribution of electronic data processing, however crude, seems likely to become ultimately an indispensable adjunct to many areas of research and scholarship. Whether or not a machine can ever be designed to have the capacity for the creative synthesis of information is of course open to question.

The problems of information retrieval have stirred the interest of individuals in such diverse fields as philosophy, psychology, linguistics, and literature, for many of the questions which have arisen are related to their traditional provinces. It seems likely that mathematical and logical conceptual tools may well exert an important influence upon these areas of specialization. Parallel with the semantic and logical research involved in the machine analysis and processing of information, engineering technology is rapidly advancing to meet the data storage and access problems which are coming to the fore. The number of bits comprising all of the documents in the Library of Congress has been estimated to be 10^{14}, or 100,000,000,000,000. New techniques for photographic storage enable 10,000,000 bits to be placed on a square inch; indications are that this may soon be increased to 100,000,000.

FUTURE POSSIBILITIES

These almost fantastic developments in memory devices, communication, and data processing cannot fail to evoke a number of exciting speculations for the future. For example, it may well be that entire libraries could be placed in these storage media, and reading stations similar to microfilm viewers made available to the public. Indeed, it may be that eventually every home will have one or more of such terminal sets connected electronically to central sources of information. Subscribers might merely have to dial the particular publication or data file they are interested in, and this information would then be made available over their viewers. The conventional telephone will perhaps be replaced by general-purpose terminals providing for both spoken and visual input and output. Present schemes to provide pay television over the telephone lines is perhaps a step in this direction.

The implications for postal service are immense. Instead of being mailed, letters could be instantaneously transmitted electronically to their destinations. The United States Post Office is already testing fast facsimile devices. The tremendous compression of information into a small space, which is becoming possible, leads to the supposition that in the future we may all carry around pocket memories containing millions of characters, just as it is now possible to carry portable radios.

TEACHING MACHINES

The implications of random access memories as educational tools have for several years been recognized. The IBM RAMAC, it will be recalled, was one of the features of the United States exhibition in Moscow in 1959. A large amount of information concerning life in the United States was stored on the disks, and tens of thousands of Russians took advantage of this opportunity to ask questions of the machine by means of the inquiry station. A number of machines have already been marketed for teaching purposes. The equipment displays a question for the student, who then answers by some mechanical method, such as pushing in a slot or pressing a button, whereupon the machine informs the student whether or not he is correct. The use of stored programs can greatly enhance the teaching flexibility of such equipment. For example, if a student gives a wrong answer, the machine can return to some previous point, and by asking questions and supplying information, could gradually lead the individual back to the correct answer.

The use of data processing techniques to substitute for teachers has been severely criticized on the grounds that it would dehumanize an important part of life and would fail to supply the warm, creative atmosphere which is necessary for true learning. One can merely hope that such equipment, if successful, would be used only for the duller parts of the educational process, and would never be employed in an attempt to supplant the inspirational and empathic aspects of the teacher-student relation.

We might well mention here the use of electronic computers in converting English texts into Braille. This system, on its elementary level, simply involves a character-for-character transcription of the English letter into the dot codes. However, most Braille publications employ a type of shorthand which uses a large number of special contractions and devices to facilitate reading with the fingertips. The conversion of textual material into this type of Braille requires the labor of a skilled transcriber. Such individuals are rare, owing to the fact that about 2 years of training are needed to acquire this ability. Electronic computers have been programmed to perform table-look-up procedures to ascertain when the special Braille characters are to be used, and can provide reading matter for the blind 100 times faster than an expert human. In this application, automatic data processing techniques are greatly improving communication on a personal level, and are enhancing the lives of a significant part of our population.

MACHINE TRANSLATION OF LANGUAGES

Closely associated conceptually with the problems of information retrieval are the dozen or so projects which have been under way in the United States to translate mechanically from one language to another. Similar research groups have also been active in other countries, particularly in the Soviet Union, where extensive studies in machine translation have been reported as early as 1954. Considerable success has been claimed by the Russians in such fields as applied mathematics.

If it were possible to discover some common logic underlying all "natural" languages such as English, French, German, etc., then it would perhaps be possible to translate from one language to another simply by giving a machine a set of formal rules and a dictionary of words and phrases in both languages. However, many of the present efforts in mechanical translation seem to be relying more upon pragmatic, empirically obtained principles for producing understandable, practical translations, rather than seeking broad syntactical concepts. Numerous workable rules can be developed by humans simply by observing themselves in the act of performing translations. Many of these principles are very general, as for example the rule that in the French language, with certain exceptions, the adjectives follow the nouns. Computers can be programmed to carry out the tests and procedures required for producing the proper linguistic patterns.

Many problems are involved in setting up a dictionary, such as whether to include all possible suffixes of a word, or to rely upon programming to decide upon tenses and cases. In translating French chemical literature, for example, the dictionary might be condensed by omitting all words ending with "ique." Terms such as "nitrique" and "sulphurique" would not be present, but the machine would be programmed to use the English equivalent of the main stem, and to substitute "ic" for "ique."

The contexts of words play an important part in translation, and one of the major problems in mechanizing this procedure is to establish dictionaries or programs to enable the equipment to recognize these contexts and to provide the appropriate translation. The presence of idiomatic expressions can be handled by instructing the machine to examine the words in the neighborhood of a specific term. By referring to a dictionary, the computer can decide whether or not an idiom is being used.

Another problem, of a technological nature, is involved in the construction of random access memories which are large and fast enough to serve as dictionaries. One such device, developed by King (formerly director of the IBM Research Laboratories), stores a vocabulary coded on a photographic emulsion on a 10-inch glass disk, which is scanned by an electronic beam. The equipment is used to translate articles from *Pravda*.

There appear to be two general approaches to machine translation: to seek to create a fully automatic, high-quality translation, or to attempt merely to produce understandable translations which require some human post editing. It may well be that the former ideal is illusory because of certain theoretical aspects of linguistic structures. It is claimed that there are many instances where it would be impossible to program a machine to perform translations, but where a human acquainted with both languages could do so uniquely and unambiguously. It would seem that scientific papers are the most amenable to machine translation, due to the stricter denotations of the words which are used. The translation of poetry and fiction involves subtleties of meaning, connotation, and context resulting from the play of imagination over a rich cultural tradition. It is difficult to envisage machines, as we now conceive of them, as capable of handling such material. These considerations involve very deep philosophical problems relating to the limitations of formal logic and the related questions as to the creative potentialities of machines.

14 THE FULFILLMENT OF SOCIAL GOAL

RATIONALITY IN SOCIETY

One of the most significant contributions which will be made by electronic computers will be to introduce rationality into many social decision-making processes which previously have been made on the basis of hunch and rule-of-thumb experience. The solution of numerous economic, sociological, and political problems has heretofore been hampered by the lack of timely, relevant information and by the absence of high-speed data processing machinery. The present availability of fast computing facilities, however, has spurred the development of the new field of *operations research*, the application of mathematical and logical techniques to decision making in complex situations.

The *transportation problem* is typical of a large class of operations, procedures, and schedules which involve a large number of interrelated factors, and which must employ some optimizing method to produce desired results. The classic example of this problem is a company which has a number of manufacturing plants located in various parts of the United States, along with various warehouses spread over the country to which shipments are made from the factories. Each warehouse serves as a distribution point for the corporation's products and, hence, must maintain a specified level of inventory. There is, of course, a limit to the capacity of every plant to supply manufactured goods. Finally, the cost of shipping products from any given factory to any particular warehouse varies as a result of geographical location and the type of available transportation facility.

The basic problem here is to decide how to allocate shipments from plants to warehouses so as to minimize the total cost of transportation.

If there is a factory in New York, it would most probably not be economical to supply a warehouse in Boston from a plant in California. However, there are many instances in which it is difficult to come to a decision as to the scheduling of shipments from factories to warehouses. For example, if there is a warehouse in Richmond, would it be cheaper to ship from a plant in New York or from a plant in North Carolina? It might appear that North Carolina is the most economical choice, but suppose that there is also a warehouse in Jacksonville, Florida, and that the other factory nearest to Jacksonville is in Dallas, Texas. Would it not be cheaper from an over-all standpoint to free the North Carolina plant to supply the Florida warehouse, even though in so doing it becomes necessary to supply the Richmond warehouse from New York? It is also possible that the capacity of the North Carolina factory is large enough so that it can meet the inventory needs at Jacksonville, having enough additional goods available to make a partial shipment to Richmond as well, thereby relieving the New York factory of some of its burden. Of course, the plant in New York has to supply warehouses in its vicinity, such as the one in Boston. It might not be able to contribute at all to the Richmond warehouse, or at best might have only a small shipment available for this purpose.

Where there are a number of warehouses and factories, a large variety of possibilities arise. It becomes increasingly difficult for a human to decide upon the cheapest way of supplying all of the warehouses from the available plants. Here is a typical problem:

	Cost of shipping each unit from plants to warehouses (in dollars)			Warehouse needs
	Plant 1	Plant 2	Plant 3	
Warehouse 1	7	3	8	10
Warehouse 2	10	2	13	20
Warehouse 3	5	0	8	30
Warehouse 4	4	9	6	80
Warehouse 5	11	1	14	100
Plant capacities	40	80	120	240

One way of allocating factory shipments to warehouses in the cheapest way would be to take each warehouse successively, and to assign its needed inventory through the cheapest available transportation route. This method is illustrated as follows, and represents a nonoptimal solution to the transportation problem.

	Units shipped from plants			Warehouse needs
	Plant 1	Plant 2	Plant 3	
Warehouse 1		10		10
Warehouse 2		20		20
Warehouse 3		30		30
Warehouse 4	40		40	80
Warehouse 5		20	80	100
Plant capacities	40	80	120	240

This solution was obtained by starting with warehouse 1, and meeting its requirements by choosing as its supplier that plant whose shipping cost is the cheapest. In this instance we see by reference to the first table that plant 2 provides the least expensive way of fulfilling the needs of warehouse 1. Since warehouse 1 requires 10 units of the product, the allocation of plant 2 for this purpose reduces plant 2's capacity from 80 to 70. Turning now to warehouse 2, whose requirements are 20 units, we again find that plant 2 is the cheapest supplier. We accordingly make this allocation, thereby giving plant 2 a remaining capacity of 50 units. Warehouse 3 has as its least costly supplier plant 2, for 30 units. Plant 2 now has only 20 units available. When we come to warehouse 4, we find the cheapest route is from factory 1 which, however, can supply only 40 units. The remaining 40 units are obtained from plant 3, reducing its capacity to 80 units. Plant 1 now is completely unavailable. In the case of warehouse 5, we are now forced to obtain manufactured goods from whatever sources as are now left. We take 20 units from plant 2, and 80 units from plant 3, thereby meeting the 100 unit requirement of warehouse 5.

The needs of all of the warehouses are now fulfilled. The total transportation cost is found by first multiplying the amount allotted to each warehouse from each factory by the cost of that shipment. For example, the cost of shipping 10 units to warehouse 1 from plant 2 is 10 × $3, or $30. The costs of all specific shipments are added together to obtain the total. In this solution to the transportation problem the total cost is $1610. Two problems arise at this point: Is this the best possible allocation; and, if it is not, how can we go about improving upon this solution?

It is apparent that by inspecting the chart of transportation rates in the first table it would be possible to shift around the allocations so as to avoid using the expensive shipment routes. Of course, each time a change is made in one part of the schedule, re-allotments must be made elsewhere to compensate for this modification. Obviously, a good deal of arithmetic must be performed each time a proposed solution is devised. If a large number of possibilities are explored, a great many multiplications, additions, and references to the rate table must be made. This time-consuming and irksome computation tends to become intolerable in big problems involving hundreds of warehouses and dozens of factories.

Another difficulty involved in the intuitive, "juggling" method for solving this type of problem is that there is no way of ascertaining when one has reached the most economical solution. The inadequacy of common sense in arriving at an optimal allocation is illustrated by the fact that the cost of supplying warehouse 3 is zero if the shipment is made from plant 2. This seems to indicate clearly that this particular choice should be made. Surprisingly enough, however, this allotment does not occur in the following, an optimal solution to the transportation problem obtained by programming a computer to carry out a mathematical procedure for solving the problem:

	Units shipped from plants			Warehouse needs
	Plant 1	Plant 2	Plant 3	
Warehouse 1			10	10
Warehouse 2	10		10	20
Warehouse 3	30			30
Warehouse 4			80	80
Warehouse 5		80	20	100
Plant capacities	40	80	120	240

The total cost of the shipments in this optimal solution is $1300. Note that three of the four lowest cost transportation routes are not utilized at all, and that the two highest cost shipping routes are employed. This demonstrates that hunch, rule-of-thumb, and intuitive methods can easily be misleading when used for making decisions in complex situations.

Mathematical models and optimization techniques are being used increasingly in diverse areas of management, administration, and economics. Many of these problems have from time immemorial been handled by a key employee with common sense, good connections, and long experience in subtle and direct coercion, troubleshooting, and expediting. One of the most frequent applications of operations research methods is in the field of inventory control, where computers have been employed to reduce capital investment in stock, minimize shortages, and decrease procedural costs. Significant achievements have been made in job shop production control, the problem of routing a variety of products through a set of different machines in a minimum of time and with a maximum utilization of economic factors.

Decisions concerning the investment of capital can also be made by automatic data processing machines. An entrepeneur has available a limited and fluctuating amount of money, manpower, and raw materials which he can invest in a number of activities. The combination of activities which will yield the maximum profit from this capital can be ascertained by programs carrying out mathematical operations. Such methods could be employed by farmers in deciding how to use their land for growing the most profitable combination of crops with their available resources.

TRAFFIC CONTROL

Another operations research application is the scheduling of freight car movements. It has been stated that every day the railroads move 12 tons of freight 1 mile for every man, woman, and child in the United States. The revenue from these shipments is in the neighborhood of $9 billion a year. In our economy enormous freight car movements from certain parts of the country recur at definite times each year. The largest of these periodic railroad operations is the transportation of the annual grain crop from the Mississippi River region. Very often there is no load available for the cars during half of their round trip from their point of origin. The result is that great numbers of empty freight cars are continually being hauled about the North American continent. The magnitude of this wastage of resources is indicated by the fact that there are in the order of 1,750,000 of these cars in operation, representing an investment of about $5 billion. The method of routing freight cars around the nation's railroad networks in the most advantageous way is similar to the transportation problem.

The use of large-scale computers for the control of automobile traffic has often been suggested. Such systems would be real-time applications with a centralized data processor receiving inputs from traffic volume sensing devices, and sending outputs to traffic control signals such as red-green lights at intersections. The machine would contain a programmed model of the entire system of city thoroughfares, and would at all times have a complete image of the concentrations of vehicles throughout the network. Mathematical-logical decisions would be made by the program as to the most efficient way to direct the automobile traffic through the system. The machine would send out appropriate signals to traffic lights to implement these choices. It is obvious that decisions made by the computer would require a complex evaluation of the effect of local changes in the traffic pattern upon the system as a whole.

Elaborate studies of air traffic control systems have been made by various organizations, and computers have already begun to take over many of the clerical problems which are involved. It seems likely that within a few decades there will exist world-wide coordination of airplane movements. Two of the major aims of such systems will be to prevent collisions by keeping aircraft in alloted positions in air lanes, and to schedule the stacking of aircraft waiting to land at airports. To perform these functions, electronic computers will maintain files of traffic movement and will establish priorities for the use of air lanes. A large number of intercommunicating data processing centers will exchange information over communications networks, and will also send and receive data from small computers in the airplanes. The large ground computing installations will carry on repetitive work such as dispatching, keeping track of the locations of airplanes, and weather forecasting. The movement of air masses will be followed by the central data processing units, and will be transmitted to the airplanes, along with other navigational information. As part of this system it is possible that radio-telephone service to all planes will be established, thereby enabling plane-to-plane or person-to-plane conversation to take place anywhere on the globe. A complete image of the air traffic situation over every airport will be maintained. The computer will continuously acquire, store, and update a large variety of facts about weather, flight plans, and traffic. When a disabled airplane requires an emergency landing, complete information and analyses of the situation will aid in redirecting the air traffic pattern so as to permit the distressed plane to land.

NATIONAL DEFENSE

The field of operations research appears to be emerging to some extent as a consequent of what might be termed a growing obsolescence of man's sensory-motor apparatus and intelligence. We have created an environment around ourselves in which data are continually being created so fast and in such enormous quantities that humans are unable to digest and evaluate this information rapidly enough to achieve their purposes in complex situations and to respond effectively to new occurrences. The most dramatic example of this state of affairs is the BMEWS (Ballistic Missile Early Warning System), a billion dollar radar and computational network set up to detect the firing of missiles aimed at the United States. Three giant radar outposts will scan the skies over all approaches from the Soviet Union. The system will sense an attack within a few seconds after it has started, and will predict where the rockets will fall. It is anticipated that BMEWS will provide the United States with at least 15 minutes warning that the missiles are on their way. The computers will be able to read and write at the rate of 3 million bits per second, and will be capable of a quarter of a million additions or subtractions each second. All radar signals will immediately be analyzed to make sure that the data do not represent peaceful satellites or meteorites. In setting up the computations, engineers have found it necessary to analyze approximately 100,000 possible trajectories which a missile launched from the Soviet Union might follow. All information acquired and analyzed by the system will be transmitted to the high commands and to NATO headquarters.

It appears that one of the main contributions of computers in the future will be to establish and maintain a continuous image of large, dynamic situations, and to provide immediate analyses and plans based upon this image. Whether or not these organismic data processing machines can ever match the creative functions of the human mind, there is no question but that they have long since outstripped their inventors in the speeds and capacities required for many decision-making processes.

WAR GAMES

Simulation techniques are being used extensively for the testing of plans in complex situations. A program is written to embody a model, or image, of the occurrence being imitated by the machine, and tapes are prepared with typical happenings. As the inputs are brought into the computer, the equipment alters the image in accordance with the effect of these changes in the situation. One of the largest simulations ever carried out is the Air Battle Model, designed by the Rand Corporation and operated for the Headquarters of the United States Air Force by Technical Operations, Inc. This model imitates an air war. Aircraft are dispatched on missions and are attacked by enemy weapons. When a plane reaches its target and drops its bombs, the result of the air raid is evaluated and the strength of the bombed installations is correspondingly reduced. A large number of missions, initiated by both belligerents, may occur at the same time. The machine keeps track of the state of all military forces, such as the position of planes in the air and the remaining capabilities of bombed airfields, updating these states in accordance with the initiation of attacks and the results of the bombing missions. The program examines the progress of the war at specified intervals, say every 15 minutes, at which times the states are adjusted. A number of factors are taken into account in the simulation, such as maintenance, fuel, and bomb-loading facilities for offensive aircraft. A variety of details may be included in flight plans, including instructions for evasive tactics, rendezvous points, refueling, intelligence communications, landing instructions, and target assignments. The simulator takes into account the using up of fuel by keeping track of the distance covered by the aircraft.

The Air Battle Model, which has been run on large-scale computers for weeks on end, is a far cry from the physical model depicting the terrain of some battlefield, surrounded by top-ranking officers pushing around figurines to represent cavalry charges. Yet even in the past the outcome of battles, according to some famous generals, was often the result of luck and the lack of adequate information concerning the progress of the battle. It need not be emphasized that the nature of modern warfare greatly increases the difficulty of making crucial decisions rapidly in the complex and dynamic situations of global conflict. The purpose of the Air Battle Model is to test out various battle procedures and to plan the proper location of defensive installations and offensive bases.

BUSINESS GAMES

Similar programs have been written to simulate decision making in business management where, as in the case of the military staff, the executives are perpetually confronted with an overwhelming mass of information on the basis of which rapid and vital decisions must be made. Of great popularity among corporate officials have been simulators which enable teams of businessmen to engage in competitive business games. The computer contains a model of an industry, and each group of contestants starts the game as a company possessing certain basic assets and operating facilities. For example, the enterprises may begin with a product selling at a specified price, with a given volume of current sales and net income, and with a certain amount of cash on hand. During the course of the game, the teams may have the opportunity to make decisions at regular intervals on production, pricing, marketing, research activities, and plant expansion. The objective is to improve their competitive position with respect to the other companies.

The machine receives as input the activities of each group of players, and evaluates the interdependent effects of these decisions in terms of the simulated economy. Operating reports are printed out by the computer to enable the contestants to appraise the current status of their company and to enable them to improve their competitive techniques.

Apart from the excitement and fun generated by these business games, it is believed that these simulations assist executives and other personnel to test new management theories and to extend their insight into the dynamic structure of the economy.

THE THEORY OF GAMES

It is interesting that one of the main contributions to economic and political theory made in the twentieth century, the *Theory of Games and Economic Behavior,* has been the work of the originator of the stored program, John von Neumann, in collaboration with the economist Oskar Morgenstern. This mathematical analysis of the functioning of strategy in games is concerned with the withholding and distortion of information in situations of human conflict such as exist in economic, political, and military behavior. Methods for deception, counterdeception, and the clarification of deliberately created uncertainties are understood mathematically. The theory provides techniques for devising optimal strategies. In particular, the theory is applicable to the central problem of economics —the formation of prices for goods in limited supply. The behavior of buyers and sellers in the marketplace is similar to a game in that each individual desires to maximize his profit in terms of his own bargaining position and what he believes is the bargaining position of the other. The *haggling* process is likened to techniques such as bluffing in poker, which aims to increase a player's power by indicating greater strength than he possesses.

The shrewd poker player realizes that his opponent is thinking, planning, and distorting information just as he himself is. In Von Neumann's analysis, a player's best strategy is to assume in advance that his own strategy has probably been found out by the other person. His basic problem is to choose a mode of behavior such that he is guaranteed a minimum result in the face of any conceivable action on the part of this opponent. Although this tactic prevents him from achieving the best conceivable outcome, it does enable him to avoid total defeat if he is discovered, at the same time yielding him the best possible result under the circumstances.

The resolution of human conflicts, according to the theory of games, results from the confluence of this *minimax* strategy on the part of all participants in the situation. Consider a family on an overnight hiking trip in the mountains. It is agreed that the site of the camp will be at the intersection of two trails. The man wishes to pitch the tent at the greatest possible height, but his wife desires to camp at the lowest available location. Let us suppose that they find that there are four trails (1, 2, 3, 4) running north and south, as well as four trails (5, 6, 7, 8) running east-west, thereby producing 16 intersections. Upon discussing the problem, they agree that the husband will be permitted to choose the latitude at which the tent will be placed, and the wife will have the option of choosing any longitude. Neither person will have foreknowledge of the other's choice at the time he or she makes a selection. The following shows the height in thousands of feet of all 16 possible locations. What are the best strategies for the man and woman to pursue?

	Heights of possible locations				Worst out-come for husband
Number of road	5	6	7	8	
1	8	2	5	1	1
2	2	2	4	2	2
3	6	3	4	4	3
4	3	2	1	7	1
Worst out-come for wife	8	3	5	7	

If the husband selects the latitude represented by road 1, he could conceivably attain the greatest possible satisfaction of his desire, i.e., an altitude of 8000 feet. However, this choice involves him in the risk of the disastrous altitude of 1000 feet, in the event that his wife "bet" upon the longitude represented by road 8. A similar catastrophe would occur if he selected road 4; here he could win a height of 7000 feet, but if his wife happened to choose road 7, the tent would have to be pitched at 1000 feet. The wisest choice the husband can make is to select road 3, which guarantees him a maximum of 3000 feet under any circumstance, and a possibility of something better.

The wife's strategy follows similar lines. Road 7 or 8 would yield the lowest possible altitude, but such a choice might involve her in a crushing defeat if her husband chose roads 1 or 4, respectively. Her shrewdest choice is to pick road 6, which affords her a maximum of 3000 feet under the worst conditions, and the possibility of an altitude of 2000 feet if her husband selects any road other than 3.

The result of these two independent strategies is that the tent is pitched at an altitude of 3000 feet, that is, at the intersection of roads 3 and 6. The theory of games is applicable to a wide variety of situations in which two or more individuals with interlocking needs are seeking to maximize their objectives in relation to each other. Among the problems considered is the desirability of entering into and withdrawing from coalitions when such actions are calculated to be advantageous. This mathematical analysis of the most opportune payoff in conflict situations has been applied to such business decisions as the choice of media in advertising campaigns, bidding for contracts, setting prices in competitive situations, and the optimization of inventory levels. The military and political implications of the theory of games are obvious, and some social scientists have heralded this mathematical accomplishment as a development comparable to the achievements of Sir Isaac Newton in the field of physics.

MASS SOCIAL DATA

Another important contribution to human knowledge will result from the application of electronic data processing equipment to the prediction of human behavior in large groups. Impressive in scope and magnitude is the employment of data processing machines by such a concern as R. L. Polk & Co. of Detroit, Michigan, which provides, among other services, statistical information on the automobile market in all regions of the United States. This company maintains a list of about 65 million names of car owners, along with such data as what type of house they reside in, whether they rent or own their home, what type of work they are engaged in, what their habits are as consumers, and what make and model of automobile they drive. This information is sold to such organizations as advertising agencies to assist them in directing their sales campaigns at specific groups of potential customers.

Automatic data processing equipment has often been used for market studies and sales analyses. One large advertising agency has recently acquired an electronic computer at a cost of almost $1 million. We may confidently expect that more and more of these machines will gradually be installed by concerns in this industry. As one executive has quipped, it won't be long before computers will be as common on Madison Avenue as gray flannel suits.

A large number of programs have been used for studies of economic trends. For example, the Department of Agriculture uses these statistical techniques extensively for predicting the future consumer demand for such farm products as wheat, potatoes, and eggs. The availability of electronic computers now makes it possible to collect, process, and analyze enormous volumes of information for forecasting purposes. The dramatic exploits of data processing machines in predicting national trends on election night is likewise an instance of the value of automatic information-handling machines in the divination of mass social behavior. These forecasts rely on mathematical models of the election, based on group characteristics of voters. The past behavior of various categories of the population, such as the farm vote, is measured beforehand, and this information is given to the machine to enable it to project early returns. It should be obvious that a poor prediction is not the fault of the computer, but is the result of inadequate human knowledge or unsatisfactory statistical techniques written into the machine's program.

The use of operations research techniques in conjunction with electronic data processing machines for the optimum allocation of resources in an economy has been studied for some years by mathematical economists. One of the most well-known methods advanced for this purpose is the *input-output* analysis developed by Professor Wassily Leontief of Harvard University. This technique sets up a model in which every unit used in any economic process is recorded and evaluated, along with every resulting product. This model permits mathematicians to obtain a dynamic, quantitative image of the entire economy, and enables them to study and analyze interdependencies among all of the factors present in the system of supply and demand.

15 THE THEORY OF AUTOMATA

COMPUTERS AND THE BRAIN

Are we basically machines? The biological and medical sciences have progressively made deeper inroads into the nature of man, showing that many occurrences in the human body once regarded as mysteries are in fact determined events, just as predictable as occurrences in the physical world. The conquest of the diseases which once decimated whole continents, and the prevention and cure of the innumerable sicknesses which once made existence miserable and short, have not been the least of the achievements resulting from the viewpoint that living processes can be understood and controlled through the investigation of their causality.

Carried further under the influence of the discoveries of Darwin, this viewpoint led scientists such as Freud to take as their cardinal tenet the assumption that all psychic events are determined. In this way, the phenomena of the human mind and emotions were opened as subject to scientific inquiry, and the communications networks which underlie society became likewise an area in which these methods could be applied. However fledgling these studies may be at present, it cannot be denied that they have already made significant advances into the understanding of the laws governing human behavior.

The possibility remains, however, that there may be activities of the intellect and realms of feeling which are not determined in the usual sense. As the Gestalt psychologists have stressed, there may be emergent patterns of cognition which are not reducible to the elements of which they are comprised, and which possess novel qualities which are unique in themselves. Moreover, certain recent discoveries in mathematical philosophy have cast an interesting and unexpected new light upon the nature of machines and their potentialities.

A machine is, par excellence, a determined system. Given all of its initial states in complete detail along with the rules governing its actions, a machine's behavior at any time in the future can be completely predicted. This conception calls to mind the famous statement of the mathematician LaPlace that, if the position and velocity of every particle in the world were known at a particular time, it would be possible to know every future motion in the universe. This assertion is of course equivalent to saying that the cosmos is a giant machine, a notion which was suggested by Newton's laws of motion.

A correspondence exists between the characteristics of any machine and the properties of deductive systems such as Euclidean geometry. Hence, by studying these axiom systems it is possible to draw conclusions concerning the nature of machines. These logical systems, also known as *formal languages,* have been investigated extensively during the last few decades. The key concepts of computational machinery can be traced back to these theoretical studies.

There are four basic constituents of any logical system. First, a set of symbols is defined which, secondly, can be combined only according to specified rules to form meaningful statements. Next, there are laws of inference which provide transformations whereby new propositions in the system can be deduced from prior statements. Finally, a deductive system possesses a set of basic axioms from which, by utilizing the rules of inference, the theorems can be derived.

A large variety of deductive systems can be constructed. Symbolic logic is one of the prime examples of such a systematization. The system is based on a set of axioms from which logical statements are derived as theorems. Deductive systems need not have any correspondence with reality. It happens that ordinary geometry and logic can be utilized for an understanding of our environment, but it is possible to construct numerous types of geometries and logics which have neither practical meaning nor relevance.

A common example of an abstract axiom system is the game of chess. Here, the symbols may be thought of as consisting of the pieces, such as the king, queen, pawns, etc., placed in relation to each other on a square board consisting of 64 boxes. The laws of inference in chess are the rules of the game, such as the prohibition against the king moving into check and the diagonal motion of bishops. The original setup of the pieces at the start of the game would be the basic axioms. New configurations of the pieces correspond to theorems in this system. They are derived from previous configurations by application of the transformation rules.

The field of *metamathematics* is the investigation of the generic characteristics of all axiom systems. This discipline studies such problems as whether there is a mechanical way of deciding whether or not any particular proposition can be deduced from the axioms of a system. This branch of mathematics and logic has attracted many of the leading minds of the twentieth century, such as Kurt Goedel.

TURING MACHINES

A. M. Turing was another of the great metamathematicians of our time. To study the nature of deductive systems, this gifted English logician conceived of an abstract automaton which he called a "Turing machine." This was purely a theoretical construct. No one has ever gone to the trouble of building equipment which would behave exactly in the manner he prescribed.

Here is a description of a Turing machine:

1. A tape of any necessary length is divided into squares containing symbols. These symbols are denoted by the letter s. A certain number of symbols are available. A square may contain only one symbol at a time.

2. The tape can be moved, one square at a time, into a machine unit which can scan (read) and write upon the tape. This device can read the symbol in a square, erase the symbol, and write a new one in its place. It can also move the tape one square either to the right or to the left so as to bring the adjacent squares into position to be scanned.

3. The internal state of the machine is represented by the letter q. This symbol is contained in a register. The various states of the machine are represented by the symbols q_1, q_2, q_3, ...

4. A logical unit takes the last s symbol read from the tape, and relates this s to the present q state of the machine. The following events now occur:

   a. The machine goes into a new q state. The new q symbol is entered into the register.

   b. The machine computes a new s symbol. This is placed on the tape square last read. The old symbol is erased.

   c. The machine instructs the tape to move one square either to the right or left.

The logical unit can also instruct the machine to stop upon reaching a certain state. The new s and q symbols formed each time are based upon a *program* within the logical unit. This program is expressed by a *transition table* which tells the machine what to do next.

The Turing machine has a definite cycle of operation: It starts by reading a symbol from a square on the tape. It then combines this symbol with the present state of the machine to produce a new machine state. When it goes into its new state, the machine computes a new symbol which is placed on the tape in place of the symbol just read. Finally, the machine commands the tape to move one square in a designated direction, after which the cycle is repeated.

As will become increasingly apparent, a Turing machine is essentially an abstract axiom system: A set of symbols is defined. Rules are specified governing the transformation of an original string of symbols on tape into another string of symbols on tape. This is a general way of conceiving of the deduction of theorems from axioms.

Any particular Turing machine can be completely described by means of a table of state transitions. For example, consider a machine whose tape squares contain either the symbol 0 or 1, and whose internal states q_1 and q_2 are 0 and 1. There are four possible combinations of symbols and states. For each combination, there is a new symbol, a new state, and an order for the movement of the tape to the right or the left. We show here a transition table. An order to move the tape to the right is represented by an R. An order to move the tape to the left is represented by an L.

State q	Symbol s	New state q	New symbol s	Direction
0	0	1	1	R
0	1	1	0	R
1	0	0	0	L
1	1	0	1	L

Thus, if the Turing machine is in state 0, and the symbol 1 is read, the machine goes into the new state 1, writes the new symbol 1, and moves to the right.

This table can also be expressed by a *transition diagram*, a chart in which the possible states of the machine are shown within circles. The four lines between the states represent the four possible transitions between states. For example, if the machine is in state 1, the symbol which will be read next must be either a 1 or a 0. The two outgoing lines from state 1 show these two possibilities. Within the rectangular box is shown the new symbol and the order for the direction of tape motion.

The transition diagram for the Turing machine we are considering is shown in Fig. 15-1 on the facing page.

Let us suppose that this Turing machine is confronted with the following tape, and is started in state 0 at the indicated square.

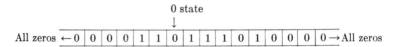

The first action of the machine is to read the designated square, which contains the symbol 0. To ascertain the next state of the machine we look at the transition diagram. This states that the machine now goes into state 1. The new symbol 1 replaces the 0 which was in the tape square. The tape is ordered to move to the right one square. At the end of the first cycle, the tape appears as

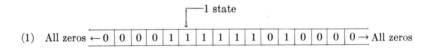

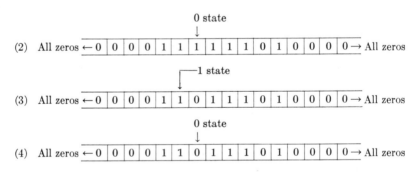

A study of these four events shows that the machine's actions at this point become periodic. From (4), the machine returns to (1), and the four transitions are then repeated indefinitely.

A Turing machine could be built to perform any computation which is carried out by modern data processing equipment.† Theoretical work by Turing and other metamathematicians has proved that there are certain limitations as to what any machine can compute. These conclusions, however, do not affect the practical engineering, scientific, and commercial uses of electronic computers.

† The Appendix shows a Turing machine for adding two binary numbers.

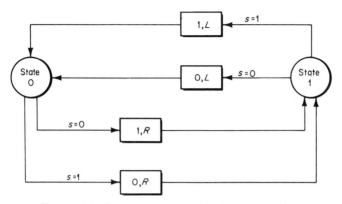

FIGURE 15-1 Transition diagram for a Turing machine.

MACHINES AND AUTOMATA

The concept of a machine is closely linked, if not identical, with that of an automaton. Both are artificially created mechanisms constructed to carry out a regular, known sequence of actions once set into motion. The conception of a predictable set of state transitions underlies the operation of these systems.

A car contains a number of these automata. The very term *automobile* means *self-moving*. The gear shift, for example, is a mechanism which

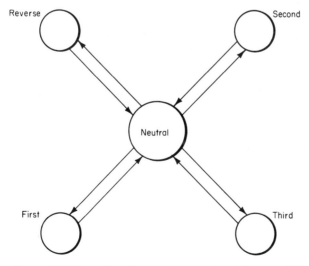

FIGURE 15-2 Transition diagram for an automobile gear shift.

can exist in any one of five possible states: first, second, third, reverse, and neutral. In all older cars, passage from one state to another required human action. The advent of modern equipment enables this mechanism to pass unaided (automatically) between certain of these states, as a function of the speed of the car. The transition diagram of Fig. 15-2 shows that to change state, i.e., to shift gears, it is necessary to pass from an initial position into neutral before another state can be entered.

One characteristic of this mechanism is that it must either be in one state or another. No intermediary states are permitted. For example, it is impossible to be in second and third at the same time. The automata with which we are concerned, namely digital computers, are of this discrete, noncontinuous variety.

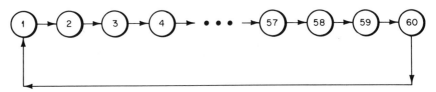

FIGURE 15-3 Transition diagram for a clock.

One of the first types of automata to attain widespread use was the clock. Once set in motion, this determined system proceeds inexorably and monotonously to pass through a set of definite, discrete states. For instance, the minute hand passes through 60 regularly spaced positions (Fig. 15-3), after which it repeats this sequence of states.

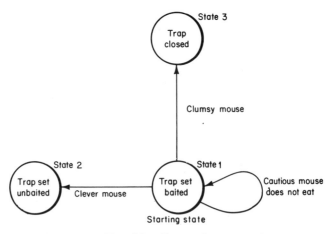

FIGURE 15-4 Transition diagram for a mouse trap.

A clock is a cyclical automation in that it iterates through a fixed succession of states. It is not very interesting from a theoretical point of view, as it is logically simple and unaffected by external happenings.

Let's consider the transition chart for a mouse trap (Fig. 15-4). This machine is influenced by its environment. However, if the rodent is clever enough to devour the cheese without springing the trap, the device remains in its original state.

There are only three possible states for this machine, and there is no way for the device to return to its original state without human intervention. The transition from the original state into the next state depends upon an external input.

Original state	External input	Next state
Set baited	Clever mouse	Set unbaited
Set baited	Clumsy mouse	Dead mouse
Set baited	Cautious mouse	Set baited

Abstract automata can be created by setting up transition tables which show how the machine goes from state to state under the influence of any external input. Figure 15-5 exemplifies an automaton with seven

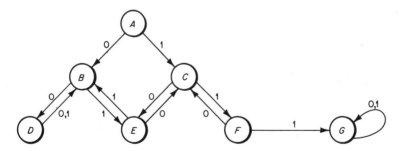

FIGURE 15-5 An automaton with seven possible states.

possible states—A, B, C, D, E, F, and G, and with two possible inputs, 0 and 1. Let's start the machine in state C. It will pass to state E if a 0 input occurs. If a 1 input is applied, it will go to F. The transition from D is to state B, regardless of whether the input is a 0 or 1. It is not possible to leave state G, no matter what happens.

Present state	Input to next state	
	0	1
A	B	C
B	D	E
C	E	F
D	B	B
E	C	B
F	C	G
G	G	G

The history of this automaton depends on its past inputs. If a sequence of inputs enters the system at regular time intervals, this history might take the form:

Time	State	Input	Next state
1	E	0	C
2	C	0	E
3	E	1	B
4	B	0	D
5	D	0	B
6	B	1	E
7	E	1	B

Of course, this history varies if there is a different sequence of inputs.

Other types of automata can be conceived which produce an output from each state. Such machines must be defined with two tables:

	Next state with input	
Present state	0	1
A	D	B
B	C	D
C	A	D
D	D	D

Present state	Present output
A	0
B	1
C	1
D	0

The transition diagram (Fig. 15-6) for this automaton includes a statement of its outputs, these being designated by the numbers in the circles following the semicolons.

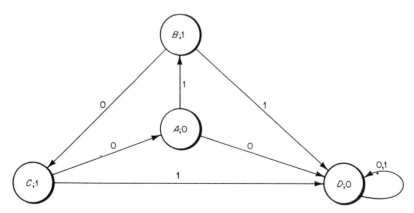

FIGURE 15-6 Transition diagram for an automaton.

Once having entered state D, the machine can never leave. Hence, it emits a series of 0 outputs if this occurs.

A combination lock may be described by an automaton. The lock opens only when a 1 output signal occurs. This output is emitted only

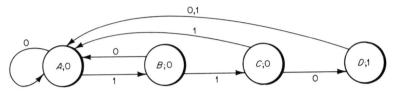

FIGURE 15-7 Transition diagram for a combination lock.

when the machine enters state D. Only one specific sequence of inputs can cause a transition to the unlocking state.

Present state	Next state with input	
	0	1
A	A	B
B	A	C
C	D	A
D	A	A

Present state	Present output
A	0
B	0
C	0
D	1

The lock's combination is the input sequence 110. Only by applying these signals in this order can a 1 output be obtained from the system. Any other sequence fails to reach D, and causes a return to state A.

THE DESIGN OF AUTOMATA

The characteristics of automata are being investigated extensively, and undoubtedly a general theory will emerge. One of the important problems in the theory of automata is the minimization of the number of states required to solve any given problem.

Let's suppose that we wish to construct a machine with the characteristics shown in Fig. 15-8.

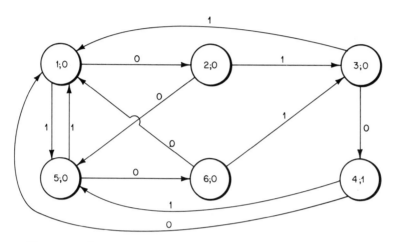

FIGURE 15-8 Transition diagram of an automaton, before minimization.

The state table is as follows:

Previous state	Next state with input		Output	
	0	1	0	1
1	2	5	0	0
2	5	3	0	0
3	4	1	1	0
4	1	5	0	0
5	6	1	0	0
6	1	3	0	0

What we mean by minimizing a machine is to develop an automaton which will produce the same outputs as the original machine, given the same inputs. We may think of the machine (Fig. 15-9) as a box with inputs entering. We don't care

FIGURE 15-9 Automaton represented as box with inputs and outputs.

what is inside the box, so long as it always has the proper outputs. If we can reduce the number of states needed to produce these required outputs from the inputs, we regard the automation as simpler. If we minimize the automaton of Fig. 15-8, we obtain Fig. 15-10.

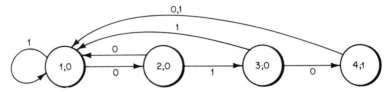

FIGURE 15-10 Automaton of Fig. 15-8, in minimized form.

This is a combination lock similar to the one discussed previously. Here the lock is opened by the input sequence 010. For any chosen sequence of input bits, this automaton will produce the same output as the more complex machine from which it was derived.

The conception of an automaton is a general notion which explains the behavior of any type of machine. The transition chart of an automaton is the set of rules, or laws, which govern the operation of any system. Both a logical circuit and an entire program can be described by transition charts. We could characterize a computer by tabulating all of the initial states of its memory units and its various internal triggers. The way in which the control system transforms these states could be described by a transition chart. This would give us a complete understanding of how the machine operates.

Of course, a modern computer consists of tens of thousands, even tens of millions of states, so this procedure would be very laborious. Perhaps some day techniques will be developed to enable this to be done efficiently. The practical value of such an undertaking would be in the elimination of unnecessary states. In the course of executing an instruction or a program, a machine passes through a number of different states. State minimization through improved logical design or programming leads to significant reductions in operating speed, efficiency, and cost of constructing and maintaining equipment. While present techniques for minimizing automata are still in the theoretical stage, it seems likely that these methods will ultimately lead to important practical applications.

IS THE MIND AN AUTOMATON?

If the human organism is construed as a machine, it follows that the brain should function as an automaton. Given its initial states, a type of "circuitry," and the laws governing the transitions which can occur, it would be possible to predict the actions of the mind.

The basic element in the central nervous system is the neuron. It has been estimated that there are 10^{10} of these specialized cells in the human brain. Leading out from each cell body are nerve fibers called *dendrites*, which form junctions, or synapses, with dendrites from other neurons. All of the cells in the brain are interconnected through tremendously complex meshes, sometimes designated as *nets*. Neurons have a threshold of excitation, which when reached causes the passage of a nervous impulse of constant intensity. This phenomenon, called the *all-or-none* law, seems to indicate that waves of nervous energy function in a binary manner, i.e., at full magnitude or not at all. Inhibition and delay are also present. After the excitation of a nerve fiber, it remains for a short period in a refractory state. During this time a second impulse is unable to pass in the normal way.

We have here a set of phenomena which resembles the operations in Boolean algebra. Mathematical logic was applied to neural activity in a classical paper published in 1943 by McCulloch and Pitts. The analogy of nerve nets to the gating systems of computers was utilized extensively by Von Neumann in the design of the first stored program machines. These conceptions are now current in writings concerned with the theory of automata. Investigators such as Rochester, Holland, Haibt, and Duda have attempted to study brain functions in learning by simulating neuron networks on the IBM type 704.

The well-known *perceptron* machine devised by Rosenblatt has learned to recognize certain patterns by using special statistical techniques. The capacity of the human mind to recognize invariances among perceptions of objects seen from different perspectives is one of the basic factors involved in intelligence. It is through this mechanism that we are able, for example, to perceive that an E is the same letter, no matter from what distance or angle we see the letter, and regardless of the type font used. An interesting feature of Rosenblatt's machine is that its memory is not localized in particular storage units, but is diffused throughout the apparatus. In this respect, the equipment is more closely akin to human memories than conventional computer information storage units.

GAME PLAYING PROGRAMS

Perhaps the most advanced attempts to simulate high-level mental functions are the programs which enable computers to play chess and checkers and to solve theorems in deductive systems.

A number of programs have been prepared to play such games as Nim. This game is played by randomly dividing a group of objects, say match sticks, into several piles on a table. Each of the two contestants successively draws as many matches as he wishes from any one pile. The aim of the game is to be the last individual to pick a match from the table. Games of this variety, however, do not require any real intelligence on the part of the machine, for a formula is known which can decide in advance the outcome of the game. Moreover, even without such a formula, a computer could examine every possible sequence of moves from any starting configuration. It could then either predict its own defeat or else select plays which would inevitably lead to victory. Of course, this would be possible only if the number of matches were small.

In the case of chess and checkers, no rule is known which could provide a mechanical evaluation of whether a particular board position will ultimately lead to victory or defeat. Nor is it possible for a computer to examine exhaustively all possible variant sequences of plays starting from a given board configuration. It is true that there is a finite number of possible games. However, there are so many possibilities that it would be inconceivable to attempt an exhaustive procedure, even with machines far faster than those now available. In checkers, the total number of continuations is in the order of 10^{40}. Dr. A. L. Samuel points out that even if three choices could be examined in every one-thousandth of a second, it would take 10^{21} centuries for a computer to consider all of these possibilities. Shannon estimated that there are in the magnitude of about 10^{120} chess games which can be played.

Samuel's checker program was written for an IBM computer, a binary machine with fixed word memory fields containing 36 bits each. Thirty-two of these bit positions represent all of the permissible positions on the checkerboard. A 1-bit stands for the presence of a piece; a 0-bit expresses the absence of a piece. Four words are required to symbolize a configuration of counters and kings on the board. Humans communicate their moves to the machine by punched cards or via the supervisory control unit. The computer replies by flashing lights on the console or by printing out messages. The basic checker playing routine is comprised of about 1100 instructions. Several thousand additional words in memory are used for associated programs and for intermediate results. The time required for the machine to make a move is in the order of a few milliseconds.

The computer plays chess or checkers by looking ahead from the starting position to possible next moves. This exploration is carried out by saving the original position, and by representing the new configurations in temporary storage locations made available for this purpose. Of course, each of the possible moves immediately following the initial position is itself succeeded by a number of possible plays. In turn, each of these second moves is followed by another set of alternatives. As has been indicated, the number of alternative moves rapidly increases. It soon becomes impractical for the machine to look ahead to all of the possible ramifications stemming from a given starting configuration. For this reason, a limit is placed upon the depth to which each particular alternative play is explored. The possibilities which are investigated by the computer form a tree structure (Fig. 15-11).

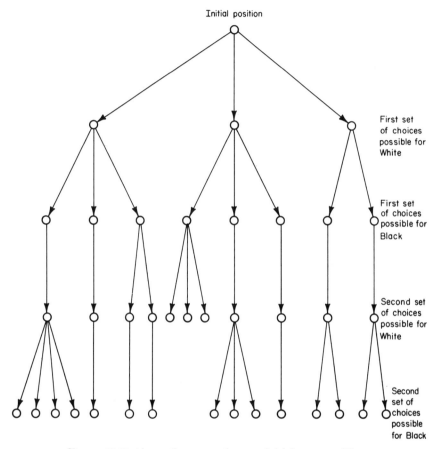

FIGURE 15-11 Alternative moves from an initial game position.

One possible procedure is to program the computer to stop examining alternatives after, say, the fourth move. However, where special board conditions are present, continuations of the tree structure are explored. In checkers, for example, when the next play is a jump, or when an exchange of pieces is possible, the machine looks into these alternatives. Apart from these situations, the depth of look-ahead is determined by the amount of machine operating time which is available and convenient, and by the fact that too shallow an exploration will cause the computer to play a poor game.

How does the program select which move to make? After establishing all of the possible alternatives within the prescribed depth, the machine evaluates these possibilities by applying various quantitative criteria. The basic goal in checkers is to prevent the opponent from moving. This objective includes the situation in which all of the other player's pieces have been captured. When this aim has been achieved, the game is won. The machine always makes preliminary tests to ascertain whether this condition has been reached by a particular group of alternatives. If a victorious termination has not been attained, the computer applies standards to test how well each possible series of moves proceeds toward this goal.

In Samuel's checker program, the most important criterion for evaluating a move is superiority in number of pieces. The machine makes the assumption that it should always play so as to cause its opponent to have less pieces than itself. An exception is made when such a move opens the possibility for exchange stratagems which would give the opponent an advantage. The criterion of a higher number of pieces of course depends upon the relative values assigned to kings and ordinary counters. This particular program equates two kings with three men. The computer will, therefore, make this trade, one way or the other, if in so doing it obtains some advantage.

The quantitative criteria applied by the computer to each alternative move consist of numerical weights. These numbers are entered into an evaluation formula which computes the merits of each of the possible plays. The *minimax* principle is then used for deciding which move to select. An example of this method is shown in Fig. 15-12. It is Black's turn to play. He can make three possible moves. Let's assume, for the sake of simplification, that the evaluation formula is able to ascertain in each case whether the continuation of the play will lead to a win, lose, or draw.

Black's three choices are designated by choices *a*, *b*, and *c*. If Black selects move *a*, White has possibilities *1* and *2*. If Black selects *b*, White has possibilities *3* and *4*. Finally, if Black picks *c*, White has the choice of *5* and *6*. Black would be foolish to select branch *a* for in this case he would lose, no matter what White did. Move *b* leads necessarily to a draw. If Black chose move *c*, the outcome would be either a victory or a defeat, depending on whether White selected move *5* or move *6*. However, Black could hardly expect White to cooperate in choosing play *5*. Black could therefore not hope for success by picking move *c*. Black's best solution is to select a strategy which will yield him an optimum result under the worst possible circumstances. He therefore selects move *b* to obtain at least a draw.

How well the machine will be able to play a game is to a large extent based upon the efficiency of the evaluation formula. This formula, in turn, is influenced by the relative weights accorded to the different criteria used to assess the value of moves. These weights can be given to the computer by the programmer. In the checker program, the machine is instructed to develop its own relative weights by analyzing the games it has played previously. As a matter of fact, the chief practical value of chess and checker programs is that they test whether or not a computer can be programmed to improve its performance, i.e., to learn. Since

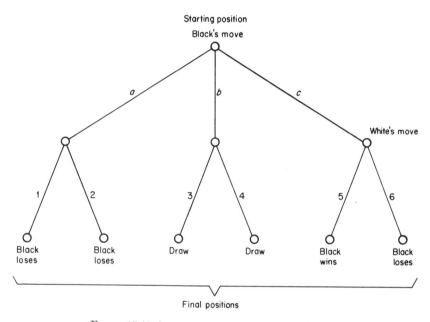

FIGURE 15-12 A game tree with evaluated branches.

the computer is increasingly winning more and more checker games from Samuel, it would appear that in some sense the machine is indeed learning.

Samuel's checker program includes a system for remembering past games. Board positions are stored on magnetic tape, and are cataloged by such factors as number of pieces on the board, the presence or absence of an advantage in pieces, and the existence or nonexistence of kings. Positions are kept on this tape in the order in which they are most likely to be needed, and the file is continually updated with new board positions. Redundant configurations are eliminated, and the program deliberately "forgets" positions which are used with a low frequency. About 50,000 board positions are available on tape for reference by the machine.

The game of chess typifies the capacity of the human mind to solve problems of great complexity. Possibly this is the reason why the effort to program computers to play this game has long fascinated many data processing theorists. An early paper by Shannon in 1949 gave direction to most later research. Turing subsequently described a machine procedure for chess playing. However, the first actual program to be written was prepared in 1956 at Los Alamos for a machine called MANIAC I. To reduce the time for moves, this program employed a six-by-six board with no bishops. Also eliminated were special moves such as castling and *en-passant* attacks.

An eight-by-eight program completed by Alex Bernstein at IBM embodied a procedure whereby the machine, instead of exploring all possible continuations, selected only those directions of play which seemed fruitful. The choice of direction was provided by subroutines which suggested plausible avenues of exploration. These approaches were based on such factors as insuring the safety of the king, developing pieces, and attacking the opponent's men.

Good selection principles reduce enormously the number of continuations which have to be explored. Accordingly, the future of machine chess playing seems to depend more on the development of such methods than simply upon increasing the speed whereby the computer looks through future alternatives. Selection procedures of this type are called *heuristic*. They are to be likened to the plausible hypotheses which a human uses when trying to solve a problem by trial and error.

Newell, Simon, and Shaw have done extensive research both in chess programs and in the machine proving of theorems in deductive systems. Both problems are essentially the same. Games such as chess are similar in nature to formal languages, in that both start with a set of axioms and rules of inference, from which theorems (or new board positions) are derived. Gelernter's program for proving theorems in high school Euclidean geometry involves basically the same problems as a game playing program. In each case, an enormous number of alternatives branch out from an original starting point. To be successful, the machine must select those paths of exploration which seem most fruitful.

As has been intimated, these advanced programming research efforts are by no means pure pastimes or challenging exercises in scholarly wit. On the contrary, such projects have the very practical goal of ascertaining to what extent machines can exercise ingenuity and creativity. One significant result of this research has been the development of new automatic programming techniques called *list* languages. These languages enable machines to process complex information structures which are similar to associated ideas in the human mind. It is to be noted that machines for playing games and solving theorems do very little arithmetic. Their power consists of the ability to manipulate symbolic relations.

If there are laws governing the formation of heuristic principles, it would seem that an automaton such as a computer could be given rules for devising fruitful hypotheses for solving problems. One form which such rules might take would be general methods of learning from experience. Whether or not the very nature of a machine excludes this possibility is a question for metamathematicians. The eminent Gestalt psychologist Kurt Goldstein once remarked to the author that all a machine can do is to bring elements into new combinations. True learning necessarily involves the creation of wholes which are not deducible from their parts.

ANALOG COMPUTERS

The machines we have been considering in this book have been *digital* computers. These are machines in which information is represented in the form of numbers (digits). It is possible that the human brain operates like an *analog* computer, or on the basis of a combined analog-digital principle.

Analog machines utilize physical devices or principles whose operation is similar to a calculation with numbers. They are less accurate than digital computers. The usual example given is the thermostat. The heat of a room causes metal in this device to expand, breaking an electrical contact, thereby shutting off the oil burner. When the house cools down as a consequence, the thermostat metal contracts until the circuit connection is reestablished. The heating system is thus self-adjusting. Flexibility in the making and breaking of the electrical contact enables the occupant of the building to regulate the temperature of the rooms as he desires. A number of little self-regulating toys have been constructed for experimental purposes. They move along a floor when activated by some stimulus such as light or heat. Some such devices have a pair of photoelectric cells as their organ of perception. The intensity of illumination activates electric motors to move the unit in the direction of the light.

The differential analyzer, first conceived by Kelvin and later designed and built independently by Vannevar Bush, is an analog computer. This machine is employed for calculating the rates of change of the different variables in a formula with respect to each other. Such equations are very common in the physical sciences. An example from sophomore calculus is a problem in which water is flowing into a reservoir at a rate determined by the size of the inlet and is flowing out through another channel. How much water will be in the reservoir a certain time after a given initial state?

A mechanical differential analyzer consists of a system of intercon- nected shafts and gears which can be arranged in any relation to each other by means of a flexible gear box. The input is provided by imparting a rotation to a particular shaft, which then drives other shafts in ac- cordance with the gear ratios. If the gear ratio is arranged to vary continuously during the process by a definite amount, then the rotation of the output shaft can measure a required rate of change. Electrical circuits can also be used for the evaluation of differential equations by utilizing networks with physical principles embodying the equations to be solved.

A simple illustration of an analog computer is provided by a multi- plying bar (Fig. 15-13). This device is a piece of steel in the form of a

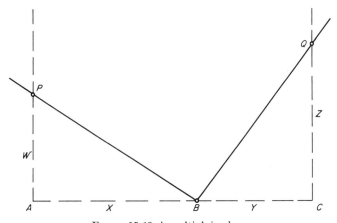

FIGURE 15-13 A multiplying bar.

right angle, constrained to rotate about a pivot at B. The distances W and Z can be set at any position by rotating the steel. Elementary plane geometry can be utilized to show that triangle PAB is geometrically "similar" to triangle QCB, and that, therefore,

$$\frac{Z}{Y} = \frac{X}{W} \quad \text{or} \quad Z = \frac{XY}{W}$$

If W is set equal to 1, then we have the product $Z = XY$, obtained by measuring the distance QC.

AUTOMATION IN INDUSTRY

The use of analog devices for controlling industrial processes is illustrated by such gadgets as the flyball governor which kept the records on the old Victrolas turning at a constant speed. Digital computers will unquestionably play a large role in future industrial automation, perhaps in conjunction with analog machines. The employment of analog-to-digital converters is very common at the present time. A number of companies have marketed devices for measuring and recording the factors occurring in productive processes. Variables such as time, weight, pressure, quantity, temperature, size, volume, and revolutions per minute can be monitored by automatic devices which transmit this data to digital computers for the preparation of management reports. One use of digital equipment for industrial control is exemplified by the employment of punched cards for the operation of rolling mills in steel plants. A rolling mill is a set of units similar to washing machine ringers through which the hot steel is passed back and forth in order to press it into the required state. Other applications have been made in the petroleum refining, chemical, metals, glass, food, and paper industries.

Considerable progress has been made in the control of machine tools by digital computers. These tools, which are used for such operations as drilling holes and for producing two- or three-dimensional contours from blocks of metal, can be operated either by analog or digital methods. The analog procedure consists of preparing templates which are inserted into the machine tool to provide it with a sequence of instructions. This method has a number of serious disadvantages. The preparation and insertion of the templates, as well as the setting up of the machine tool, are long and arduous procedures. Where a large number of identical products must be manufactured, as in the automobile industry, these factors are not important. But where only several units of a kind are to be turned out, the time and labor required become excessive.

The use of digital equipment for controlling machine tools provides a number of striking advantages. The instructions take the form of cards or tape which can be changed easily when a different product is scheduled to be manufactured, or when a modification of design is to be introduced. There is no bound to the accuracy which can be specified by digital commands, other than the limitations of the machine tool itself. In addition the manual time and skill needed for the preparation of the templates is eliminated. Furthermore, a greater variety of control functions can be carried out, such as applying temperature regulation and turning the tool on and off. Finally, the rate of operation of the machining process can be controlled to a much greater extent than with the analog procedure.

One of the main difficulties which has arisen in the numerical (digital) control of machine tools has been the translation of engineering drawings into the detailed instructions, or program, to be executed by the machine. The blueprint may call for various geometrical shapes such as straight lines, circles, arcs, and other curves. To solve this problem, an automatic programming language has been developed which enables such diagrams to be transcribed easily into a sequence of instructions. The program, written in a language close to ordinary English, specifies the coordinates involved in each machine tool operation. It includes statements such as the geometrical characteristics of the surfaces, the cutting instructions, and the mode in which the cutting is to take place. The compiler of this program produces the detailed commands for the accurate, proper positioning of the machine tool and for the cutting and drilling motions needed. Such shapes as flanges, pockets, and grooves can be programmed with this language. Engineers can specify all of the planes, cones, cylinders, spheres, ellipsoids, and other solid curves which are required for the production of the desired object.

16 INTELLIGENCE IN THE COSMOS

PHILOSOPHICAL IMPLICATIONS

"What hath God wrought?" This first message sent by Samuel Morse over his telegraph line seems strange to our modern ears. Entering as we are an era in which intercommunicating artificial intelligence systems will span the surface of the planet, the transmission of information by a human opening and closing a switch to form dots and dashes at 35 words per minute cannot but appear archaic. It is curious to note that Thomas Alva Edison, whose inventions and discoveries were to a large degree responsible for the electronic age, earned his living as a young man by working as a telegraph operator.

Like the apparatus used, the sentiment expressed by Morse in his famous message seems incongruous in our present setting, for little trace remains in the contemporary world of science and engineering of the religious philosophy which once encompassed all of the varied entities and events in the universe. This world view taught that all phenomena were part of a divine scheme in which the power which moved every object was the love of God, a power which kept all things forever aspiring to fulfill their prime purpose in existence. Indeed it was the abandonment of this teleological viewpoint that all things must be understood in terms of their purposes which helped give rise to modern science. Many philosophers feel that the intellectual development leading from Newton through Darwin to Freud has culminated in a mechanistic conception of society which provides no basis for a higher meaning of life. Man stands alienated from the great traditions which once dignified human life and which motivated individuals to consecrate their lives to nobler causes.

The rebuilding of our inherited spiritual capital on a foundation which is congenial to our scientific outlook is hence necessary for heightening the life-affirmation of individuals and for strengthening the vigor of representative democracy. In setting out upon this task, we cannot turn our back upon the fact that man is an animal who has arisen in the course of evolution, and whose motivations are the product of the natural forces which have caused this species to arise on our planet. What can the emerging theory of automata contribute to our understanding of the nature of human life, society, and the universe in which these phenomena have appeared?

THE ROLE OF COMPUTERS IN SOCIETY

It seems likely that mathematical techniques for maximizing the allocation of resources and for studying the interrelations of costs and prices in the economy will be found increasingly useful in formulating long-range goals for economic enterprises. According to Adolph A. Berle, Jr., there is at the present time enough detailed information continuously flowing into various agencies of the Federal Government in Washington, D.C., to provide, if coordinated, an excellent image of the workings of the entire economy of the United States. The analysis of this picture could perhaps provide valuable policy-making assistance to the 500 large corporations which own two-thirds of the industry of the United States.

It has long been the dream of many thinkers that the application of scientific method to human society would result in benefits as vast and as startling as the incredible transformations of our environment which have become possible through the physical sciences. The new technology of electronic data processing will unquestionably play a major part in this introduction of rationality into social affairs. Real-time machine systems can gather data quickly and accurately for the analysis of the events and trends occurring in a complex, dynamic society. High-speed computational units and very fast random access memories could be located in cities throughout the country, and could remain in continuous communication through information-transmission networks. These data handling facilities could be programmed to remember and organize sociological and economic data according to elaborate mathematical models. Their outputs could enable human policy makers to make rapid, far-reaching decisions based on the rational evaluation of adequate, timely information.

Such decisions, as we have previously emphasized, are not concerned with lifeless, abstract symbols. On the contrary, they intimately affect the emotional depths of almost every individual in the world. The interrelated costs and prices of economic goods constitute a mechanism for establishing wage scales and for distributing consumer goods. These monetary values thus provide a system of incentives and rewards for all of the people contributing to the well being and progress of society. The price structure is a method for allocating material enjoyments, status gratifications, and opportunities to engage in creative work. From the broad standpoint of ethical and political philosophy, the economic system is society's attempt to administer justice to its members. Its aim is to enable each individual to actualize his potentialities to the maximum degree commensurate with the needs of others.

A similar function is performed by skills inventories which aid in the selection of individuals for positions within organizations. The recognition and reward of deserving people becomes increasingly difficult as the size of a group becomes large. Possibly electronic computers will enable more sophisticated techniques to be used for the evaluation of job performance and the assessment of ability.

COMPUTERS AND UNSKILLED LABOR

One of the short-range effects of automatic data processing has been to reduce the number of unskilled workers needed in industry. This trend will unquestionably continue with the growth of the new technology. In the long run, everyone will probably have to be highly trained in some craft or profession.

Of course, the revolutionary effects of data processing machines cannot be measured merely by employment statistics. We must consider the impact upon individuals. Automation may bring painful personal readjustments, uprooting some people from their homes, their accustomed skills, and their positions of prestige, compelling them to recommence their careers in new surroundings. But this has its bright side. Exciting new opportunities come into view. The taking over of routine clerical jobs by electronic computers frees men and women for more interesting work and more challenging use of their capacities.

ORGANISMS AND MACHINES

Most of the machines we have considered so far have simply been devices for receiving, processing, and sending out information to and from sensing and display units. A system such as SAGE-BOMARC is more advanced, in that it can innervate "muscles" to perform actions in the environment, and can control these motions through perceptions of concurrent events.

The analogy to human behavior is even closer in the instance of computers used for industrial process control. These machines can be likened to the functioning of the central nervous system in regulating and activating the internal states and movements of the organism. The human body contains a large number of remarkable controls for maintaining the stability of its physiological processes. These homeostatic mechanisms maintain constant levels of water, salt, sugar, proteins, fat, and calcium in the blood, and call into play various processes for attaining a constant level of body temperature. The assuring of an adequate supply of water is provided by a deficient secretion of saliva by the salivary glands when the body is lacking water, thereby producing the motivation of thirst. Hunger is the result of powerful periodic contractions of the stomach when it is empty. The appearance of these drives causes the central nervous system to energize the skeletal muscles to move the body around in search of water and food.

Analogously, it seems probable that manufacturing plants in the future will be, to a large extent, run by central data processing units in continuous communication with monitoring and control devices. The computers will no doubt make optimizing decisions, and will perhaps be able in some sense to learn by experience. Possibly a number of subcontrol stations corresponding to such organs as the heart will be utilized to regulate normal operations, and will only rarely be brought under the direction of the higher guidance center. The digestion of raw materials by the factory will be controlled by automatic devices. The computer will transmit orders for the replenishment of inventories when supplies run low.

In the living animal, the organs of perception and the muscular apparatus developed around the mouth, a device which became necessary for the intake of food into multicellular organisms. The evolution of the human face is a fascinating aspect of the emergence of the head from the structures which formed near the mouth to enable the organism to obtain a better awareness of a new environment. Effective seizing and chewing gave rise to the jaw. Early shark-like organisms were among the first to have teeth. The development of the eyes and ears gave animals greater power over their environment by enabling them to sense objects at a distance. Such perceptions were less possible with the organs of smelling, tasting, and touching. Problems in body support and spatial movement gave rise to the skeleton and the external musculature, the arms and legs. The need for coordinating perception and locomotion, as well as the necessity for regulating internal states, was responsible for the emergence of the nervous system.

While data processing machinery has hardly begun to rival the human brain in functional complexity, computers are far faster in the direct communication of information than our central nervous system. Our nerve impulses are conducted at velocities in the magnitude of 250 miles an hour, whereas the speed of electronic transmission approaches 186,000 miles a second. One of the differences between organisms and machines is that the latter do not go through a long process of evolution in attaining their present capacities, whereas living creatures have undergone, and presumably will continue to undergo, an evolution into different species.

THE BIRTH OF NEW MACHINES

The logic of reproduction in automata was considered by Von Neumann. For true reproduction to take place, it is not sufficient for an original machine to produce another machine which can merely operate in the same way as itself. The offspring automaton must also be able to reproduce itself just as its parent did. There must be an identity between grandfather machine and grandchild machine. No decrease in complexity should result from the reproductive process.

To conceive of reproduction in automata, let us imagine an automaton immersed in some environment which contains all of the various parts which are needed for the construction of other machines. Just as a biological creature can obtain inert matter from its surroundings and use this material to reproduce itself in entirety or to regenerate parts of itself, so our hypothetical automaton can obtain a selection of tubes, wires, tapes, transistors, etc., from its environment, and utilize these components for duplicating itself. The logic of the reproduction is a trifle involved:

Consider an automaton A which when furnished the description of some other automaton, will produce that other automaton. Automaton A contains within itself the capacity for receiving this description—a program for preparing another machine. When A fabricates another automaton, that offspring will contain, like A, the capacity for receiving a program about how to produce an offspring.

Let's also consider an automaton B. This machine is to be conceived as similar to the everyday punched card reproducer. When given a deck of program cards, it can make a copy of this sequence of instructions.

Conceive now of a combination of automata A and B, with a controlling device C, which initiates the following sequence of operations: Automaton A is given the instructions for creating an offspring. Then C commands A to produce the automaton described in this program. C now orders B to duplicate the program, and to give it to the new automaton just created by A. Finally, C disengages the newly constructed automaton from its parent.

Let us designate the automaton composed of A, B, and the control mechanism C by the symbol D. For D to commence its functions, it must receive, as we have seen, a program, placed in its A part. Assume that this description, a program for constructing the machine D, is placed into the A component of D. Denote the resulting automaton as E.

The aggregate E is now a full-fledged self-reproductive automaton. As soon as the program for creating D is entered into the machine, it can commence to fabricate other machines identical with itself. It is apparent that this program, or pattern of information, performs a function analogous to the genes in a living organism.

No working model of Von Neumann's hypothetical reproducing automaton has as yet been made, but some simple self-reproducing mechanical systems have been devised. Perhaps the most interesting is that of Homer Jacobson. He used a model railroad in which certain types of moving cars joined together to produce combinations which in turn acted so as to produce additional combinations. L. S. Penrose has also devised a model consisting of blocks which under certain conditions can combine into groups which produce more combinations of blocks.

INFORMATION PATTERNS IN LIFE

Considerable progress has been made during the last decade in understanding the mechanisms operative in the growth of living organisms. It has been ascertained that the basic element in the structure and functioning of all organic tissues is the coordinated activity of protein molecules. The types of protein molecules which a living being creates determine how it works and grows. What governs the synthesis of these particular molecules? The pattern of information, or program, which directs the formation of the specific number and class of protein molecules is located in the genes. Within the genes exist certain large molecules of deoxyribonucleic acid (DNA), which contain the plan for the animal which is to be generated. These DNA molecules are transmitted from parent organisms to offsprings over millions of years, and in this way the continuity of a species is preserved. During the growth process of a particular creature, the program carried by the DNA is brought from the genes to the cells of the body by means of ribonucleic acid molecules (RNA).

The pattern of information contained in the RNA molecules is certainly analogous to a sequence of instructions. The wonderful embryological process whereby the germplasm continually reproduces itself, grows through a series of well-defined states, and differentiates itself into the structures characteristic of a particular species of organism is a type of program, albeit one incredibly more complex than any as yet envisaged. Indeed, the capacity of living beings for creative activities— their ability to leap to daring intuitive hypotheses, to synthesize disparate ideas, and to devise systems of abstract imagination—indicates that life operates upon principles of much greater profundity than deductive logic. Perhaps some calculus of creativity underlies the functionings of organisms, a language of control embodying ideas and generative powers which we have yet to glimpse.

In any event, the physical basis for the storing and processing of the programs for the reproduction and development of living creatures is of a totally different nature from the components used for the memory and logical units of our present automata. It is true, however, that solid-state components now being utilized for electronic computers are increasingly operating on the molecular level. The living tissue constituted by the DNA molecules is a pattern of information, an organized structure of control which has been passed from plant to plant, from animal to animal, and from human to human over the vast millennia during which life has existed on this planet. Each individual is but the temporary bearer of a program which he has received from his ancestors and which he strives to transmit to his descendants. Cyclically through the ages, the germ cells formed during reproduction have surrounded themselves with somaplasm and directed these cells to differentiate and grow, and the matured organisms have in their turn created new germ cells to repeat the cycle.

The science of physics has long been concerned with the transformations of energy in the physical world, and in the nineteenth century the German scientist Rudolf Clausius coined the term *entropy* to describe the loss in available energy whenever one form of energy is converted into another. The classic example of this process is the radiation of light and heat by the sun, a continuous dispersal of potential energy into empty space. A small fraction of this kinetic energy is captured by plants on earth which, through photosynthesis, convert this energy into starch. We are now rapidly using up the vast supplies of energy stored by plants during the Carboniferous Age, during which enormous jungles of vegetation were converted into our coal deposits. The second law of thermodynamics states that the amount of energy in the universe is constant, but that its entropy is always increasing. Some day, in other words, all of the potential energy in the universe will be transformed into kinetic energy, and there will result a uniform level of energy throughout all space. This state has been popularly called "the heat death of the universe."

The study of the transmission of messages for the purposes of control has given rise in recent years to a new science of *information theory*. As we have seen, the same information can be represented in a variety of ways, as for example a written letter, a voice over a telephone, a sequence of dots and dashes, or a group of magnetized spots on a tape. The core characteristic of information is the presence of a pattern; the medium in which it exists is not essential. Form, not content, is important. It is apparent that a haphazard arrangement of some sort, such as a random sequence of noises, does not constitute a message. The presence of an orderly structure existing by itself has a low probability, for the second law of thermodynamics states that while a system tends to lose its pattern, it almost never gains in order and regularity. The existence of information is therefore a measure of the orderliness of an arrangement.

It would seem that living beings constitute a reversal of the universal trend toward the increase of entropy, for organic life is basically a pattern of information which persists, in an improbable way, in a physical world where order tends to decrease. The emergence of organisms, and their evolution into higher forms, indicates the presence in the cosmos of a force which opposes the second law of thermodynamics, and which continually struggles to produce more complex systems of creative control. The reproduction of living creatures has further advanced the amount of orderliness in the universe, and the development of civilization has introduced further form into a structureless cosmos. The great dams, buildings, and communication networks which we have created exemplify the formation of higher levels of control on this planet. Our science and technology represent storehouses of information which seem destined to yield measureless power over our environment.

ENTROPY IN SOCIETY

Man's increase in knowledge and power can be regarded as a manifestation in nature of a force opposing entropy, and the maintenance of social order is a necessary condition for the continuation and promotion of a species. In the words of the political philosopher Hobbes, a state of society in which every man is every man's enemy results in a life which is "nasty, brutish, and short." The continuing progress of civilization requires the maintenance of justice to encourage men to strive and create by properly rewarding each individual for his contributions to society. Where disorder and injustice exist, men's energies are continually occupied in fighting for self-preservation and struggling in envious malcontent.

The development of social institutions to implement a state of justice is necessary for the advancement of technology, science, and culture. A highly developed specialization of activity is required for social progress. One of man's major problems is the framing of institutions to enable the products of this division of labor to be equitably distributed, and to provide procedures to facilitate the acceptance of new ideas and techniques into industrial, scientific, and cultural activities. In the absence of utopian conditions, the function of law is to render effectual the institutions which perpetuate and promote the creative growth of civilization.

There seems to be little disagreement among commentators upon the contemporary scene that we are rapidly approaching a state of affairs in which almost all aspects of life will be engulfed by giant industrial, governmental, and educational organizations. As Thurman Arnold long ago emphasized, the idea that our economy is composed of a large number of small, independent enterprises is a fictitious myth. Even conservative spokesmen concur on the fact that ambitious and intelligent young men must now increasingly seek careers in big companies rather than in the formation of their own ventures. The key problem which faces the modern world is the preservation and extension of democracy, freedom, and opportunity within the large organizations which control the lives of members of our society.

The most effective form of social organization is one in which each individual is capable of evaluating his ability relative to others, and is willing to accept his merited position without outward or inward rancor. This attitude is possible when every person feels that he is part of some larger social whole to which he contributes according to his merits, and by which he is rewarded according to his contributions. Where this frame of mind is absent, there tends to result a situation in which all men are dissatisfied, and are continually plotting, scheming, and struggling for immediate selfish advantage, instead of devoting themselves to creative activities.

A species can be regarded as a type of self-organizing, reproducing, and optimizing program existing in nature. All of the past, present, and future members of a species are variations on the same basic plan. Each individual's life serves to perpetuate this program. Insofar as a person contributes creatively to society, he is an agent of history, an agent of a natural process which tends to increase order and to decrease entropy. The deeper meaning of life is derived from the realization that each person is part of a larger energy in which he is not submerged but to which he can devote himself in a unique and individual way.

The growth of civilization and the contribution of the individual to its continuation is a victory of the life force over that of disintegration. Man is an expression of a creative energy existent within the cosmos, and the triumph over disorder is inwardly experienced as an emotional commitment to a positive attitude of life affirmation. Possibly we can identify Freud's conceptions of Thanatos (the death instinct) and Eros (a force of universal love) with the physical principles of increasing and decreasing entropy.

It seems likely that life exists in similar or other forms in many other parts of space. We might speculate that there is a cosmic power which causes the emergence of these programs under appropriate conditions in various regions of the universe. Can it be said that there is a master program underlying all forms of life wherever it exists—some universal power of love which exerts control over the cosmos? Possibly, as the philosopher Henri Bergson suggested, physical phenomena should be regarded as degenerate or lower manifestations of biological phenomena. The principles of operation of these higher forces have yet to be discovered by humans. However, there is a long tradition in mathematics, stemming from Pythagoras and expressed in geniuses such as Kepler, Newton, Pascal, Descartes, and Leibnitz, which is based on an intuition that mathematical thought mirrors the working of a divine mind. Possibly some higher type of logic is the key to the essence of the cosmos. What form this language of control takes we cannot at this point say.

APPENDIX: A TURING MACHINE FOR ADDING TWO BINARY NUMBERS

The two numbers to be added will be stored on the tape as follows:

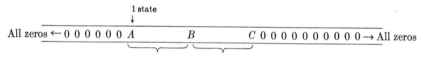

At each end of the tape there is assumed to be an indefinitely long sequence of zeros. Three symbols, A, B, and C on the tape are used to mark off the binary numbers to be added. One number is between A and B; the other between B and C. After the machine has finished its computation, the tape will contain all zeros, except for the symbols D and E. The answer will be between D and E.

To take a concrete example:

$$0\ 0\ 0\ 0\ A\ 1\ 1\ 0\ B\ 1\ 1\ C\ 0\ 0\ 0\ 0\ 0\ 0\ 0\ 0\ 0\ 0$$

becomes

$$0\ 0\ 0\ 0\ 0\ 0\ D\ 1\ 0\ 0\ 1\ E\ 0\ 0\ 0\ 0\ 0\ 0\ 0\ 0\ 0\ 0$$

Here we performed

$$\begin{array}{r} 110 \text{ number in } AB \\ \underline{11} \text{ number in } BC \\ 1001 \text{ sum in } DE \end{array}$$

269

To avoid cumbersome expressions in describing this Turing machine, let's establish some conventions.

We will want the machine to move the tape in search of a particular symbol. The machine will not alter any of the symbols it reads while hunting for this needed symbol. We'll designate this activity as shown in Fig. A-1. This means that the machine stays in state q, moving in direction R, without replacing any symbols on tape until it reaches the symbol s for which it has been searching. The box convention, it will be recalled, designates the new symbol, and the direction the tape is ordered to move. For example, the illustration of Fig. A-2 means that the new symbol is D, and that the tape is to move one square to the right.

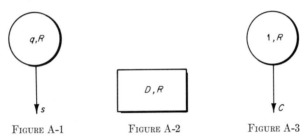

FIGURE A-1   FIGURE A-2   FIGURE A-3

The over-all plan the machine pursues is to find the next pair of binary digits to be added, to form their sum, and to deposit this sum elsewhere on the tape. If a carry is produced, this is taken into account when the next pair of bits is added. A large part of the machine's activities is concerned with the problems of demarcating the numbers on the tape. The following transition diagram, adapted from a flow chart prepared by Professor John McCarthy, shows in detail how the process is carried out.

As indicated above, the machine starts in state 1 at the number A on the tape. The symbol shown in Fig. A-3 means that the machine keeps moving to the right. It leaves all symbols unaffected until the symbol C is reached. At this point the machine enters state 3 (Fig. A-4). The symbol C is not affected.

The machine has now located the right-hand bound of the first binary number to be added. It now moves to the left. There are two possibilities at this point: the first binary digit may either be a 1 or a 0. In the example given, the bit is a 0, so the machine follows the 0 path in the diagram. This 1 is replaced by an X (for reasons to be given shortly). The machine continues to the left, entering state 6.

Having found the first member of the pair of bits it will add, the machine hunts for the B, the left-hand bound of the number. It passes over any other bits which happen to be present (in this case, the other 1). Upon finding B, the machine enters into state 10. It is now ready to obtain the first bit from the second number to be added. Again, there are two possibilities: the first binary digit could be a 0 or a 1. In this instance it is a 0. This 0 is replaced by an X, and the machine enters state 14. The machine has now found both digits comprising the pair to

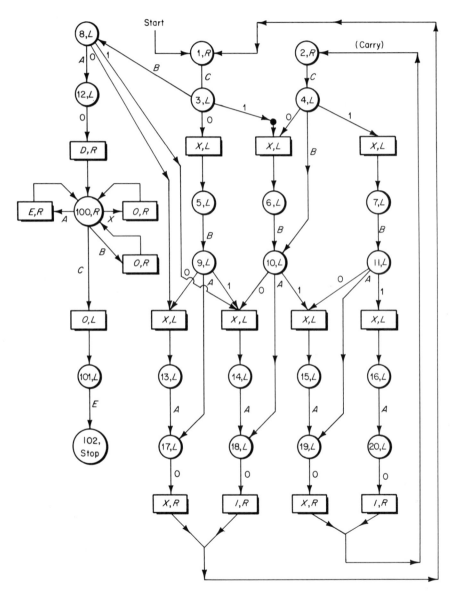

FIGURE A-4 Transition diagram for a Turing machine for adding two binary numbers.

be added. It seeks for the end of the second number, namely for the symbol A, after which it enters state 18.

The first digit of the sum is a 1. This digit is deposited immediately to the left of the A. The 1 replaces the first 0 to the left of the A.

The machine has now completed its first addition cycle. It repeats the procedure by moving to the right again until it finds C. This time the machine must obtain the second pair of bits to be added. It now hunts for the second bit in the first number. The last time, it will be recalled, the first bit was replaced by an X. It is now apparent that the reason for this was to enable the machine to locate the second binary digit in the course of its second addition cycle.

After the machine has completed its first addition, the possibility exists that it has used all of the bits in one or both of the numbers. Hence, after state 3, a path is provided for the machine to take when it reaches the end of the first number. When this occurs, the machine encounters the B, and enters state 8.

We shall not trace the operations of this machine any further in detail. However, a few general comments on the over-all procedure may be helpful.

Note that various states and transitions are provided to take care of carries. For example, if the machine is in state 10, it must either have encountered a 1-bit in the first number, or else there must have been a carry from the addition of the previous pair of bits. If now the machine encounters another 1, it is apparent that there will be a carry, and the machine will perform the appropriate actions after entering state 15.

If there is a second carry after a prior carry, the machine enters state 2. It will remain in the carry procedures if a 1 is reached, otherwise it will return to the noncarry procedures at the left of the diagram.

The end of the problem occurs when the machine exhausts both numbers, i.e., when it immediately reaches a B followed by an immediate A. This circumstance can arise only when all of the bits comprising both numbers have been replaced by X's. Upon entering state 12, the machine demarcates the left-hand boundary of the answer by placing a D in this position. Now the machine must go to the right, replacing X's in the sum with 0's. The X's were used here originally to enable the machine to differentiate between a 0-bit belonging in the sum, and a 0-bit which was merely one of the indefinite number of 0's to the left of the original A.

The machine continues to the right, replacing A with E, thereby establishing the right-hand demarcation of the sum. Now the machine merely replaces everything to the right of the E with 0's. It then returns to the E, where it enters state 102, and stops.

REVIEW QUESTIONS

CHAPTER 2

1. What are *intermediate results* in a computation? How are intermediate results handled by a person using a modern desk calculator?

2. Describe *branching*. How does it occur in an automatic data processing machine?

3. What is a *loop*? Why is it necessary?

4. Briefly define a *program*.

5. Draw a schematic abacus containing the number 872.

6. What are the advantages and disadvantages of punched-card machines?

7. What were the contributions of Babbage and Von Neumann to automatic computing?

8. Briefly describe a *stored program*.

9. What was the first electronic computer?

CHAPTER 3

1. Obtain a punched card or draw a schematic punched card. In columns 8 through 20, inclusive, indicate how the characters COLUMBUS 1492 would be punched. Place a blank column (no punch) after the S, as indicated.

2. Explain the terms *field*, *brushes*, *hubs*, *print positions*, and *armature*.

3. How are positive and negative numbers usually differentiated on punched cards?

4. What is a *cycle* in a punched-card machine?

5. How are punches in a card sensed by the machine?

6. Describe how a sorter processes cards. What is the output of this machine?

7. What is the general purpose of a plugboard? What is its basic principle of operation?

8. How would you wire the plugboard of a reproducing machine so as to duplicate the information in columns 45-50 into columns 30-35 of a blank card?

9. How do punched-card machines carry out comparisons?

10. What makes a relay open and close?

11. How would the number 2 be represented by a mechanical counter? How would the number 4 be added to this counter?

CHAPTER 4

1. What is the chief value of electronic data processing machines? Exemplify the differences between information handling and computing.

2. What are the four levels of understanding the operations of data processing machines?

3. Where does input data go when it enters an electronic data processing machine? Where does the machine keep intermediate data and constant factors?

4. Referring to Fig. 4-4, explain what happens when operation 2 is carried out.

5. What is the function of *control circuits*? What is their relation to a *program*?

6. What is meant by *machine logic*? What is the control system composed of?

7. Describe the two parts of an instruction.

8. Explain the two phases in the operation of the control system.

9. What function is performed by switching circuits?

CHAPTER 5

1. Explain the terms *number base* and *positional notation*. What is a *bit*?

2. Express the decimal number 83,948 as powers of ten. Add 3 to this number, and express the results as powers of ten.

3. Write out the binary equivalents to the decimal numbers 18 through 27.

4. The octal numbers 10 and 11 are equivalent, respectively, to the decimal numbers 8 and 9. Can you write the octal equivalents to the decimal numbers 10 through 17?

5. Express the binary number 1101 as powers of 2.

6. Perform the following binary additions:

001	011	0111
010	010	0001

Check your results by converting all of the binary numbers and the answers to the decimal system.

7. Represent the decimal number 64 in binary coded decimal.

8. What is the function of *zone* bits? Since B is the next alphabetic character after A, how do you think B is represented as a code?

9. What is the purpose of a *check* bit in a code? Assuming that a check bit must make the sum of the 1-bits an even number, what check bits would be used with the codes

$$1 \quad 0 \quad 1001 \quad \text{and} \quad 1 \quad 1 \quad 0001?$$

10. How are bits represented by electrical pulses? What is a *bistable* physical device? In what sense are magnetic drums and magnetic cores bistable units?

11. Explain the difference between serial and parallel relay circuits.

12. Enumerate all of the conditions under which the circuit in Fig. 5-9 is closed.

CHAPTER 6

1. Name the four essential operations underlying machine logic.

2. There are eight possible different input combinations to the following *and* gate. Enumerate all eight possibilities. Under what conditions, if any, will there be a 1 output from the gate?

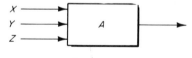

PROBLEM 6-2

3. Under what conditions, if any, will there be a 1 output from the following *or* gate?·

PROBLEM 6-3

4. Under what conditions, if any, will there be a 1 output from the following system?

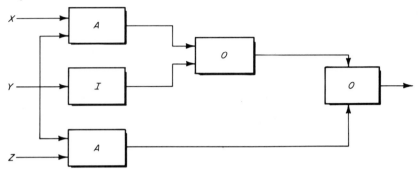

PROBLEM 6-4

5. Construct a gating circuit with six inputs which will emit a 1 only if a binary 9 (001001) enters the network.

6. Trace the four different input combinations through the half-adder. Do the proper outputs occur?

7. What is the difference between a combinatorial and a sequential circuit?

8. If an input enters the following circuit at time t_1, at what time will there be an output?

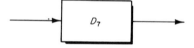

PROBLEM 6-8

9. Consider the following sequential circuit:

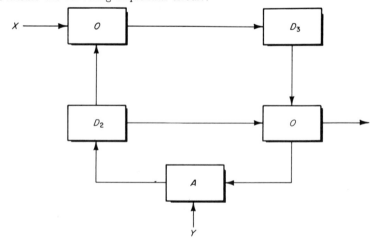

PROBLEM 6-9

Assume that a 1-bit enters X at time t_1. Between t_1 and t_{20}, when will there be 1 outputs? What is the effect during this period of introducing 1-bits at Y?

10. What are the characteristics of a trigger?

11. Consider the following network:

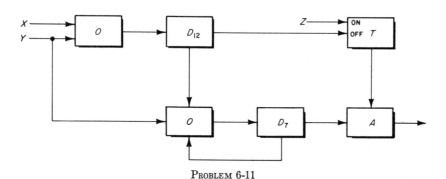

PROBLEM 6-11

Assume that a 1-bit enters at Z at time t_1. At time t_2, 1-bits enter at X and Y. What outputs, if any, occur between t_2 and t_{30}?

12. Trace the following addition through the full adder. Does the proper output occur?

$$\begin{array}{r} 011 \\ \underline{101} \end{array}$$

13. Compare the two binary numbers 0010 and 1111, using the *comparator* in Fig. 6-25. Does the proper output occur?

14. Assume that the binary number 100 is initially stored in the right shift circuit shown in Fig. 6-26. After the shift, verify that the number represented is 010.

15. What is the purpose of a memory *address*? Show in Fig. 6-27 how memory locations M_1, M_2, and M_3 are *reset* (turned to zero). If the binary digits 1, 0, and 1, enter, respectively, on X, Y, and Z, how are they stored in M_1, M_2, and M_3?

16. What is the function of a routing signal?

17. Perform the binary multiplication

$$\begin{array}{r} 11001 \\ \underline{10111} \end{array}$$

Check your answer by converting the binary numbers and the answer to the decimal system.

18. How are partial products used in performing a multiplication?

19. What is the function of the *complement* in subtraction?

20. Perform the division $73/9$ by repeated subtractions.

21. In the example of machine multiplication given in this chapter, what is the basic four-step cycle which is repeated? How does the control system send out routing signals for each step?

CHAPTER 7

1. In the expression pqr the variables p, q, and r can be either true or false. There are eight possible combinations. In which case is the entire statement true?

2. In which cases is the entire statement $p \lor q \lor r$ true?

3. Is $p \lor \bar{q}r \equiv q \lor \bar{p}r$?
Prove your answer by means of a truth table.

4. Is $pr \lor pq \equiv p \overline{(qr)}$?
Prove your answer by means of a truth table.

5. What is the Boolean expression for the following circuit?

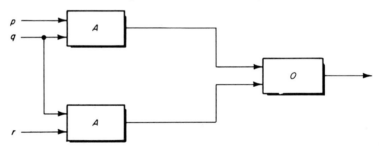

PROBLEM 7-5

Can this circuit be further simplified?

6. Construct a gating circuit which meets the following conditions:

p	q	Output
0	0	1
0	1	0
1	0	1
1	1	0

Can this circuit be further simplified?

7. The output of the following circuit can be expressed by the conjunction *KL*.

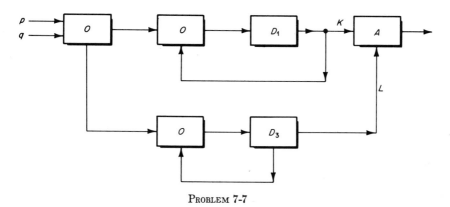

PROBLEM 7-7

Explain why, in terms of time relationships, this circuit can be expressed by the equation

$$(p^{n-1} \vee q^{n-1})(p^{n-3} \vee q^{n-3})$$

8. If the output of a circuit is fed back into the network, as in Fig. 7-18, why is the present functioning of the system a function of its history?

CHAPTER 8

1. Describe the machine units comprising a typical data processing system.

2. What is meant by the *automatic sequencing of instructions*?

3. How are memory locations identified?

4. What is the function of the *operation code* and *address* in an instruction?

5. Using the simple computer described in this chapter, add the numbers contained in memory locations 098 and 233. Place the sum in memory location 900.

6. Show how the instructions you used in Question 5 would look if stored in the memory locations starting with 301.

7. Assume that the instruction L 500 is stored in memory location 100. Assume that the number 4 is in location 999 and that the number 2 is in location 998. Multiply the contents of location 999 by the contents of location 998. Add this product to the contents of location 100. Store the answer back in location 100.

8. Show how the instructions you employed in Question 7 would appear if stored in the memory locations starting with 000.

9. Assume that some number is stored in location 500, and that some other number is in location 501. Compare these numbers. If the number in 500 is higher than the number in 501, transfer control to a command located in 000.

10. How is comparison used to enable a machine to decide which program branch to take?

11. There are two punched cards in the card reader, each containing a 10-digit number. Using the simple READ instruction described in the text, read the first card into memory location 500 and the second card into location 600.

Compare the two numbers. If the number in the first card is higher, stop the machine. If the number in the first card is not higher, add the two numbers, place the sum in location 700, and stop the machine.

12. Assume 100 numbers are stored in memory locations 400-499, and that another 100 numbers are stored in 500-599. Perform the following additions:

(400) + (500).   Place sum in 600.
(401) + (501).   Place sum in 601.
etc.

Use the loop technique. After the 100 additions have been executed, stop the machine.

13. Explain *instruction time* and *execution time*. What is the purpose of the control counter and the memory address controls?

14. How is a GO command executed by the machine logic?

15. A royal flush in poker is the sequence of cards "10, jack, queen, king, ace," all cards being of the same suit. Suppose you were asked to program a computer to examine a deck of 52 cards, to determine if a royal flush were present. Prepare the flow chart for this search program.

16. What happens when the operator of a data processing machine presses the start key?

CHAPTER 9

1. What is the purpose of the *erase* head on a magnetic tape unit?

2. How would the number 823 appear on magnetic tape?

3. What is the purpose of the interrecord gap on tape?

4. How is information on punched cards placed on magnetic tape?

5. It is desired to sort a deck of playing cards into the order: 2 of spades, 2 of hearts, 2 of diamonds, 2 of clubs, 3 of spades, 3 of hearts, 3 of diamonds, 3 of clubs, 4 of spades, etc. How could this sort be accomplished using the technique shown in Fig. 9-2?

6. How would the numbers 43, 99, 07, 13, 83, 98, 52, and 50 be sorted, using the technique of the table on page 126?

7. Sort the numbers in Question 6, using the method described in the table on page 127.

8. What is the value of grouping records on magnetic tape?

9. How does buffering reduce input time?

10. What is the function of carriage control characters when printing outputs?

CHAPTER 10

1. How can the code number of an inventory item be used to look up its record in memory?

2. What is the function of a master file? What operations are performed upon it?

3. What are *utility* programs? How does a loading program work?

4. What types of errors are made by programmers?

5. What is a *subroutine*?

6. What is a *supervisory* program?

7. Why are assembly programs necessary?

8. Differentiate between a *source* program and an *object* program. What is a *programming language*?

9. Describe the main function of a compiler.

10. How would you go about programming $7x^3 + 3x^2 + 4x - 1$, using the nesting technique?

11. Describe two types of inaccuracies resulting from computational methods.

12. What is *parallel addition*?

13. What is an *instruction format*? Describe two different types.

CHAPTER 11

1. Approximately what percent of all commercial transactions make use of checks? About how many checks are written each year?

2. What is a *source document* for a data processing system? Exemplify.

3. In fixed-asset accounting, how are new acquisitions entered into the master file?

4. What is a *run* on a data processing machine?

5. What is the purpose of *pre-edit* runs?

6. Why is it desirable to alternate tape units when making use of a large master file?

7. Why is the order of records on the master file and the changes tape important? How is information in the changes tape entered into the master file?

8. What is the function of *character sensing* equipment?

9. Name the objectives of inventory control.

10. What is the purpose of FOSDIC?

CHAPTER 12

1. What functions do computers perform when a space vehicle is launched?

2. Describe in general how computers help to track satellites.

3. Name and briefly describe eight scientific, engineering, and industrial applications of computers.

4. How could computers assist in medical diagnosis?

CHAPTER 13

1. Distinguish between *batch processing* and *real-time* processing.

2. What is a *random access* memory, and why is it important in many applications?

3. How is data stored and obtained from a random access disk unit?

4. Why is the random access concept important in banking applications?

5. What are the over-all data processing problems in SAGE and SABRE?

6. What initiates an input in SABRE?

7. Explain *queuing* and its affect on the operation of a real-time system. What factors influence *response time*?

8. Using Fig. 13-9, assume a third transaction starts at time 20. Ascertain where this new transaction is delayed.

9. How do priorities among inputs affect the operation of a real-time system?

10. What is the basic problem in *information retrieval*? Exemplify applications of this type.

11. In what respects are teaching machines similar to real-time systems?

CHAPTER 14

1. Describe the essential characteristics of the *transportation problem*.

2. Give examples of *operations research* problems.

3. How could data processing machines aid in automobile and air traffic control?

4. How are computers used in playing war games?

5. What are the general characteristics of business games?

6. Describe and exemplify the minimax principle in game theory.

7. How are computers used in market research?

CHAPTER 15

1. What is a determined system? Are humans determined systems? Is *free will* an illusion?

2. What are the four properties of any logical system?

3. Describe the characteristics of a Turing machine. Add two binary digits, using the Turing machine described in the Appendix.

4. Give an example of a mechanism which goes through transitions from state to state.

5. Suppose the automaton in Fig. 15-5 starts at state *A*, and the following sequence of inputs occur: 0, 1, 0, 1, 1, 0. In which state does the automaton end?

6. Construct the transition table for the following automaton:

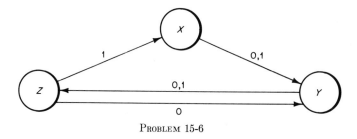

PROBLEM 15-6

7. Construct the state diagram for this automaton's transition table:

Present state	Input to next state	
	0	1
W	Z	Z
X	Y	Y
Y	W	W
Z	Z	Z

8. Test whether a sequence of inputs other than 110 can cause the combination lock in Fig. 15-7 to go from state A to state D.

9. By applying the same input sequences in both cases, test whether the automaton in Fig. 15-8 is essentially identical with the simplified automaton in Fig. 15-10.

10. In what respects is the behavior of neurons similar to the operations in Boolean algebra?

11. Can a computer predict the outcome of a chess or checker game by a formula or by an exhaustive search of all possible moves?

12. What is a *game tree*? What limits the exploration of a game tree by a computer? How are moves evaluated by a machine? What are *heuristic* principles?

13. How is the minimax principle used in playing games such as chess and checkers?

14. How do analog computers differ from digital computers?

15. How are computers used to control the operation of machine tools?

CHAPTER 16

1. How does the mechanistic conception of the universe differ from the pre-scientific world-view?

2. In what ways could computers be used to control large scale social phenomena? Is this desirable? What problems would it raise?

3. What are the problems caused by automation? What are the social and economic advantages of automation?

4. In what respects is an organism similar to a machine's control system? How do the two differ?

5. Describe the logic of reproduction of automata.

6. Compare genetic information with a computer program.

7. What is the second law of thermodynamics? What is *entropy*? How is information related to entropy? Are evolution and the expansion of knowledge related to entropy?

INDEX